Strength
FOR TODAY

I can do all things through Christ who strengthens me !

Phil 4:13

Brenda Walsh

Strength
FOR TODAY

ONE-MINUTE DEVOTIONS
to encourage, inspire,
and
spiritually change
YOUR LIFE

BRENDA WALSH

Graphic Designer: Chrystique Neibauer | cqgraphicdesign.com
Copy Editor: Mellisa Hoffman
Cover Image: shutterstock.com/Jes2u.photo

Scripture marked ERV are taken from the Easy-to-Read Version. Copyright © 2006 by Bible League international.

Scripture quotations marked ESV are from The Holy Bible: English Standard Version® (ESV®), copyright © 2001 by Crossway, a publishing ministry of Good News Publishers. Used by permission. All rights reserved.

Scriptures marked KJV are from the King James Version of the Bible.

Scripture marked MSG are taken from THE MESSAGE, copyright © 1993, 2002, 2018 by Eugene H. Peterson. Used by permission of NavPress. All rights reserved. Represented by Tyndale House Publishers, Inc.

Scripture quotations marked NASB are taken from the NEW AMERICAN STANDARD BIBLE®. Copyright © 1960, 1962, 1963, 1968, 1971, 1972, 1973, 1975, 1977, 1995 by The Lockman Foundation. Used by permission.

Scripture quotations marked NIV are from the HOLY BIBLE, NEW INTERNATIONAL VERSION®. Copyright © 1973, 1978, 1984, 2011 by Biblica, Inc®. Used by permission. All rights reserved worldwide.

Scripture marked NKJV is from the New King James Version®. Copyright © 1982 by Thomas Nelson. Used by permission. All rights reserved.

Scripture quotations marked NLT are taken from the Holy Bible, New Living Translation copyright © 1996, 2004, 2007, 2013 by Tyndale House Foundation. Used by permission of Tyndale House Publishers, Inc., Carol Stream, Illinois 60188. All rights reserved.

Scripture texts credited to NRSV are from the New Revised Standard Version of the Bible, copyright © 1989 by the Division of Christian Education of the National Council of the Churches of Christ in the USA. Used by permission. All rights reserved.

Scriptures marked RSV are from the Revised Standard Version of the Bible, copyright © 1946, 1952, and 1971 the Division of Christian Education of the National Council of the Churches of Christ in the United States of America. Used by permission. All rights reserved.

ISBN 978-0-9864-2911-8

July 2019

Additional copies of this book are available through:

brendawalshbooks.com

Adventist Book Centers®: Call toll-free 1-800-765-6955 or visit www.adventistbookcenter.com.

Amazon: www.amazon.com

For there is hope for a tree,
if it be cut down, that it will sprout
again, and that its shoots will not cease.

Job 14:7

Acknowledgments

A special thanks to my friends who have been an inspiration and strength to me personally ~ I deeply appreciate your love and friendship. There is not room to list everyone, but here are a few whom God has used specifically to lift me up during some of my darkest days and most challenging trials. For you I am eternally grateful.

Jerry & Karen Arnold
Wendine & Christine Austin
Dr. Royce & Judy Bailey
Ted & Peg Bernhardt
Jack Blanco
Ashton Botha
Truby Bowen
Don & Carole Bretsch
Frank & Martha Brown
Julie Douglas
Steve & Kari Duffy
David, Gayl & Marleta Fong
Sam & Ellen Godfrey
Stephanie Griffin
Vicki Griffin
Peter & Eva Griffith
Ray & Madlyn Hamblin
Dr. Andrew & Karen Harewood
Cory & Christal Herthel
Mellisa Hoffman
Gary & Cori Hollingsead
Dr. Buddy & Tina Houghtaling
Dan & Donna Jackson
Dr. Alvin & Jewel Kibble

Sanja Kitevski
Dona Klein
Kay Kuzma
Kevin & Jenny Maevsky
Rick & Cindy Mercer
Fred & Sandy Miller
Chrystique Neibauer
Dick & Lucy Neuharth
Haziel & Lichelle Olivera
Ruthven Phillip
Gordon & Marie Pifher
Ken & Cheryl Rogers
Zenobia Seward
Bill & Bonnie Shuris
Nancy Sterling
Dr. Calvin & Irina Taylor
Justin & Charissa Torossian
Reed & Gerda Von Maur
Curla Walters
Andrea Ward
Vince & Mele Williams
Eric & Joy Whipps
Surangel & Marilyn Whipps
Ron & Betty Whitehead

Special Thanks

I want to thank my Lord, Savior, and best Friend, Jesus Christ, for His grace, mercy, and amazing love. It doesn't matter how many times I have failed Him—He has never failed me! He has wiped away my tears, lifted me up in His arms when I was too weak to go on, and comforted me during some of the darkest days of my life. And through it all, He was not only kind, patient, and long-suffering, He has always loved me.

There are not enough words or ways to express how very much I love Jesus, and I want to spend the rest of my life praising Him and sharing Him with others. I treasure our special time together each day in worship and studying His Word, and the longer I remain in His presence, the more I want to be there.

It is my deepest desire that each of these devotions will inspire others to not only develop a closer relationship with God but to prepare them to spend eternity with Him in heaven, where all of the trials of this earth will be over—no more tears, sorrow, or death, but each day will be more glorious than the day before. Oh, how excited I am for that day—to see Jesus face to face!

Choose today, and every day, to make Jesus first in your life, and claim His promise in James 4:8, "Draw near to God and He will draw near to you," and then you will receive His "Strength for Today."

Dedication

I dedicate "Strength for Today" to the talented ministry
team that God has called together to reach His children through
"Kids Club for Jesus Studio and Leadership Center."

To my esteemed colleague, Dr. Andrew Harewood: Thank you for
answering God's call to be president of our children's leadership
center, training children to be leaders for Christ. You are an amazing
man of God, and it is a privilege to work with you, introducing
children around the world to Jesus.

To our chief financial officer, Zenobia Seward: I'm so grateful to
have such a godly woman on our team who believes in honesty and
transparency and being a good steward of God's money.

To my awesome assistant and operations manager, Mellisa Hoffman:
Thank you for your dedication to the Lord's work all these years and
for supporting me through thick and thin. God has blessed you with
so many talents and you are one of the hardest workers I know.
I thank Jesus for you!

To our creative director of print and web, Chrystique Neibauer:
You are unbelievably gifted and one of the fastest designers in the
industry. (Thank you for designing our logo!) Your commitment to
excellence is a real blessing, and I am truly grateful for the many years
you have dedicated to this ministry.

To our technology director and leadership coordinator,
Ben Calderon: You are an innovative visionary, who is always
striving to get the best results in the most efficient ways. But most
importantly, you are passionate about youth ministry and saving
souls for God's kingdom.

To our executive board members not listed above, Howard Bishop,
Sam Godfrey, and Kevin Maevsky: Thank you for answering God's
call to be a part of this worldwide children's ministry. You provide
competence, integrity, insight, and wisdom, and your leadership is
valued and appreciated. May God bless you and our entire team with
Holy Spirit guidance and direction as we work together to introduce
children to their best Friend, Jesus.

Happy New Year

Therefore receive one another, just as Christ also received us, to the glory of God.

Romans 15:7 (NKJV)

Today is the first day of a new year, and it's not too late to make one more New Year's resolution: be more accepting of others. This resolution alone will make the world a better place, and will also make us personally happier, more at peace, and most of all, draw us closer to Jesus.

When we approach life with the position that *we know it all*, we are *always right,* and *only our opinion matters,* we alienate those around us. This "better than thou" attitude destroys every kind of relationship, from the most casual acquaintance to friends, family, and, yes, even spouses! When we expect someone to look the way *we* want them to look, talk the way *we* want them to talk, or even act the way *we* think they should act, that person immediately builds a wall. Our expectation sends out a strong judgmental message.

Pretty soon, the wall is so high and thick, there's no communication at all! We need to accept each other's differences, embrace the qualities that make each of us unique, and, above all, love as Jesus loves! All throughout the Bible, God tells us to love . . . love . . . love . . . each other! Resolve this year to *tear down the walls* that are keeping us from being more like Jesus! Make this year the year to be more loving, more patient, and more accepting of others!

Does Jesus Care?

O give thanks to the LORD, for he is good, for his
steadfast love endures forever.

Psalm 136:1 (NRSV)

There is an old but precious song by J. Lincoln Hall that goes like this: "Does Jesus care, when I've said 'goodbye' to the dearest on earth to me, And my sad heart aches till it nearly breaks, Is it aught to Him? Does He see?" The answer is found in the chorus: "Oh, yes, He cares, I know He cares, His heart is touched with my grief; When the days are weary, the long nights dreary, I know my Savior cares."

Absolutely, positively, Jesus cares! In fact, He loves us so much that He died on a cross to save us—yet why is it so difficult to comprehend love that deep? Some people have never experienced love from family or friends here on earth, so they especially struggle with knowing the depths of God's love! Others suffer from poor self-esteem and hate themselves so much that they have trouble believing anyone loves them! But we serve a God who has equal love and compassion for *all* His children, even those who are poor, lonely, and broken!

God doesn't play favorites! Even if we reject God and choose not to love Him, He *still* loves us! When we are going through the toughest trials of our lives, and it seems like we are all alone, we can rejoice knowing we are never alone! Jesus loves us with an everlasting love . . . and yes, He cares!

Sticks and Stones

For we all stumble in many things. If anyone
does not stumble in word, he is a perfect man, able
also to bridle the whole body.

James 3:2 (NKJV)

Words are powerful! They can cut like a knife and leave painful wounds that can lead to a lifetime of self-doubt, poor self-esteem, and self-loathing! The old expression, "Sticks and stones may break my bones, but words can never hurt me," is quite simply . . . just not true! How you use your words can either help or hurt others. The sad thing about hateful words is, that once spoken, they can never be taken back! The damage is done.

That's why it's so important to choose your words carefully, speak with kindness, and always consider how your words will be received. A kind, gentle word can do wonders to lift someone's spirits and bring joy and healing to a broken heart. The Bible says in Proverbs 15:23 (NIV), "A person finds joy in giving an apt reply—and how good is a timely word!"

The most powerful words come from the Bible—God's Holy Word. When we truly listen to what He is saying, we'll find that God promises to give us the instruction, courage, strength, and wisdom that we need to speak in such a manner that will represent Him. As long as Jesus is shining through, you'll never have to worry about saying the wrong thing!

Spiritual Power

*Teaching us that, denying ungodliness and
worldly lusts, we should live soberly, righteously,
and godly, in this present world.*

Titus 2:12 (KJV)

Choosing God's commandments over sinful urges not only demonstrates your love for Him but strengthens your relationship with Him as well. When you seek God's will for your life, He will lead and guide you around all the things that pull you away from Him. And the closer you are to Jesus, the more you will want to please Him by living a godly life.

Whenever temptation raises its ugly head, God is there to give you the victory—all you need to do is ask. In other words, God will give you spiritual power to win the battle over sin! In 1 Corinthians 15:57 (NIV), we're told, "But thanks be to God! He gives us the victory through our Lord Jesus Christ." When you fall in love with Jesus, you no longer have the same worldly desires, and as you grow spiritually, your eyes are open to danger. Those once "harmless" temptations no longer have the same appeal. Bottom line—there's no sinful pleasure on this earth that is worth missing out on eternity with Jesus!

The Bible says in 1 John 2:17 (NIV), "The world and its desires pass away, but whoever does the will of God lives forever." Claim this promise for your own and choose to live a godly life. Resist temptation by using God's spiritual power to overcome sin, and prepare to live with Him in heaven for all eternity.

Enjoy Today

*The LORD will give strength to His people; the LORD
will bless His people with peace.*

Psalm 29:11 (NKJV)

After the holidays, when everyone has gone, decorations are put away, and the house is quiet, you may start to feel sad that it's all over. Then comes the worry wagon full of credit card bills from gifts purchased that you really couldn't afford. Top that all off with a good portion of anxiety and guilt and the stress levels soar off the charts! Now is the time to evaluate your spiritual life.

Ask yourself a few questions: *How is my relationship with God? How much time do I spend each day in prayer and worship? Do I go to God "first" with my problems? Do others see Jesus in me? Am I a good witness to others?*

Instead of being discouraged, use this time to jump-start your relationship with God. Listen, and you'll hear God's voice in the midst of your troubles. He will give you the courage and strength to face whatever life throws at you, and through it all, He will sustain you with His peace!

Claim God's promise in Isaiah 43:2 (NKJV): "When you pass through the waters, I will be with you; and through the rivers, they shall not overflow you. When you walk through the fire, you shall not be burned. Nor shall the flame scorch you." Don't spend another minute sinking in the holiday blues—instead spend time with God and enjoy today.

Best Inheritance

*"Therefore you shall lay up these words of mine in
your heart and in your soul . . . You shall teach them
to your children, speaking of them when you sit in your
house, when you walk by the way, when you lie down,
and when you rise up."*

Deuteronomy 11:18-19 (NKJV)

———◦◦◦———

Satan is hard at work trying to steal, kill, and destroy our children, and he is using every trick in the book to accomplish his goals: alcohol, drugs, sex, movies, video games, and anything else that will take their minds off Jesus! These worldly influences make raising Christian children more challenging than ever before.

Make no mistake, there is only one way to fight the enemy, and that is to allow God to fight the battle! The Bible says in Isaiah 49:25 (NLT), "For I will fight those who fight you, and I will save your children." That is a promise from God that we can claim for our children. Many times parents fail to introduce their kids to Jesus, and then when their children grow up and turn from God, they suffer with guilt.

Instead of wallowing in guilt and despair, pray this prayer: "Dear Heavenly Father, please forgive me for not being the parent you wanted me to be and don't allow my mistakes to cause my children to rebel against you. Oh Lord, I plead with you to save them." God will honor the heartfelt prayers of parents—even long after they have passed away. Praying for our children is the best inheritance we could possibly leave them!

No Perfect Prayer

*I cry out to the LORD with my voice; with my voice to
the LORD I make my supplication.*

Psalm 142:1 (NKJV)

❧

There are some who feel awkward when they pray, as if God is judging them on how eloquent their prayers are. They believe in God, but they can't really visualize or feel connected to Him. Because they are not comfortable praying, soon they stop trying altogether and drift further and further away from the very One who gave His life to save them!

The truth is, there is no such thing as a *perfect* prayer! God just wants you to talk to Him heart-to-heart, friend-to-friend, and He truly listens, hears, and answers. You're not just an insignificant little human here on earth! Your voice matters in heaven! When you call out to Jesus, He gives you His full attention. He's not listening for perfect grammar, nor does He condemn you for stuttering or stumbling over your words.

Jesus loves you with an everlasting love, and everything you say is important to Him. So, the next time you think that God doesn't hear you or that your prayers go no higher than your ceiling—think again! Jesus loves you and cares about every aspect of your life—and He wants to hear from you!

Humble Pie

*For You will save the humble people, but will
bring down haughty looks.*

Psalm 18:27 (NKJV)

If you're all puffed up with pride and arrogance—sooner or
later you'll find yourself eating a slice of humble pie! Proverbs
16:18 (NKJV) says, "Pride goes before destruction, and a
haughty spirit before a fall." Bottom line—God will not honor
arrogance and self-centeredness, and, in fact, God despises a
prideful heart. He wants His children to be humble and think
of others first.

There are even instances in the Bible where God gave His
people grace and spared their lives—because they humbled
their hearts. Check out 2 Chronicles 34:27 (NIV): " 'Because
your heart was responsive and you humbled yourself before
God when you heard what he spoke against this place and its
people, and because you humbled yourself before me and tore
your robes and wept in my presence, I have heard you,' declares
the Lord."

There are over one hundred verses in the Bible about humility and just how important it is to God. The Bible even says
in Psalm 37:11 that there is a special reward for those who are
humble. When you are tempted to take all the credit, take over a
conversation, or act like you are better than everyone else, stop
and consider how God feels about a heart full of pride—then
cut yourself a slice of humble pie, and, remember, if you want
to be like Jesus . . . be humble!

Fight the Volcano

*"Be angry, and do not sin": do not let the sun go down on
your wrath, nor give place to the devil.*

Ephesians 4:26-27 (NKJV)

There are some people whose personalities run hot and cold
and the least little thing can upset them. The sad thing is
that when pushed too far . . . they explode like an erupting
volcano! These eruptions are usually followed by shame, regret,
and remorse. Unfortunately, words once spoken can never be
taken back and actions can never be undone. Most people, if
they waited and calmed down, would not respond in the same
way. The Bible gives wise advice in Psalm 4:4 (NLT): "Don't
sin by letting anger control you. Think about it overnight and
remain silent." And Proverbs 14:29 (NLT) says, "People with
understanding control their anger; a hot temper shows great
foolishness."

The plain truth is, anger ruins relationships, and, worse,
separates us from our Lord and Savior. Lives can be destroyed
over one impulsive action caused by a bad temper, and, let's
be honest, whenever anger rears it's ugly head, there is usually
selfishness involved. If we really want to be more like Jesus and
reflect His unselfish character, we need to pray for His sweet
spirit to dwell within us. The Bible says in Nahum 1:3 (NKJV),
"The Lord is slow to anger and great in power."

There is truth to the saying "You will attract more bees
with honey than with vinegar." Responding with an outraged
temper will not only affect you spiritually, but you won't be a
good witness to others, so give all that anger to God and let
Him fight the volcano!

Top of Your Priority List

But his delight is in the law of the Lord,
and in His law he meditates day and night.

Psalm 1:2 (NKJV)

Many Christians struggle finding time to spend alone with God. There are many theories about why people who profess to love God with all their hearts can't carve out time in their day to worship Him. It's not that they don't *want* to, but rather they feel their lives are too busy—so time for worship becomes something they aspire to, but don't view as a necessity.

One of the reasons is simply because people lose sight of just *who* God is. If you view God as anything less than who He is—a loving, caring, all-powerful, King of the Universe God—then the level of importance to spend time with Him is greatly diminished. God isn't a *scorekeeper* who bases His love for you on how much time you spend with Him.

God loves you more than you could possibly comprehend, and when you truly understand the depths of His love for you, worshiping Him will not be a chore but a privilege that you look forward to. In fact, instead of trying to *fit time in*, spending time with Jesus will climb to the top of your priority list!

It is during alone time with your heavenly Father that you gain wisdom, patience, and love for your fellow man. Your soul is also refreshed, giving you everything you need to face your day. The Bible says in James 4:8 (NKJV), "Draw near to God and He will draw near to you."

Ready and Waiting

When I am afraid, I put my trust in you.
In God, whose word I praise, in God I trust;
I am not afraid; what can flesh do to me?

Psalm 56:3-4 (NRSV)

Do you remember how scary it was when you first learned how to ride a bicycle? Once your training wheels were removed, your confidence level hit a new low the minute you realized how quickly you could fall. But when Dad or Mom was running behind you with a firm hand on your bicycle seat . . . all of a sudden you became a lot more confident, and that fear of falling disappeared, giving you time to learn how to balance on two wheels. So it is with God.

As long as He has you firmly in His grasp, all fear goes away, because you know God has your back! He's not going to let you fall! Proverbs 3:5 (NKJV) tells us, "Trust in the LORD with all your heart, and lean not on your own understanding." If you are depending solely on yourself, you will fall every time! But Jesus never fails! He is 100% reliable . . . 100% of the time!

If fear starts to raise its ugly head, declare unto God as David did in Psalm 13:5 (NIV): "But I trust in your unfailing love; my heart rejoices in your salvation." When you're trusting in Jesus, there's no need to push the panic button or be afraid, because He's right there beside you—ready and waiting to catch you *before* you fall!

Hope in the Lord

*Now may the God of hope fill you with all joy and peace
in believing, that you may abound in hope by the
power of the Holy Spirit.*

Romans 15:13 (NKJV)

Christians and non-Christians think quite differently when it comes to the word *hope.* Non-Christians usually think of hope as hoping for something they want and regard it more like a *maybe* or it *might* happen. They even think of it as something they wish for, such as "I *hope* I don't get the flu this year," or "I *hope* it doesn't rain tomorrow." But Christians know that real hope is in the Lord!

If you find yourself saying, "I hope so," start praying for God to give you more faith and trust in Him. Remember, when you pray, "God's will be done," you can count on God to do what is best for you—rather than *hope* He will. Sometimes what you *think* you want—isn't what you really want at all. When you hope in the Lord, you *know* with absolute certainty that God keeps His Word.

You can believe it when Jesus says He loves you and wants you to spend eternity with Him. The Bible says in Psalm 147:11 (NIV), "The LORD delights in those who fear him, who put their hope in His unfailing love." One of the best things about having Jesus as your best Friend—is that you never have to *hope* so . . . because you *know* your hope is in the Lord!

Life Is a Gift

Jesus said to him, "I am the way, the truth, and the life.
No one comes to the Father except through Me."

John 14:6 (NKJV)

There are some people who take life for granted, especially those who are young and still trying to figure out how they fit in this great big world. But somehow, the days have a way of turning into years very quickly, and, in a blink of an eye, you'll suddenly realize that more than half your life is gone.

Of course, it doesn't seem possible because only yesterday you were looking at gray-haired people and couldn't even imagine being that old. It is usually at this point, you look in the mirror and realize that the person looking back isn't even someone you recognize! Your memory isn't what it used to be, you have aches and pains, and your opinion doesn't seem to matter very much to anyone anymore. Reality forces you to evaluate and take stock of your life—thinking of past accomplishments as well as the regrets.

But the biggest regret of all is waiting until the end of your life to realize you need a Savior—that you had lived your whole life just going through the motions of being a Christian. Whatever is done for self will pass away—but what you do for Christ will last forever!

Life is a gift from God and how you choose to live it will determine whether or not you'll spend eternity in heaven! Time is running out. Choose today to serve Jesus!

Doing the Right Thing

For it is better, if it is the will of God,
to suffer for doing good than for doing evil.

1 Peter 3:17 (NKJV)

God wants us to obey Him and do His will, regardless of the consequences. And the truth is, doing the right thing is not always easy. Sometimes as Christians, we have the false expectation that if we are doing what God wants us to do—then everything will be easy in our lives! But that could not be further from the truth.

Jesus set a wonderful example for all of us to follow. When He was here on earth, He was ridiculed, plotted against, spied on, and lied about—but He kept doing the will of His Father! There will be times when we are doing what we *know* God wants us to do, and yet we will suffer rejection, persecution, and hardship. Just because we feel *uncomfortable* or don't like being tormented for something we don't deserve should not deter us for even a moment from doing God's will.

Jesus warned us that there would be troublesome times. He says in John 16:33 (NKJV), "These things I have spoken to you, that in Me you may have peace. In the world you will have tribulation; but be of good cheer, I have overcome the world." We need not worry or fear when we are *doing the right thing*, because God will stand by our side—even in the midst of our toughest trials!

A Bitter Heart

Bear with one another and, if anyone has a complaint against another, forgive each other; just as the Lord has forgiven you, so you also must forgive.

Colossians 3:13 (NRSV)

Walking around with a heart full of resentment, anger, and bitterness because of an injustice that you've experienced . . . is a recipe for pain! It's simply impossible to experience joy in your life if you are burdened with a bitter heart. You might be able to stuff all those feelings deep down inside where you think no one will notice—but the longer you keep them bottled up within, the more damage they will do.

You may not even realize it, but unforgiveness has a way of coming out in negative ways and affects your words, deeds, and actions. But even worse than that, harboring all that bitterness will separate you from Jesus, causing you to miss out on eternal life. The Bible tells us in Mark 11:26 (NKJV), "But if you do not forgive, neither will your Father in heaven forgive your trespasses."

It doesn't matter who or what caused the pain—nothing is worth missing out on heaven! Ask God to put forgiveness in your heart for those who have done you wrong and experience the vibrant life God wants you to have.

Let God Decide

But as for me and my house, we will serve the Lord.
Joshua 24:15 (NKJV)

Other than choosing Jesus, choosing your spouse is the most important decision you will make in life. Listed in the order of importance, here are three basic rules to follow if you are considering getting into a relationship.

1. *God first*: Do they love God above all else, including you? Are they just attending church because you want them to? If they don't have a strong relationship with Jesus, walk away, for without God there is *no* love—because God *is* love!

2. *Family*: How much do you like their family? If you don't get along with the family, walk away! Remember, when you get married, you marry the family too! If you can't stand the potential in-laws, that will be a problem that will cause misery, heartache, and division.

3. *Equal energy*: Are you always the one who has to *do everything*? Do you put more energy into the relationship than they do? If you don't call, will they? If you are the one giving 80% and they are giving 20% on a consistent basis, it won't work—walk away! If it's already this way *before* marriage, it will be much worse *after* marriage!

God knows you better than you know yourself, and He always wants what is best for you, so when choosing your mate, don't take chances with what you *think* you want—let God decide!

Did You Say Thank You?

Oh, give thanks to the Lord, for He is good!
For His mercy endures forever.

1 Chronicles 16:34 (NKJV)

Whenever you do something nice for someone, it always feels *good* to receive a response of thankfulness. Although that should not be your reason for giving, your human nature wants to hear that the receiver of your kindness was indeed grateful. If you sent someone a birthday gift and never received a thank-you or even an acknowledgment that they received your gift, the next year you probably wouldn't send one at all.

There's a story in the Bible about ten lepers who were healed, yet only *one* leper came back to thank Jesus. The Bible says in Luke 17:15 (NIV), "One of them, when he saw he was healed, came back, praising God in a loud voice." And then Jesus answered in Luke 17:17 (NIV), "Were there not ten cleansed? But where are the nine?" It's very clear how God views thankfulness.

How thankful are you for what God has done in your life? Do you remember to thank Him when your prayer is answered and your cancer is gone, or do you say, "Wow, that chemo really worked"? When you're having car trouble and you cry out for God to help you, then all of a sudden your car starts, do you shrug it off as a coincidence or do you praise God for starting your car? Before ending your prayer where you listed all the things you want God to do for you, don't forget to say, "Thank You," for what He has already done.

Blessed Assurance

*But I trusted in your steadfast love; my heart shall
rejoice in your salvation.*

Psalm 13:5 (NRSV)

Everyone needs a little assurance from time to time. No matter how hard you try, there's always someone out there who wants to see you fail and is eager to tear you down. It's surprising how quickly one negative comment can influence how you feel about yourself. But positive comments have the total opposite effect. It makes a huge difference in your day if your boss tells you you're doing a good job, a friend compliments you on how good you look, or someone tells you how much they love you.

It's amazing how reassurance from someone you care about will go a long way to build up your self-esteem and help you regain your confidence! One thing you can know with absolute certainty is . . . God loves you! In His Holy Word, He reassures you over and over again just how much He cares about you—so much so that He sacrificed His only Son to die on a cross so that you could be with Him forever—throughout all eternity! Love just doesn't get deeper than that!

You never have to feel insecure about God's love! The Bible says in Hebrews 13:5 (NKJV), "I will never leave you nor forsake you," and God always keeps His promises. Praise God for His blessed assurance!

Hating Our Own Sin

*How many are my iniquities and sins? Make me know
my transgression and my sin.*

Job 13:23 (NKJV)

———◆———

Why is it easier to see someone else's faults and shortcomings than it is to see our own? When our friend brags about selling his car without letting the buyer know it was going to need more repairs than what the car was worth, we might feel the need to point out his sin of dishonesty. But the next day, we don't have any trouble at all exaggerating our accomplishments on our resumés in order to get that big job we wanted! Somehow, we were able to see our friend's sin—but not our own.

The Bible has quite a bit to say about pointing out the faults of others. In Matthew 7:4 (NIV), Jesus said, "How can you say to your brother, 'Let me take the speck out of your eye,' when all the time there is a plank in your own eye?" Yes, it's tempting to want to correct or fix someone else, but the reality is, no one is perfect, and we all make mistakes.

We're told in Romans 3:23 (NKJV), "All have sinned and fall short of the glory of God." We are all sinners, so we need to leave the fault-finding to God! Instead of criticizing others, let's ask God to apply eye salve to our eyes that we might see our own sins before we point out the sins of anyone else. Imagine what a better world this would be if we could just learn to hate our own sins more than we hate the sins of others!

Praying for Discernment

Rejoice always, pray without ceasing, in everything give thanks; for this is the will of God in Christ Jesus for you.

1 Thessalonians 5:16-18 (NKJV)

Every day, there are people who are forced to make life-changing decisions, and many ask the question, "How do I know if I'm making the right choices?" Some want answers so desperately that they search out their horoscopes, while others pay psychics to tell them what to do. Looking to the stars for answers won't help—you must ask the Maker of the stars!

Christians know that the only way to make the *right choice* comes from following God's advice. But even Christians sometimes struggle with discerning God's voice and often find themselves asking questions, such as *How can I be certain it is God leading and not my own selfish desires? Is it even possible to know for sure that it's God's voice and not man's or Satan's?* And the answer is a definite *yes!*

The Bible tells of many men and women who knew God's voice—Abraham, Moses, Esther, and the list goes on and on. In John 10:27 (NKJV), we're told, "My sheep hear My voice, and I know them, and they follow Me." However, to discern God's will for your life, you must have an active prayer life, talking with Him heart to heart . . . all throughout your day! The more time you spend in prayer, the closer you will be to God—and the more you will *hear* and *know* His voice.

No-Drama Life

*Put on the whole armor of God, that you may be able to
stand against the wiles of the devil.*

Ephesians 6:11 (NKJV)

Someone once asked, "How ya doin' today?" and the quick reply was, "Doing great!" Immediately, the response was given, "Shame on you! You don't have the devil worried—you need to do more for Jesus!" That may make you smile, but the truth is, if things are going smoothly in your life and everything is great, chances are you are not active in ministry. If you think committing your heart and life to God is your ticket to a perfect, no-drama life, think again!

Satan is never happy when you are working for Jesus and will push every button he can to discourage you! In fact, the more you do for Jesus, the more trials and troubles you will have! As you draw closer to your Lord and Savior, you can count on the devil to increase his efforts to separate you from the only one who can save you! He will try to deceive and discourage you and make you think that he is more powerful than God, but don't fall for the enemy's lies for even one moment!

You don't have to worry about what the devil will do, because you know what God will do! Just stay close to Jesus and keep your eyes on Him. Don't strive for a perfect, *no-drama life* here on earth, but focus on *eternal life* with our heavenly Father!

In Need of a Savior

*But when He saw the multitudes, He was moved with
compassion for them, because they were weary
and scattered, like sheep having no shepherd.*

Matthew 9:36 (NKJV)

People watching is fast becoming a favorite pastime. It's quite interesting to just sit and watch people as they go by. Some are busy talking on their phones, while others walk with purpose at a fast pace, and then there are those who just saunter along as if they have no place to go. You'll see people smartly dressed, others are in casual attire, and then there are those with the *thrown-together* look, as if they just rolled out of bed. But look closely as they pass by—look past the polite smiles and the head nod, then think about the story that lies behind the face.

Outward appearances are deceptive—often masking pain, heartache, anxiety, fear, or hopelessness. Everyone has a story and a burden to bear. If only we could see each other through God's eyes, perhaps we would treat each other differently—having more compassion, patience, and love for our fellow men. People need to know that God loves them and has a purpose for their lives.

Pray that God will help you judge less—and love more! Remember that there is no such thing as *perfect* people on this earth for we are all sinners . . . in need of a Savior!

One-Way Monologue

I call upon you, for you will answer me, O God; incline your ear to me, hear my words.

Psalm 17:6, (NRSV)

If you want a relationship with God, it starts with prayer. Most people think that prayer comes easy for Christians, but, for some, it may feel strange to talk to someone they can't see, hear, or touch, so praying can be awkward. The best way to feel comfortable is to just start praying!

It may feel like a one-way monologue at first, but the more time you spend talking to God, the more comfortable you'll feel. And then before you even realize it, you'll hear His voice. Somehow your monologue has become a two-way conversation! As you grow spiritually, praying becomes as natural as breathing. However, when you allow the hustle and bustle of your life to diminish your prayer time—that is when your life starts to fall apart. You simply can't enjoy the abundant life God wants you to have if you shortchange your time with Him.

Coming into the presence of God allows you the privilege of having Him lead and guide you through this journey of life. When tempted to skip prayer time, remember this: there is nothing in this world that is worth missing out on your appointment with the King of the Universe!

Appearance of Evil

"But he who does the truth comes to the light, that his deeds may be clearly seen, that they have been done in God."

John 3:21 (NKJV)

———◆———

It's not enough to *do the right thing*—it's also important to make sure you avoid even the appearance of evil. For instance, suppose the person you've been giving Bible studies to happens to drive by just at the very moment you are coming out of a tavern. They will probably judge you as a hypocrite and you may never know why they suddenly ended the studies—and they may never know that you had just gone in to use the restroom.

If you're a single girl traveling across country with a couple of your guy friends, you may be completely innocent, staying in separate hotel rooms, but there will be those who will think you're less than pure. The Bible says in 1 Thessalonians 5:22 (KJV), "Abstain from all appearance of evil."

God wants you to live your life as a living example of Christ abiding in you. To do that, you need to be conscious of how others will see you and strive to reflect Jesus in all your actions. You can't win others to Christ if you are not living a righteous life yourself. In all cases, avoid appearances of evil and choose to be a living witness for Christ in all that you do and say!

People Are Not Perfect

*Though he fall, he shall not be utterly cast down; for the
LORD upholds him with His hand.*

Psalm 37:24 (NKJV)

———◆———

We've often heard the old expression, "If at first you don't
succeed, try, try, again," and it's not a bad creed to live by
as no one really wants to be a quitter. But if things don't turn
out the way we want them to, we tend to feel like a "failure," and
often just want to *give up*! Sometimes, we even fail ourselves
by making bad choices or not living up to what we know to be
right. When a relationship fails, we're fired from a job, or our
children don't turn out the way we hoped, we get all discouraged
and start blaming ourselves or others for why we failed.

It's not a good feeling, but the truth is—we all fail at some
time or another. People are not perfect, nor do they live perfect
lives! We are all human, and it's inevitable that we will make
mistakes from time to time. In fact, there's only one guarantee in
life and that is God's love for us! His love will never change, for
He loves us no matter what—with an unending, unconditional,
unfathomable love.

God hates the sin, but loves the sinner! The good news is,
we serve a God who is a *forgiving* God, and, despite our failures,
He lovingly embraces us when we repent and leads us in the
direction that we should go. The only *real* failure . . . would be
to refuse God's help!

Cure for Anxiety

*Be anxious for nothing, but in everything by prayer and
supplication . . . let your requests be made known to God.*

Philippians 4:6 (NKJV)

There are some people that question the need for prayer,
wondering why they should pray when God already knows
their thoughts. And it is true—God does know your thoughts,
but He *responds* to your prayers! God wants you to come to
Him and lay out your petitions before Him, and one thing you
can be sure of is that God will always answer and will always
have your best interests at heart.

One of the blessings of being able to communicate directly
with God is that prayer is the best cure for anxiety. When you
pray about your problems, you are talking to someone who
actually has the power to do something about it. No matter
how big or small the problem, God can solve it! When you're
troubles seem too heavy to bear, give them to Jesus and allow
Him to embrace you in His arms of love, giving you comfort
and peace of mind.

The Bible says in Psalm 107:9 (NKJV), "For He satisfies the
longing soul, and fills the hungry soul with goodness." And
in John 15:7 (NKJV), we're told, "If you abide in Me, and My
words abide in you, you will ask what you desire, and it shall be
done for you." So the next time you start to feel anxious, there's
no need for pacing the floor—instead get on your knees and
you'll quickly discover the cure for anxiety.

Victory Over Temptations

*No temptation has overtaken you except such as
is common to man; but God is faithful, who will not
allow you to be tempted beyond what you are able, but
with the temptation will also make the way of escape,
that you may be able to bear it.*

1 Corinthians 10:13 (NKJV)

There are times when we may struggle with being tempted to do things that we know are not right, and we've fallen so many times that it seems we're on a losing streak against the devil. It might even be a sin that is considered *no big deal* in the eyes of the world and we're comforted by knowing that *no one else could possibly know*. But God knows! And when we're walking the Christian walk, our conscience will give us no rest. The Holy Spirit pleads with us to surrender our secret sins, and if we keep ignoring God's voice, the devil wins!

Temptation is all around us and can't be avoided because we live in a world of sin. We may have even prayed for the temptations to be taken away—but if the temptation was just removed, we would not be leaning on God for strength. Consider this: every temptation is an opportunity to overcome and obtain the victory over sin! With God's strength, we can always resist temptation! Philippians 4:13 (NKJV) tells us, "I can do all things through Christ which strengthens me." Jesus wants us to choose to serve Him with our whole hearts, and when we do, we will have gained the victory over temptation!

Refresh, Reboot, Restart

*"For I, the LORD your God, will hold your right hand,
saying to you, 'Fear not; I will help you.'"*

Isaiah 41:13 (NKJV)

When your heart is heavy and you're weary, discouraged, and feel all alone—it's time for some inner soul-searching and prayer. In other words, it's time to refresh, reboot, and restart. Begin your reboot by reading Matthew 11:28-30 (NKJV), and accept God's invitation to "Come to Me, all you who labor and are heavy laden, and I will give you rest. Take My yoke upon you and learn from Me, for I am gentle and lowly in heart, and you will find rest for your souls. For My yoke is easy and My burden is light."

Choose a quiet place where you can be alone with God. Share with Him all your worries, cares, and concerns, and then ask Him to take control of each one. Don't forget to pray, "Thy will be done," and then ask God to fill your heart with joy! The next step is critically important . . . and that is to truly trust God to do what's best. Don't try and tell God what to do! Remember, His plan is always the *best* plan!

When you get off your knees, don't try and pick up those heavy burdens again! Instead, walk away with a heart full of joy knowing that God is in control! The Bible says in Psalm 55:22 (NKJV), "Cast your burden on the LORD, and He shall sustain you." So, it's time to push the *restart* button and trade in your heavy heart for a new heart singing praises to God . . . all day long!

Hypocritical Christians

He who says he abides in Him ought himself also
to walk just as He walked.

1 John 2:6 (NKJV)

The world looks at *Christians* differently and holds them up to a higher standard. After all, the meaning of the word "Christian" is to be *Christlike*, and even atheists know that Christians are supposed to be loving, kind, and thoughtful. It's one thing to *say* you're a follower of Christ—but it is your daily actions that prove it. When non-believers see a *professed* Christian act selfish, mean, or rude—instead of drawing others *to* Christ, it drives them further away! The Bible says in Matthew 7:21 (KJV), "Not every one that saith unto me, Lord, Lord, shall enter into the kingdom of heaven; but he that doeth the will of my Father which is in heaven."

To be a Christian is to be connected with Christ and to do His will. It's not about what *we* want to do, but what *God* wants us to do! If there is one thing that hurts Christianity more than anything else, it's people who profess to be Christians, but their words and actions don't show it. In other words, they are being hypocrites!

They may go to church and even be leaders, but if they are not filled with the Holy Spirit, it is all for nothing! In fact, to all hypocritical Christians, God will say He never knew them! Ask God to come into your heart and life—striving everyday to be more like Jesus.

Chosen for Leadership

Be diligent to present yourself approved to God,
a worker who does not need to be ashamed,
rightly dividing the word of truth.

2 Timothy 2:15 (NKJV)

God wants all of His children to be *spiritual leaders*. You may not think of yourself as a *leader*, but in Mark 16:15 (NKJV), God has commissioned you to "Go into all the world and preach the gospel to every creature."

There are different kinds of *preaching* and *witnessing*, but the strongest and most effective way of sharing your faith is to lead *by example*! Your daily actions will go further to influence others than anything else! When you react with humility to hostile situations instead of using angry words, people notice! When you act with kindness instead of indifference, people notice! And when you are honest, people notice!

The Bible says in 1 Timothy 4:12 (NKJV), "Be an example to the believers in word, in conduct, in love, in spirit, in faith, in purity." And the secret to being a good leader is found in Matthew 20:26 (NLT), "Whoever wants to be a leader among you must be your servant." Unless we have Christ living within us, we can't lead anyone . . . anywhere! Your example can either lead people *to* Christ or *away* from Him, so it's critically important that your every move is guided by the Holy Spirit! Yes, God has chosen you for leadership—the question is, what kind of leader are you?

Practicing Self-Control

Whoever has no rule over his own spirit is like a
city broken down, without walls.

Proverbs 25:28 (NKJV)

Whenever you have behaved poorly, are you truly remorseful, or do you easily excuse your actions with the
thought, *That's just the way I am*? Making excuses for your bad
behavior does not make it right in God's eyes. The truth is, you
do have the power to change! Through the strength of Jesus
Christ, everyone has the ability to live a godly life, exercising
discipline and self-control. The choice is yours!

You can be victorious over selfish desires by claiming
Philippians 4:13 (NKJV), "I can do all things through Christ
who strengthens me." When you practice self-control, you
reflect God's own character. He doesn't make rash decisions,
nor does He make mistakes! His plan is perfect and so is His
timing. Remember, He never gets in a hurry, but He always gets
there on time!

It doesn't matter if you are struggling with appetite, gossiping,
lying, cheating, anger, or any other character imperfection—
whatever it is, God will give you a fresh start, just as if you've
never sinned! Thankfully, God doesn't rub your face in your
transgression, or say, "I told you so." Pray and ask Jesus to give
you more self-control, and with His Holy Spirit power, you will
begin to change . . . one thought, one word, one action at a time!

You Belong to Me

Commit your way to the Lord;
trust in him, and he will act.

Psalm 37:5 (NRSV)

———◆———

It's important for your Christian growth to stop and read your spiritual thermometer from time to time, so that you can assess where you are in your walk with God. It's far too easy to get so caught up with the business of life that your time with Him starts to decrease. Without even realizing it, morning devotions fall to the wayside and even your prayers are few and far between. It isn't long before you find yourself sleeping in instead of attending church, and before you know it, God isn't on your mind at all!

When God seems distant and you have lost the joy of loving and serving your heavenly Father, you are in a vulnerable and dangerous place! You need to stay so close to Jesus that nothing can separate you from Him! You are weak, but He is strong, and He invites you to lean on Him for courage and the determination to resist temptations in this world.

Ask God to open your eyes and allow you to see what He sees. You can't change if you don't know what's broke! So ask yourself, *Who do I belong to—God or Satan?* If you truly don't know the answer, go to your Bible and you will hear God speak to you in His kind and loving voice . . . "You belong to Me!"

No Class Distinctions

And walk in love, as Christ also has loved us.

Ephesians 5:2 (NKJV)

A ll throughout the Bible, God asks us to love each other—as He loves us! When Christ was here on earth, He set a wonderful example of how to live our lives, including how to *love*! Jesus loved everyone! He loved the dirtiest beggar in the street to the richest man in the land! He made no class distinctions as to race, wealth, or positions of importance when He gave a kind word, stopped to listen, or performed miracles.

Every decision God makes . . . is made out of love! In fact, Jesus loves us so much that He died on a cross to save us from our sins. Love just doesn't get deeper than that! This should be our criteria as well. Before making a decision, we need to ask ourselves, *Am I motivated by love, or am I influenced by power because I have the right and the authority to make this decision?* In the judgment day, we will have to answer for every decision we make!

The only way to know if we are making wise choices is to be led by the Holy Spirit! We need to ask God to place more love in our hearts! Decisions made for love's sake will give us joy and happiness such as we have never known and draw us even closer to Jesus! God wants us to love as He loves . . . unconditionally!

Live in the Present

*But seek first the kingdom of God and His righteousness,
and all these things shall be added to you. Therefore
do not worry about tomorrow, for tomorrow will
worry about its own things.*

Matthew 6:33-34 (NKJV)

People miss out on so many blessings because they haven't learned to live each day to the fullest! If they are depressed, they are usually living in the past, moping about the *good ole days* and how wonderful they used to be. There are those who find change difficult and so they wallow in the pit of depression, not knowing how to climb out.

Then there are those who are on the opposite end of the spectrum who live in the future. They dream and plan for the day when all the wonderful things will happen to them, certain that only then will they finally be happy! They are usually anxious, worried, and live in a constant state of stress!

But as Christians, we know that God wants us to plan for the future, but live in the present, making the most of each day as if it were our last! We can only do this by trusting our past, present, and future to Jesus! He knows the end from the beginning and what is best for us. He will never let us down! As long as we are holding God's hand, we don't have to worry about tomorrow . . . or ten years down the road. Nor do we need to be all sad and depressed because life isn't like it used to be! Every day with Jesus . . . is sweeter than the day before!

Forgiveness Required

And be kind to one another, tenderhearted, forgiving one another, even as God in Christ forgave you.

Ephesians 4:32 (NKJV)

———◆———

Whenever someone has hurt our feelings, done us wrong, or has treated us unfairly, it's human nature to dislike that person and even become bitter and angry. The longer all those ugly feelings are allowed to remain in our hearts, the stronger the weeds of hate grow, until eventually, they destroys any hope of happiness. God wants us to live the abundant life He has planned for us and that's the reason He has commanded us to *forgive*.

In fact, the Bible says in Matthew 6:14 (NIV), "If you forgive other people when they sin against you, your heavenly Father will also forgive you." Notice the requirement of the forgiveness of *our* sins: *if* you forgive others. God also commands us in Colossians 3:13 (NIV), "Bear with each other and forgive one another if any of you has a grievance against someone. Forgive as the Lord forgave you."

When we are hurt so deeply that it's not possible for us to forgive, we can pray and ask God to put forgiveness in our hearts, and He will give us Holy Spirit power to do just that! And when we do, His sweet peace will flow through us, melting all that bitterness and anger away.

Powerful Weapons

Take the shield of faith, with which you will be able to quench all the flaming arrows of the evil one.

Ephesians 6:16 (NRSV)

Just as God has a special plan for your life, don't forget that Satan has one too! In fact the Bible says in John 10:10 (NKJV), "The thief does not come except to steal, and to kill, and to destroy." The devil's plan is downright lethal, which is why God gave you powerful weapons of mass destruction to strike down the enemy!

When Satan tries to discourage you, hit him with the weapon of *praise*! It's impossible to sing praises to God and be discouraged at the same time! When the devil tries to pressure you to go against God's Holy Word—fight back with *obedience*! God will give you the victory—all you need to do is allow Him to fight your battles!

Another powerful weapon is *faith*! Putting your full faith and trust in God is an amazing defense against the devil's doubt-filled arrows. Equip yourself with the *whole* armor of Christ and you will win an awesome victory! And let's not forget the most effective weapon of all—the ammunition of *prayer*! Nothing can penetrate your shield of faith if you are directly connected to your heavenly Father!

Remember, God will give you the power to fight the enemy no matter what he throws at you! So put your spiritual armor on and get ready for battle against the devil's attacks . . . using the powerful weapons God gave you!

Reading God's Word

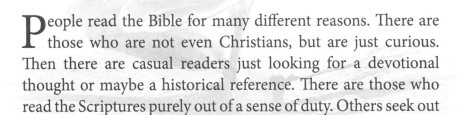

*Apply your heart to instruction, and your
ears to words of knowledge.*
Proverbs 23:12 (NKJV)

People read the Bible for many different reasons. There are those who are not even Christians, but are just curious. Then there are casual readers just looking for a devotional thought or maybe a historical reference. There are those who read the Scriptures purely out of a sense of duty. Others seek out passages of Psalms for praise and worship. Some read because they are despondent, at the end of their rope and reach out for some kind of *hope.*

There are those who out of sheer boredom have picked up a Bible from a drawer of their hotel room and gave their heart to Jesus. God's Holy Word is the most printed book in all the world and has also caused the most controversy. It is the most powerful, insightful, inspiring book you could ever read. Even though there are numerous reasons *why* people are motivated to read it, the most important reason is for inspiration and instruction! It is an incredible source of insight and wisdom, for no one is a better teacher or counselor than God! His complete fail-proof plan for your journey through life is all detailed in His Word, including His full plan of salvation.

But before you even open your Bible to read, pray and ask for Holy Spirit guidance and understanding. Pick up your Bible today and you'll soon find that the most valuable time of your day is the time you spend alone in God's Word.

Key to Your Heart

*My child, give me your heart, and let
your eyes observe my ways.*

Proverbs 23:26 (NRSV)

Understanding just *who* God is and how much He loves us is directly related to our desire to serve Him as Lord and Savior. Simply put, it's really *all about the love*! If we didn't truly know that God *is* love and that no one could possibly love us more, then why would we want to give our hearts to Him? But when we start to understand the depth of His love, we can't help but want to give our hearts to Him and serve Him!

Sometimes we hold back on fully surrendering *our* will to *His* will, because there is something in our lives we just don't want to give up! We're afraid that giving our hearts to God will force us into losing something precious that we are not willing to live without—such as an unhealthy relationship, a successful career, or a cherished lifestyle. But when we are clinging to our treasured sins, it is usually because we don't have a clear picture of just *who* God is! We don't fully acknowledge that He is a loving and just God! If we knew that, then it would be easy to turn our hearts over to Him, trusting fully that He is a powerful God who wants only what is best for us and has the power to take care of us.

Give God the key to your heart and surrender your troubles, weaknesses, and, yes, your secret sins to Him. He will replace your pain and heartache with His gift of joy—it's life-changing!

Accepting Grace

"My grace is sufficient for you, for My strength is made perfect in weakness."

2 Corinthians 12:9 (NKJV)

There are many Christians who don't fully realize the meaning of God's grace. They believe that they need to be perfect before becoming a candidate for mercy. But God's grace and mercy is extended to all those who ask for it. No matter what the devil wants you to think—you simply cannot earn grace.

The definition of grace is "to get something you do not deserve; unmerited favor." Too often though, people wait and suffer through horrible guilt, agony, and remorse before drawing upon the grace of God. Their self-worth is too low to even imagine how much God loves them. Satan fills their minds with self-loathing thoughts: *I'm not important. I don't matter, it's like I'm invisible. I'm a nobody, why would anyone love me?*

But don't listen to the devil's lies. He wants to make you feel like a worthless, no-good idiot, but God wants to remind you that you are a highly loved and treasured child of the King of the Universe! Oh, how much better it would be if you reached out to God for His mercy . . . at your very time of need. He will give you the strength to face each trial, no matter how bad you messed up or how terrible you feel about yourself.

Regardless of what kind of trouble you are in, call upon Jesus today and accept His gift of grace.

No Regrets

*For godly sorrow produces repentance leading to salvation,
not to be regretted; but the sorrow of the world produces death.*

2 Corinthians 7:10 (NKJV)

Wouldn't it be wonderful if we could live each day with *no regrets*? Can you imagine what that would be like? We wouldn't have to be sorry for saying the wrong thing, acting out in anger, or being unkind. There would be no cutting someone off in traffic, getting impatient with a sales clerk, or snapping at a loved one. And there would be no need to feel ashamed, guilty, or bitter—because there would be . . . no regrets!

Well, there is a place of *no regrets*, and that is our heavenly home. Oh, how awesome it will be to live for all eternity where we will have pure minds and motives and we won't say or do things we'll be sorry for. Just think for a moment what that will be like! There will be no more sin in our heavenly home— no pain, tears, sadness, or death. No disappointments, worry, arguments, or frustration! No auto accidents, killings, or terrorist attacks. It's downright mind-blowing!

Oh, how glorious that will be! And we won't have to wait long, because Jesus *is* coming soon! We need to make sure our hearts are fully surrendered to Him and let nothing stand between us and our Savior! Jesus loves us so much that He doesn't want anyone to be left behind! I can't wait to be neighbors with you in heaven soon and live our lives with *no regrets*!

Interceding for Others

*Confess your trespasses to one another, and pray for one
another, that you may be healed. The effective, fervent
prayer of a righteous man avails much.*

James 5:16 (NKJV)

It's all too easy to go to the Lord in prayer about our own
wants and needs, but how often do we actually lift someone
else up in prayer? There are people in our lives who are not only
struggling physically and emotionally, but spiritually as well.
Instead of hearing the pitiful tale of woe, shaking our heads
thinking, *That's so sad*, and walking away . . . we need to *pray*
for that person!

Yes, we can intercede in prayer for others, including our
loved ones, friends, and even strangers. To *intercede* means
to lift someone up in prayer when they are too weak to pray
for themselves—when we present their needs and plead their
case before the throne room of God! Jesus set an example of
intercessory prayer when He was on the cross praying for God
to forgive those who were crucifying Him.

We have the privilege of interceding for others in prayer and
expecting that God will respond! Oh, how important it is to
pray for each other. We need to intercede, for each time we pray
for someone else, we are inviting Jesus to work in their life. It
is the most important way to minister to others, and in return,
our own lives will be blessed! Praying for someone is the most
important act of love you could possibly do for them!

Guarding Your Heart

Because Your lovingkindness is better than life,
my lips shall praise You.

Psalm 63:3 (NKJV)

People who hide behind their protective walls will never enjoy close and meaningful relationships with others. To be close to someone requires communication, and not just the superficial talk that most people resort to. If you want a relationship with someone, you must *share your heart*. Confide your fears as well as your hopes, joys, and dreams.

The more you open up, the closer you will become and the more comfortable you will feel about telling what's on your mind. Sharing details of your life creates a bond of friendship, such as telling your friend about what happened at work, describing the delicious entreé you ate at lunch, or relating a witnessing experience you just had. But, let's face it—*sharing* can be scary. There is always the risk that the person you trust will betray your confidence, so it's good to *go slowly* in your relationship and build trust before you bare your soul.

But the one person that you never have to worry about is your best Friend, Jesus! He will never sell you out, throw you under the bus, or hurt your heart. Jesus is 100% trustworthy! He loves to hear all about what makes you happy as well as your worries, heartaches, and disappointments. He wants you to come to Him for the little things *and* the big things! Falling in love with Jesus is the best relationship that you could possibly have, and best of all . . . you never have to guard your heart!

Alone with God

Give unto the LORD the glory due to His name;
worship the LORD in the beauty of holiness.

Psalm 29:2 (NKJV)

————◇————

When it comes to daily devotions and *being alone* with God, we tell ourselves there is simply not enough time in our day. But if we're really honest, we do have the time, we just choose to do other things! Everyone has the same hours in a day, but we all make different choices as to what we do in those hours. Most often, we choose to spend our time doing all the things that are most important to us!

Trying to balance all the demands of our busy lives can be exhausting, but, oh, how sad that almost everything else takes precedence over spending time with our Creator, King of the Universe! We tell ourselves that *tomorrow* we'll make time, but tomorrow never comes! Whenever we lose sight of *who* God is and what He has done for us, we lose our desire and motivation to spend time with Him.

When someone is *really* important to us, we make time for them, and so it is with God! The more we love Him, the deeper our desire to be close to Him. Reading the Bible and praying becomes precious time that we guard fiercely. God wants us to love Him so much that we long for time in His presence! And when we truly fall in love with Jesus, spending time with Him won't be something we feel we *have* to do, but rather something that we look forward to. We'll count it a privilege to have *alone time* to communicate directly with our Lord and Savior!

Paper-Plate Mentality

I know what it is to be in need, and I know what it is to have plenty. I have learned the secret of being content in any and every situation.

Philippians 4:12 (NIV)

———◆———

Some people live just waiting for the day when something wonderful will happen and falsely think that *then* they will finally be happy! Instead of enjoying life and giving thanks to God for today, they go through the motions of living, waiting for that *special* moment, when they marry the *perfect* person, get that *perfect* job or their *perfect* dream comes true.

Instead of being content to use paper plates while your fine china sits in the cabinet, choose to live life to the fullest! Get rid of your paper-plate mentality and enjoy each and every day that God gives you. Don't wait for your life to be perfect before you choose happiness. Allow God to plan your future, knowing and trusting that He loves you more than anyone else possibly could and He wants what is best for you.

It's dangerous to travel life's journey without Jesus as your Navigator. He wants to give you the desires of your heart, and there's no safer person to trust than your Lord and Savior! James 4:14-15 warns us that life is short, and the most important thing is to do God's will! More than anything He wants you to spend eternity with Him in heaven where each day will be more glorious than the day before! Real happiness and joy comes from making God first in your life and doing His will. Start today by praying, "Lord, what would You have me to do? I'm Yours!"

Freedom of Being Loved

*How priceless is your unfailing love, O God! People take
refuge in the shadow of your wings.*

Psalm 36:7 (NIV)

Fear of being unloved is the basic reason for poor self-confidence, inability to move forward, and lack of motivation. The old expression "Love makes the world go round" is absolutely true, because God *is* love, and without Him, life is empty, meaningless, and downright scary!

Knowing with absolute certainty that you are loved gives you power to go forward with confidence and holy boldness! It allows you to open the door of uncertainty without fear and trepidation, because you know God loves you and is with you! You can throw fear out the window and relax, enjoying each day . . . because you are loved!

Everyone wants to be loved by family and friends, but there is no one who will love you more than Jesus! If you increase your time praying and studying God's Word, the more you will know and understand just how much God loves you.

Basking in the joy of His unconditional, deep, and abiding love will help you discover new courage and confidence that you never knew before! The freedom of *being loved* will allow you to change who you are today . . . and become the person God created you to be!

Never Alone

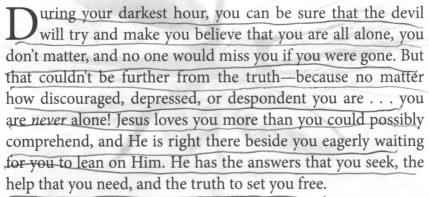

Be strong and of good courage, do not fear nor be afraid of them; for the LORD your God, He is the One who goes with you. He will not leave you nor forsake you.

Deuteronomy 31:6 (NKJV)

During your darkest hour, you can be sure that the devil will try and make you believe that you are all alone, you don't matter, and no one would miss you if you were gone. But that couldn't be further from the truth—because no matter how discouraged, depressed, or despondent you are . . . you are *never* alone! Jesus loves you more than you could possibly comprehend, and He is right there beside you eagerly waiting for you to lean on Him. He has the answers that you seek, the help that you need, and the truth to set you free.

It's important to always stay close to Him because God alone is your strength and the source of power to fight the enemy. The Bible says in John 15:4 (NIV), "Remain in me, as I also remain in you. No branch can bear fruit by itself; it must remain in the vine. Neither can you bear fruit unless you remain in me." In other words, when Jesus says, "Remain in me," He is asking you to stay close to Him, because He wants to protect you.

In Isaiah 30:21 (NIV), we're told, "Whether you turn to the right or to the left, your ears will hear a voice behind you, saying 'This is the way; walk in it.'" God wants you to know that no matter what, you don't have to be afraid, because He is with you—you are never alone!

Toxic Friendships

*A friend loves at all times, and a brother is
born for adversity.*
Proverbs 17:17 (NKJV)

Having a friend you can count on and who will love you no matter what is a wonderful blessing. Life is more enjoyable when shared, and it's easier to deal with heartache and burdens when a friend is there to help you through. A *real* friend is someone you can confide in, lean on, and can trust will share your joys as well as your sorrows. But if jealousy rears its ugly head, even the best of friendships can be destroyed in an instant.

People who have been friends for years suddenly no longer speak—all because of pride, hurt feelings, blame, and misunderstanding. When a friend resents your success or is jealous of the attention or recognition you receive, love cannot survive, and it is hard to build back trust. Some friendships are so toxic, they need to be severed completely. When that happens, you still need to *love* and *forgive* that person, even if they haven't asked for forgiveness, but it doesn't mean that God expects you to be close friends again.

Thankfully, Jesus is your *best* Friend, who loves you with an everlasting love. He knows your heart more than your closest earthly friend. He knows where you come from, your thoughts, your feelings, the person you used to be, and who you are today! He will never turn on you, talk behind your back, or resent your accomplishments. Most of all, God's friendship and love will last for eternity!

Change the World

*Only fear the LORD, and serve him faithfully
with all your heart; for consider what great things he
has done for you.*

1 Samuel 12:24 (NRSV)

———◆———

You may think you are too small and insignificant in this world to make a difference, but that's simply not true. Everyone has the opportunity, with Holy Spirit power, to *change the world*—but only if you are willing to allow God to take charge of your life. With God's power and strength, there is nothing that you cannot do!

The problem is that most people are too afraid to give up control and they refuse to follow God's leading. But you never have to be afraid to go where God takes you. He *is* trustworthy and He will never call you to do a task without giving you everything you need to accomplish it successfully! Proverbs 16:3 (NIV) tells us, "Commit to the LORD whatever you do, and he will establish your plans." And in Colossians 3:23 (NIV), we're told, "Whatever you do, work at it with all your heart, as working for the Lord, not for human masters,"

When you surrender your heart and life to Jesus, you become changed. You no longer see life the same way. You look at situations and challenges differently, because God has equipped you to handle them with grace, integrity, loyalty, and tender mercy. And when you become obedient, God is able to use you to change the world around you. Listen for God's voice calling you today—and answer saying, "Here am I Lord, send me."

Wake-Up Call

*I sought the LORD, and He heard me, and
delivered me from all my fears.*

Psalm 34:4 (NKJV)

———◈———

It's not God's desire that we live in fear, for fear is the opposite of *faith*. However, there are times when God uses fear to wake us up to face our own faults and failures. This was certainly the case for Jacob when he heard his brother, Esau, was coming to see him, along with 400 men. Jacob was absolutely terrified and quickly put a plan into action. The Bible says in Genesis 32:7-8 (NIV), "In great fear and distress Jacob divided the people . . . into two groups . . . 'If Esau comes and attacks one group, the group that is left may escape.'"

God responded to Jacob's passionate prayer for protection and touched the heart of not only Jacob, but his brother as well. Jacob was impressed to send his brother gifts and ask for forgiveness, and Esau's heart was softened, forgiving the sin his brother committed so many years before.

The fear that had been in Jacob's heart actually helped him see his own faults, and God gave him the strength and courage to make things right. Instead of allowing fear to destroy you, let it be a *wake-up call* to examine your life, making the changes God wants you to make and turning your fears over to God.

Knowing God's Will

Trust in the LORD with all your heart, and lean not on your own understanding; in all your ways acknowledge Him, and He shall direct your paths.

Proverbs 3:5-6 (NKJV)

If you're faced with a potentially life-changing decision and you just don't know which way to turn, it can be quite frustrating—especially when you've prayed and prayed and still don't have a clue what God has in mind. You may even feel a bit irritated because you can't seem to get an answer from God. Unfortunately, if you're looking for a delivery from heaven or the sound of God's voice on your voicemail, you will be sorely disappointed. So, the question comes to mind: Can anyone actually really know God's will? The answer: Absolutely!

In fact, there are many people mentioned in the Bible who knew God's will, such as Enoch, Abraham, Moses, Peter, Paul, Joseph, and the list goes on and on. One thing that all of them had in common was they spent time communicating with God! If you develop a consistent and frequent habit of prayer and study of God's Word, you'll find your heart opened, with a clearer vision of where God is leading you.

The Bible says in James 1:5 (NIV), "If any of you lacks wisdom, you should ask God, who gives generously to all without finding fault, and it will be given to you." It's also important to trust God's perfect plan and you'll find He will reveal His will in His perfect timing—just listen to the Holy Spirit's guiding.

Thankful for Life

May He grant you according to your heart's desire,
and fulfill all your purpose.

Psalm 20:4 (NKJV)

If you're complaining because you don't have the perfect life you always dreamed of just *stop* . . . and count your blessings! Make a list of all the things you're unhappy about, and then make a list of all your blessings. Without a doubt, your blessing list will be much longer!

Don't forget to list *all* your blessings, starting with the fact that you woke up this morning! Yes, being alive is definitely a privilege that is denied to many. Just imagine all the young people who died too soon? Wouldn't they count it a blessing to have kicked cancer and watched their children grow, or to have escaped an auto accident and graduated college, got married, have kids, and enjoyed living?

Sometimes people can be so busy complaining about what they *don't* have, that they fail to appreciate what they *do* have! Instead of hating your life, embrace it. Hatred never solves problems—it only creates them. Ask God to come into your heart and live a life that is pleasing to Him. You'll find that you'll no longer feel like a failure for not measuring up to your own expectations. Instead, you'll feel loved, appreciated, and cherished by God—someone who loves you more than anyone else ever could! So when you open your eyes each morning, before even getting out of bed, pray, "Thank you, God—I'm alive!"

State of Hopelessness

He gives power to the weak, and to those who have no
might He increases strength.

Isaiah 40:29 (NKJV)

———————

It seems everywhere you turn there is sorrow, tears, suffering, and death. It can be so overwhelming that your soul grows weary from the weight of discouragement and your body screams out for strength to go on. But before you are tempted to succumb to a state of hopelessness, cry out to Jesus to give you strength.

The Bible says in Isaiah 41:10 (NKJV), "Fear not, for I am with you; be not dismayed, for I am your God. I will strengthen you, yes, I will help you, I will uphold you with My righteous right hand." As long as you are walking with Jesus, you have nothing to fear, for God will provide you with everything you need to face each day.

So be patient and wait upon God, that you might receive His strength as promised in Isaiah 40:31 (KJV): "But they that wait upon the LORD shall renew their strength; they shall mount up with wings as eagles; they shall run, and not be weary; and they shall walk, and not faint." Ask God to take away all discouragement, doubt, and fear and replace them with His strength to make it through every challenging and stressful situation. All you need to do is pray, "Lord, give me strength."

God Rewards Obedience

You shall not add to the word which I command you, nor take from it, that you may keep the commandments of the Lord your God which I command you.

Deuteronomy 4:2 (NKJV)

There are Christians who work hard in church activities and are even well known for doing acts of kindness in their communities, but they have never once asked God what *He* wants them to do. Sometimes you want to settle into your comfort zone just going through the motions of being a *good Christian,* not wanting to fully trust in God's plan. But it doesn't matter how much time you spend witnessing, passing out Bibles or feeding the homeless, unless God asked you to do it, it's for nothing!

The Bible makes it very clear in Matthew 7:21-23 (NKJV), "Not everyone who says to Me, 'Lord, Lord,' shall enter the kingdom of heaven, but he who does the will of My Father in heaven. Many will say to Me in that day, 'Lord, Lord, have we not prophesied in Your name, cast out demons in Your name, and done many wonders in Your name?' And then I will declare to them, 'I never knew you; depart from Me, you who practice lawlessness!' "

It is not enough to be willing to serve Jesus, you must pray and ask God to show you what He wants you to do for Him. You can trust Jesus with your life, for He loves you more than anyone else possibly could! And when you surrender *your* will to *His* will, that's when God can use you the most! And don't forget, God rewards obedience . . . with eternal life!

Brokenhearted

*The Lord is near to those who have a broken heart, and
saves such as have a contrite spirit.*

Psalm 34:18 (NKJV)

We live in a world full of heartache and pain, and unfortunately, that will not change until Jesus comes. One of the worst forms of heartache is the pain of losing a loved one. Of course, when someone dies, it especially hurts knowing they are no longer there to share your life with, and just the thought that they won't be there for all the special moments and milestones in your life feels unbearable.

The pain of a lost relationship can be just as painful. It's devastating when an engagement is broken or your marriage partner walks away and leaves a terrible, deep hole in your heart that it seems no one can fill. Love that is not returned leaves a hurt so deep, you might feel that you will never love again! You may even start building a high wall around your heart just to prevent ever feeling that pain again.

Fortunately, there is someone who loves you with an everlasting, unending, unmeasurable kind of love, and that *someone* . . . is God! He not only loves you, but He is building a mansion for you right now so that you can live with Him in heaven forever, where there will be no more broken hearts, but only joy and happiness. When your heart is breaking, remember that Jesus is the *only* Healer of hearts, and He is waiting to wrap you in His comforting arms of love!

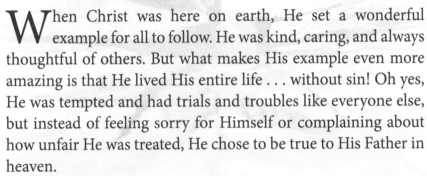

Jesus, Our Role Model

For to this you were called, because Christ
also suffered for us, leaving us an example, that
you should follow His steps.

1 Peter 2:21 (NKJV)

When Christ was here on earth, He set a wonderful example for all to follow. He was kind, caring, and always thoughtful of others. But what makes His example even more amazing is that He lived His entire life . . . without sin! Oh yes, He was tempted and had trials and troubles like everyone else, but instead of feeling sorry for Himself or complaining about how unfair He was treated, He chose to be true to His Father in heaven.

Jesus was so closely connected to God that He never considered acting in a sinful manner, even for a moment. Christ should be our role model, for as long as we commit our lives to Him, He will give us the strength and the power to overcome sin!

Some may say, "As long as I'm a good person, I obey the law, and I don't hurt anyone . . . then I'll go to heaven!" However, they are sorely mistaken—being a *good* person is not our ticket to Paradise. We need to *know* our Savior and surrender our hearts and lives to Him. Don't wait any longer—allow Jesus to be your role model starting right now and plan to spend eternity with Him in your heavenly home!

Cookie-Cutter Christian

"He who is without sin among you, let him
throw a stone at her first."

John 8:7 (NKJV)

———◆———

Why is it that the world judges Christians so harshly? There's an unspoken standard of excellence that is set the moment you give your heart to Christ. All of a sudden, you are supposed to be *perfect*, and if you fall below the expected line of perfection, then you are suddenly no longer a *Christian* in the eyes of others. This includes fellow Christians as well as non-believers. Even atheists know that a professed Christian is *supposed* to "turn the other cheek," keep the temper in check, and act in a *godly* manner, and if you stumble and act differently, then you are judged. But what the world seems to forget is that there's no such thing as a *cookie-cutter Christian*.

God created His children to be different—each with a unique personality. And each Christian reacts differently to the temptations of this world because everyone's measure of faith is different. The more time you spend with Jesus, the more you become like Him. Some are *baby* Christians as they begin their new walk with God, while others have had a close relationship with Him for years, daily spending time in prayer and studying His Word. It's only natural that baby Christians will not react in the same way as someone who has *always* held God's hand. Instead of judging, lend a helping hand, lift up the weak, and ask God to use you to help others along this life's journey.

Crossroads of Life

If any of you lacks wisdom, let him ask of God, who gives to all liberally and without reproach, and it will be given to him.

James 1:5 (NKJV)

Whenever we are at the crossroads of life, trying to decide which way to turn, the best thing to do is go to God for wisdom. Only He knows the end from the beginning and what is best for us! But sometimes, trying to decipher what is God's will from what is ours can be quite confusing.

The Bible gives the best advice in Jeremiah 6:16 (NIV), "Stand at the crossroads and look; ask for the ancient paths, ask where the good way is, and walk in it, and you'll find rest for your souls." Sometimes God's answers come through a friend, a certain sign, or just a strong impression from the Holy Spirit. One thing you can be sure of is that God will never ask you to do anything illegal, immoral, or that would go against His Holy Word.

Be patient and wait for God's perfect plan and His perfect timing. You will know God's will because your mind won't be in turmoil thinking you made a mistake, but rather you will feel a peace come over you, confident that you made the right decision. If after making a decision you are awake all night, tossing and turning, chances are it was the wrong decision!

When standing at the crossroads of life, pray and ask God not only to *know His will*, but for the strength and courage to carry it out.

Juicy Gossip

*Let no corrupt word proceed out of your mouth, but
what is good for necessary edification, that it may
impart grace to the hearers.*

Ephesians 4:29 (NKJV)

No sugar coating, no glossing over the facts—there will be no gossipers in heaven. Gossiping is the first thing people do when they get angry with someone because they want to tear down that person's reputation to all who will listen.

And social media has made spreading lies happen at an astonishing speed! Getting even by gossiping might momentarily provide a morbid sense of pleasure, but that evil satisfaction quickly disintegrates and is replaced with guilt. It's that horrible feeling when sin separates you from God! Pure and simple, destroying the reputations of others will destroy your own relationship with your heavenly Father!

Words you speak have the ability to either tear someone down . . . or lift someone up! Anytime you talk bad about someone, spread juicy gossip about them, or manipulate the minds of others by planting false ideas or exaggerated facts—it is a sin—whether you are the one who is spreading the gossip or the one listening. The Bible says in Proverbs 20:19 not to even associate with someone who gossips!

Pray this prayer in Psalm 141:3 (NKJV), "Set a guard, O LORD, over my mouth; keep watch over the door of my lips." Determine in your heart to always speak kindly of others and when someone starts to tell you some juicy gossip, walk away!

An Uphill Battle

Therefore encourage one another and build up each other,
as indeed you are doing.

1 Thessalonians 5:11 (NRSV)

———◆———

Sometimes you may feel life is a constant struggle. It's as if you are always climbing uphill, tripping over rocks and debris along the way. No matter what you do, it seems you just can't get a break! Someone or something is always knocking you down. During these times, it helps to know you are not alone, and that a friend is there to strengthen and encourage.

It is a blessing to have Christian friends who will lift you up, not bring you down. The last thing you need is friends like Job had . . . who told him to curse God and die! And don't forget about your best Friend, Jesus, who will never leave you or forsake you.

When you pray, be honest with God. Tell Him how you feel—your innermost fears and concerns. Some people question why they have to pray when God knows everything anyway! And the truth is, God does know our thoughts, but He *responds* to our prayers! Life doesn't have to be an uphill battle when you pour your heart out to God, for He is full of grace and mercy. No one loves you more than He does, and He will listen with a heart of love and give you the strength, courage, and ability to face every challenge. And best of all—He can do more than just listen. He alone has the power to save!

Calling the Shots

But blessed is the one who trusts in the LORD,
whose confidence is in him.

Jeremiah 17:7 (NIV)

———◆———

People that work in the television industry know just how hard it is to produce a film and that it takes a talented team of people to make it happen. Few people read the long list of credits at the end, but in addition to the actors, there's wardrobe personal, makeup artists, set designers, audio technicians, lighting crew, camera operators, directors, and the list goes on and on. But of all the crew, the producer is the one with the vision and calls the shots. The crew members might all have different opinions on how it should be done, but if the actors listened to everyone else, it would only be mass confusion and end in disaster. Many times the actors have no idea *why* the producer insists on a certain way of doing things, but when they listen and carry out the instructions, the production runs smoothly! It's a *win-win*!

There are days when we wake up and wish we had a crew to help us get things done. We would make a lot less mistakes if someone else was telling us the right direction to go and writing our scripts of what to say and do! Life would be so much easier wouldn't it? The good news is, we *do* have that option available to us right now! That's because God is the master Producer and stands ready to lead, guide, and direct us in all that we do and say—we need only to ask and trust Him to *call the shots*!

God's Trusted Friends

*You are My friends if you do whatever I command you.
. . . I have called you friends, for all things that I heard
from My Father I have made known to you.*

John 15:14-15 (NKJV)

The Bible mentions many times special people that God chose to be His trusted friends—those with whom He shared things that He didn't share with everyone. He gave them His plan of action, His motives, and even revealed His desires. He chose friends who *chose* Him and He was close to because of all the time they spent together.

God knew their hearts and that they were loyal and trustworthy. There is only one way to become one of God's trusted friends and that is to spend time with Him every day! Talk to Him and allow Him to be your very *best* friend!" There is no better friend you could ever have! He listens to the prayers of His children and takes into consideration their requests and heart's desires as He moves forward with His answers.

The Bible tells of times when God even altered His original plans because of the persistent prayers of His friends who had proved worthy of His trust. Every real and true friendship has two main requirements: loyalty and trust. Without those two characteristics, there is no real friendship.

So it is with God—He values your friendship, which is demonstrated by an unselfish, relentless pursuit of His will . . . no matter the cost! Won't you decide today to become one of God's trusted friends?

Our Amazing God

The LORD your God in your midst, the Mighty One, will
save; He will rejoice over you with gladness, He will quiet
you with His love, He will rejoice over you with singing.

Zephaniah 3:17 (NKJV)

No matter how much time you spend with God, you will never reach the end of what you can learn about Him. You can read the Bible cover to cover a hundred times and you will still learn and discover new Bible truths. That's because God's wisdom is beyond anything we can possibly comprehend and His mind more vast than the universe.

In Proverbs 4:11 (NIV), we're told, "I instruct you in the way of wisdom and lead you along straight paths." The same goes for the power of God, which knows no end. You'll never hear of an instance where God's power was not enough to accomplish His will. God never *lacks* power, but rather, He *gives* power! The Bible says in Isaiah 40:29 (NIV), "He gives strength to the weary and increases the power of the weak." But here is the best news yet about our amazing God: His love never fails and you will never reach the limits of His love!

This has been the case since the beginning of time! There are those who have rejected God's love, but He has never rejected them. He loves all His children so much that He can't imagine heaven without them! There's a beautiful promise in Isaiah 54:10 (NIV) that you can claim for your own: "'Though the mountains be shaken and the hills be removed, yet my unfailing love for you will not be shaken nor my covenant of peace be removed,' says the LORD, who has compassion on you."

The Spirit Is Willing

*When He came to the place, He said to them, "Pray that
you may not enter into temptation."*
Luke 22:40 (NKJV)

When you become a *Christian*, you make a commitment to
live a life fully surrendered to God. But no matter how
hard you try, there may be times when your spirit is willing,
but your flesh is weak. You *want* to do the right thing, but the
second you take your eyes off Jesus, you fall and end up in
Satan's trap. The apostle Paul struggled with this as he stated
in Romans 7:15-17 (NIV), "I do not understand what I do. For
what I want to do I do not do, but what I hate I do. And if I do
what I do not want to do, I agree that the law is good. As it is, it
is no longer I myself who do it, but it is sin living in me."

If you make a mistake or do something wrong, God doesn't
want you to be filled with guilt, darkness, and hopelessness.
Because He loves you, He gave His life for your transgressions
and thus provided freedom from sin. Romans 8:1-3 (NKJV)
says, "There is therefore now no condemnation to those who
are in Christ Jesus . . . For what the law could not do in that it
was weak through the flesh, God did by sending His own Son in
the likeness of sinful flesh, on account of sin: He condemned sin
in the flesh." Avoid Satan's pitfalls by keeping your eyes focused
on Jesus Christ. Mark 14:38 (NKJV) says, "Watch and pray, lest
you enter into temptation. The spirit indeed is willing, but the
flesh is weak."

Blessing of Contentment

Now godliness with contentment is great gain.
1 Timothy 6:6 (NKJV)

We are living in a world that places a high value on wealth, fame, and prestige. It doesn't help that television and movies give people a false sense of what happiness is all about. We watch our favorite characters jet set to exotic vacations, wear designer clothes, drive fancy cars, and live the life of luxury. Without even realizing it, the desire to have all those things that we don't have is implanted into our minds! But herein lies the danger: we can be so focused on getting what we *think* we want that we lose sight of the blessings we already have!

Keeping our minds set on earthly goals is Satan's plan to distract us from our *heavenly* goal. As long as we measure happiness in terms of obtaining *the impossible dream*, we will never be happy, nor will we be preparing to spend eternity with our Savior! The Bible tells us in Philippians 4:11 (NRSV), "I have learned to be content with whatever I have."

There is great danger in developing a love for worldly pleasures because it takes our focus from spiritual things. We're told in Philippians 4:19 (NKJV), "And my God shall supply all your need according to His riches in glory by Christ Jesus." All we need to do is keep our eyes on Jesus and trust Him to provide. Instead of wishing for an expensive home, a position of power, or great wealth, learn to be content with what God has already given and discover the joy and blessing of contentment!

The Devil's Table

Behold, children are a heritage from the LORD,
the fruit of the womb is a reward.
Psalm 127:3 (NKJV)

———◆———

Raising children to love Jesus is more challenging today than ever before. Satan knows his time is short and is desperately devising evil plots to lure kids away from Jesus. He doesn't care how he does it—as long as children turn their backs on God, he wins! The Bible says in 1 Peter 5:8 (NIV), "Be alert and of sober mind. Your enemy the devil prowls around like a roaring lion looking for someone to devour."

It's critically important to remove all the obstacles and roadblocks the devil puts up, so that we keep our children's eyes focused on Christ. Today's world provides more than enough satanic distractions with messages of hate, violence, and sex—all cleverly disguised and delivered in a neat little package via video games, smartphone apps, television, books, music, and so much more.

And surprisingly enough, parents are falling for it. They ignorantly give their children whatever they want without even a thought about the evil influence that comes with it. It's no wonder kids think church is boring and have trouble paying attention. Parents, guard your children's hearts by feeding them spiritual food and getting rid of anything that comes from the devil's table! Matthew 19:14 (KJV) says, "But Jesus said, 'Suffer little children, and forbid them not, to come unto me: for of such is the kingdom of heaven.'"

Two Choices and Only Two

The name of the Lord is a strong tower;
the righteous run to it and are safe.

Proverbs 18:10 (NKJV)

If you are walking around with a heavy heart, chances are you are hanging on to a lot of heavy emotional baggage. And as long as you keep lugging it around, it will destroy you. Perhaps it's something you haven't forgiven yourself for, hard feelings in your family, a business deal that went wrong, the death of a loved one, or someone who has done you wrong—but whatever it is, let it go and give it to Jesus!

No human is strong enough to bear this load—only Jesus can take this burden from you. Go to Him *first*, instead of dragging your burdens around until you fall from the weight of your heartache. Oh, how much better it is to trust Jesus than trying to manage alone. It all comes down to this: you have but two choices and only two! 1) Trust in God, or 2) Don't trust in God. It's that simple! You must decide, for there is no state of neutrality.

You are either for Christ or against Him. The Bible says in Matthew 12:30 (NIV), "Whoever is not with me is against me." Choose Jesus today and give all your emotional baggage to Him. God will always be there for you . . . in the good times and in the bad! Choosing Jesus as your personal Savior is a lifelong choice and it is your *only* choice for everlasting happiness—not only on this earth, but for all eternity!

God Sees Your Tears

You number my wanderings; put my tears into
Your bottle; are they not in Your book?

Psalm 56:8 (NKJV)

It may seem that no one cares, as if you didn't matter at all ... but Jesus cares! When you feel all alone, thinking that no one would notice if you fell off the face of the earth ... Jesus is there! You could be in the depths of despair, feeling that there's not a person in the world that truly loves you ... but Jesus does!

There's a beautiful song by Gordon Jensen that goes like this: "God sees the tears of a brokenhearted soul, He sees your tears and hears them when they fall. God weeps along with man and takes him by the hand. Tears are a language God understands. When grief has left you low, it causes tears to flow. And things have not turned out the way that you have planned. But God won't forget you, His promises are true. Tears are a language God understands."

Remember that no matter how *all alone* you feel, you are never really alone, because Jesus is always with you. *Help* is only a prayer away! You may feel unlovable, but God loves you so much He gave His life just so that you could spend eternity with Him in heaven! You may think you're unworthy, but Jesus makes you worthy! God sees your tears and longs for you to run into his arms of love, where He will wipe away each tear and fill your empty heart with His joy!

Eyes Straight Ahead

They will have no fear of bad news; their hearts are steadfast, trusting in the LORD.

Psalm 112:7 (NIV)

If you watch the news, read the newspaper or use the Internet, it's impossible to avoid learning about all the bad things going on in our world: domestic violence, sexually-abused children, gang violence, rapes, murders, and the list goes on and on. And to make matters worse, now there are daily reports of terrorist attacks that are leaving people so frightened they are afraid to leave their homes.

But if you continue to fixate on the ugliness of this world, you will miss out on the peace that only God can bring. The Bible says in Psalm 25:15 (NKJV), "My eyes are ever toward the Lord." Instead of concentrating on what the devil does, be like David and keep your eyes straight ahead—focused on Jesus Christ. He is the only one who can save you from the horrendous pain and horror of this world and give you the strength you need to face each day.

It won't be long before Jesus comes again to take you to live in heaven with Him forever—where He will give you a life that is so wonderful, your human mind can't begin to comprehend it. So don't live in fear. Lean on Jesus to lead, protect, and guide you through this difficult journey of life, and He will give you comfort, joy, and peace such as you never thought possible. All you need to do is keep your eyes straight ahead . . . looking at your Savior.

Turn the Other Cheek

"Vengeance is Mine, I will repay," says the Lord.
Romans 12:19 (NKJV)

———◆———

Have you ever wondered what the Bible means in Luke 6:29 (NIV): "If someone slaps you on one cheek, turn to them the other also." When others mistreat you, call you names, or ridicule you, it's human nature to want to retaliate or get even. But that's not God's way! Turning the other cheek means that even when someone does you wrong, you don't try to even the score! When someone screams at you in disgust, pray for Holy Spirit power and respond in a gentle and kind manner. When you are ridiculed and laughed at, rely on God's strength to reflect His character in every situation. And when you are talked about, and slandered, ask God to put forgiveness in your heart so you will react with Christian love.

When Christ was here on earth, He was treated unfairly, gossiped about, and even spit upon, yet He took it all in loving silence. He never once spoke in anger to defend himself, and God wants us to follow His example. The Bible says in Colossians 3:13 (NIV) "Bear with each other and forgive one another if any of you has a grievance against someone. Forgive as the Lord forgave you."

The next time your friend turns on you, your spouse yells in anger, or your boss tells you you're worthless, instead of welling up inside with righteous indignation and getting ready to have a volcanic eruption, turn the other cheek and give all that anger to Jesus. Ask Him to replace it with an extra measure of His love . . . and He will.

Praise God!

Therefore by Him let us continually offer the sacrifice of praise to God, that is, the fruit of our lips, giving thanks to His name.

Hebrews 13:15 (NKJV)

———◆———

There are days when your life is filled with so much joy, you just can't help but praise Jesus for His goodness! But the moment when everything seems to go wrong, it's a whole different story! All of a sudden you become bitter and angry and start blaming God! But, let's be clear—just because you are a Christian does not mean that everything will go smoothly in your life! Remember, calm seas don't make better sailors! In other words, if you've never experienced the challenges and difficulties of life, you would never learn to lean on Jesus! If people were always blissfully happy, they would never know their need of a Savior! So instead of being bitter, thank God for your trials!

The Bible says in James 1:12 (ESV), "Blessed is the man who remains steadfast under trial, for when he has stood the test he will receive the crown of life, which God has promised to those who love him." Remember, Job stood the test and remained faithful to God even though he lost literally everything! He lost all his wealth, his home, his children, and even his friends! Yet, through it all, Job praised God! It doesn't matter what heartache or trials you are experiencing—in all things . . . praise God!

Mood Changes

Oh, satisfy us early with Your mercy, that we may rejoice and be glad all our days!

Psalm 90:14 (NKJV)

When God created human life, He gave each of us a wide variety of emotions. Depending on life circumstances, our moods can change in an instant! If someone cuts us off in traffic, we immediately get angry. If someone gives us an unexpected compliment, all of a sudden we feel like smiling. Our day can start out great, until we find out we just got fired. That brings on a whole bucketload of emotions, including shock, denial, anger, and the list goes on.

It's not wrong to feel anger. After all, God created that emotion, but definitely not okay to stay angry. Our emotional buttons get pushed in our spiritual life as well. If we like the pastor and feel warmly accepted by church members, then we look forward to going to church. But when the first member upsets us or does us wrong, we all of a sudden find excuses not to go anymore because of feelings of resentment, hurt, and bitterness.

That's why God doesn't want us to allow our emotions to rule our spiritual lives—especially our faith in Him. If we allow our faith in God to diminish because someone hurt our feelings, then our faith is based on people, not God! Our moods can change like the wind, but God never changes! He is the same yesterday, today, and tomorrow!

No Wrong Way to Pray

Likewise the Spirit helps us in our weakness. For we do not know what to pray for as we ought, but the Spirit himself intercedes for us with groanings too deep for words.

Romans 8:26 (ESV)

Some people pray beautiful, eloquent prayers, while others pray short, awkward prayers, and still others don't pray at all because they simply don't know how. But here's the truth: there is no *wrong* way to pray! Prayer is simply communicating with your Creator God, and however you would normally talk with your best friend is a good way to pray. Just share what is on your heart, in your own words, the way you would normally say things!

God doesn't expect you to have a degree in communications before you approach His throne room. Nor does He only listen to or answer the *beautiful* prayers! In fact, the most powerful prayer you could ever pray consists of only three words: "Jesus, save me!" That prayer alone can send thousands of angels to your side for *divine intervention*.

It's important to pray with faith. The Bible says in Matthew 21:22 (NKJV), "And whatever things you ask in prayer, believing, you will receive." Pray about everything, pray often, and pray with faith, remembering, there is no wrong way to pray!

Speck of Sawdust

Do not speak evil of one another, brethren. He who speaks evil of a brother and judges his brother, speaks evil of the law and judges the law. . . . Who are you to judge another?

James 4:11-12 (NKJV)

Whether we like to admit it or not, we are all guilty of being judgmental. We see someone walking by with tattoos or a ring in their nose and immediately make a judgment call about their character. If someone is talking with a hillbilly accent, we assume they're not very smart, and if someone walks by without saying hello, we are insulted and label them as stuck up, conceited, or full of themselves.

Even worse, we judge people's relationships with God based on our own criteria of what we think they should do or how they should act. The Bible says in Luke 6:41 (NIV), "Why do you look at the speck of sawdust in your brother's eye and pay no attention to the plank in your own eye?"

In other words, before pointing out the faults of others, or judging them harshly, we need to examine our own lives and ask God to show us our own weaknesses. We soon realize that we are not better than anyone else. The Bible says in Romans 3:23 (NKJV), "For all have sinned and fall short of the glory of God."

No one is perfect, except God. Instead of looking for the faults in others, look for the good. And if you see your brother fall, instead of judging . . . lend a hand!

Live Life to the Fullest

Beloved, I pray that you may prosper in all things and be in health, just as your soul prospers.

3 John 2 (NKJV)

———◆———

From the moment you are born, you begin to die! That's just the natural progression of life. Genetics aside, maintaining a healthy lifestyle plays a big role in how long you will live, as well as the quality of your life. That's why it's important to take good care of your body, getting plenty of rest, healthy food, water, exercise, and abstaining from drugs, alcohol, and tobacco. But in addition to those basic needs, if you want to live a rich, vibrant, and well-balanced life, you need to take care of your spiritual health as well. The best way to do that is to spend time each day in God's presence, studying His Holy Word.

Communicating with God gives you the wisdom, comfort, strength, and direction you need to face each day. Without Jesus, your life is but an empty shell, without real joy or purpose. The Bible says in Psalm 73:26 (NLT), "My health may fail, and my spirit may grow weak, but God remains the strength of my heart; He is mine forever." You see, your body won't last forever here on earth—but because of Christ's death on Calvary, you have the opportunity to spend eternity in heaven with a new body, where there will be no more sickness, pain, or death. Oh, what a glorious day that will be! Determine today to keep your spiritual life healthy by walking hand-in-hand with Jesus each day!

Secrets Tell the Truth

Every way of a man is right in his own eyes,
but the LORD weighs the hearts.

Proverbs 21:2 (NKJV)

Some Christians believe God has a check list for the number of good deeds you must accomplish in order to enter into heaven. They start feeling guilty if they perceive themselves not measuring up to what everyone else is doing. It is then that their reasons for performing acts of kindness become selfishly motivated—trying to earn *the key to eternal life*. But the truth is, there is no such checklist or special key. The door to grace and mercy is open to all. Eternity with Jesus is not a reward for accomplishing the required amount of good deeds. If heaven was available only to *perfect* people, no one would be there, because no one is perfect.

The Bible says in Ecclesiastes 7:20 (KJV), "For there is not a just man upon earth, that doeth good, and sinneth not." God knows your heart and whether your motives are pure or selfish. He wants you to be kind to others—not just your friends, family, or people you love, but to strangers as well, without looking around to see who's watching or for some expectation of a reward! Hebrews 6:10 (NIV) says, "God is not unjust; he will not forget your work and the love you have shown him as you have helped his people and continue to help them." Show kindness—not because you have to or because you want to get brownie points with God. You simply can't fool Him, for your secrets tell the truth about what's in your heart!

A Calloused Heart

"For the hearts of this people have grown dull. Their ears are hard of hearing, and their eyes they have closed."

Matthew 13:15 (NKJV)

Do you profess to love and believe in God, yet turn on Him the moment things don't go your way? Perhaps you are disappointed that you didn't have your prayers answered the way you wanted, stressed because the bills are piling up, or suffering from a devastating loss. Oh, how quickly you fall out of love with Jesus, yet He is the only one who can solve your problems. How sad it is when our love for Christ becomes so shallow and conditional!

It's easy to trust God and walk the Christian walk when things are going great, but it is when you experience the first sign of trouble that your faith is really put to the test. How you react during the hard times shows how deep your love is for your Savior.

Anger and bitterness are the perfect ingredients to form a calloused heart so thick that no one can penetrate it. But Jesus is the Healer of hearts! The Bible says in Psalm 51:10 (KJV), "Create in me a clean heart, O God; and renew a right spirit within me." Stop blaming God and feeling sorry for yourself, —instead trust Him to solve your problems, and don't forget to ask Him for a clean heart today!

Suffering with Depression

The righteous cry out, and the LORD hears, and delivers them out of all their troubles.

Psalm 34:17 (NKJV)

Many people suffer from depression, including Christians. Sadly, fellow brothers and sisters in Christ can be quite judgmental, which only causes more suffering. No one but God can know the pain another person is going through, and although doctors can prescribe medicines to help, that is not enough. Leaning on Jesus to get through the dark days is critical to recovery.

If you are suffering from depression, go to Jesus for help. The more time you spend in prayer and the study of His Word, the better you will feel. Sometimes depression causes you to feel inadequate to spend time in God's presence, so you back away. But when Jesus died on Calvary, He made you worthy to come to Him any time of the day or night. He has given you full access to the most powerful physician in the world—God!

When you are sinking in the quicksand of depression and approaching God's throne room seems impossible, *get up*, don't *give up*. Run to Jesus—He will welcome you with His outstretched arms of love and hold you close!

The Bible says in Deuteronomy 31:8 (NIV), "The LORD himself goes before you and will be with you; he will never leave you nor forsake you. Do not be afraid; do not be discouraged." There is an answer for those suffering with depression, and it is ... Jesus Christ, your Lord and Savior, the only Healer of hearts!

Your Memory Bank

*I will call upon the Lord, who is worthy to be praised;
so shall I be saved from my enemies.*

Psalm 18:3 (NKJV)

———◈———

It's good to remember all the wonderful things that God has done for you, but, sadly, all too often His grace and mercy is quickly forgotten. It's even worse if you rationalize an answered prayer as a mere coincidence, not even giving God the credit for His divine intervention. To ensure you remember all the great things God does for you, store them in your memory bank! For instance, when the doctor gave you no hope and yet you recovered from an illness, remember the miracle often, and don't forget to praise Jesus each time you think of it.

Thinking about all the good things God does for you is faith-building! Keep each blessing stored in your memory bank, and whenever you're discouraged or Satan tempts you to think that God doesn't love you and has forgotten you, stop and make a visit to your memory bank. You'll be refreshed and overflowing with joy just thinking about how good God is to you. If you suffer from chronic forgetfulness, then perhaps a daily journal would be good. Write down each and every time God intervened on your behalf or blessed you in a special way. Then read your *book of blessings* often, reflecting on what an awesome God you serve! On every page, you'll be reminded just how very much Jesus loves you!

Slipping Away

But this I say: He who sows sparingly will also reap sparingly,
and he who sows bountifully will also reap bountifully.

2 Corinthians 9:6 (NKJV)

When you first fall in love with Jesus, you are exuberant, excited, and on fire for Him, but it's far too easy to let the flame go out. In order to hold on to your rich love relationship with Him, you must stay connected through prayer and the study of His Word. There is also another element that keeps you from slipping away . . . and that's active evangelism! There's no better *spiritual high* than helping someone come to know your Lord and Savior. When you put your faith in action, it is one of the most rewarding experiences you can have.

In Titus 3:8 (NKJV), the apostle Paul admonished believers with these words: "This is a faithful saying, and these things I want you to affirm constantly, that those who have believed in God should be careful to maintain good works. These things are good and profitable to men." There is bound to be some highs and lows in this journey of life, but God wants you to keep doing good works. And a life lived for Jesus results in a life filled with good works, which not only benefits others but strengthens your faith as well. Even if you don't *feel* like doing good works, do them anyway, and don't allow bitterness, anger, depression, or anything else cause you to slip away from God.

Pursue the Lord with all your heart, for when you do, your love relationship with Jesus will grow and good works are sure to follow.

Value of a Soul

*And keep the charge of the Lord your God: to walk
in His ways, to keep His statutes, His commandments,
His judgments, and His testimonies, as it is written in the
Law of Moses, that you may prosper in all that you
do and wherever you turn.*

1 Kings 2:3 (NKJV)

People spend their whole life trying to achieve *success* through fame, fortune, or power. But what is the real measurement of success? For some, it's how much money they have in the bank, driving a fancy car, sending their kids to the best schools, or having power and influence. But no matter how high a status you reach in the eyes of man, nothing is more important than the value of your soul!

The Bible says in Mark 8:36-37 (NLT), "And what do you benefit if you gain the whole world but lose your own soul? Is anything worth more than your soul?" The devil uses the trappings of this world to blind you from what really matters, and that's . . . staying close to God! You can't begin to even imagine how much you mean to our heavenly Father, until you think of His great sacrifice on Calvary. Only then can you start to comprehend just how much He loves you.

Are you wondering how much your is soul is worth? Well, Jesus loves you so much that He left the splendor of heaven to give His life, dying on a cross so that you can live with Him for all eternity. You just can't pay a higher price than that!

Setting Goals

*Therefore we make it our aim, whether present
or absent, to be well pleasing to Him.*

2 Corinthians 5:9 (NKJV)

———◆———

It's good to have goals, something we want to achieve and strive for, but it's also important to enjoy the time leading up to the moment we actually achieve that goal. It's very easy to become so *goal-oriented* that we don't enjoy the special moments we spend getting there.

Setting goals for ourselves can be stressful—worrying whether or not we can accomplish such a feat and fearing the embarrassment of failure. But we can avoid all the unnecessary stress if we first present our goals before God and ask for His blessing. We need to know if our goals line up with God's goals for us, because when *our* will becomes *God's* will, we have nothing to worry about! We can trust that everything will turn out the way God wants it to!

God knows our strengths and weakness, and even more importantly, He gives us everything we need to accomplish *His* goal for us. There is one goal that all Christians should have, and that is our heavenly goal! So go ahead, dare to dream, challenge yourself, and set realistic goals—just be sure to consult with the *Master Planner* first!

Power Source for Patience

Do not hasten in your spirit to be angry, for anger rests in the bosom of fools.

Ecclesiastes 7:9 (NKJV)

Why is it that people seem to have more patience with perfect strangers than they do for their own family or loved ones? If walking down a crowded grocery store aisle and someone accidentally bumps into us, as soon as they start frantically expressing how sorry they are, we're quick to forgive and assure them, "It's all right, no harm done!" But if a loved one was to do the same thing, often the response is a disgusted tone and cutting words, "Watch where you're going," or "Why do you always have to be so clumsy?"

But usually the person we have the least amount of patience with is . . . ourselves! When we make a mistake or do the wrong thing, it's harder to forgive ourselves than it is to forgive others. That's because we expect more, so whenever we feel like a failure, we can be pretty hard on ourselves.

As Christians, we understand the importance of forgiving others, but we also need to learn to forgive *ourselves*. When we are tempted to get frustrated, upset, or angry, instead of totally losing it, tap into the power source for patience . . . by praying for an extra outpouring of God's Holy Spirit. With God's power working through us, we will have the strength to face whatever comes our way, and do so with kindness, dignity, strength, and patience. With God's Holy Spirit power, we can conquer any storm. Yes, even the storm within ourselves!

Me-First Mentality

*No one should seek their own good,
but the good of others.*

1 Corinthians 10:24 (NIV)

There's something sorely missing in our world today and that is the inability to put others first. We've become a selfish society where we are so focused on what we want that stepping on someone else to get there just doesn't seem to matter. But God is very clear on how He views selfishness. The Bible says in James 3:16 (NIV), "For where you have envy and selfish ambition, there you find disorder and every evil practice." And in Philippians 2:3 (NIV), we're told, "Do nothing out of selfish ambition or vain conceit. Rather, in humility value others above yourselves."

Being *self-centered* never brings happiness. Real joy comes from Jesus and becoming more like Him. When Christ was here on earth, He was always thinking of others and went out of His way to be kind and helpful. Without ever complaining, He spent countless hours healing the sick, sharing words of encouragement, and doing acts of kindness, all the while enduring hunger, lack of sleep, and the constant pushing and shoving of the crowds.

When He was beaten, bruised, bleeding, and dying on a cross, He wasn't thinking of himself. Instead, He thought of His mother, His friends, the thief next to Him on a cross, and each one of us that we might live eternally with Him! So, toss out the *me-first mentality* by implementing a *Christ-first mentality*, and strive to become more like Him!

Spiritual Family

*Finally, all of you be of one mind, having compassion
for one another; love as brothers, be tenderhearted, be
courteous; not returning evil for evil.*

1 Peter 3:8-9 (NKJV)

Everyone needs to feel loved, wanted, and accepted—it's just the way humans are made. God created man to have families and to love and take care of each other. The Bible says in 1 Timothy 5:8 (NKJV), "But if anyone does not provide for his own, and especially for those of his household, he has denied the faith and is worse than an unbeliever."

God makes it very clear that families are to love and take care of each other! Without the sense of *belonging* to a family, there is a deep feeling of emptiness and loss, as if there were no purpose for living. Many are alone in this world, with no one to call and say, "I arrived safely," or "I'll be home late—just didn't want you to worry!" Some have families that are so dysfunctional, it's not healthy to have any type of relationship with them. And still others are lonely because their family members have passed away.

But the good news is, God has given you a spiritual family to love, support, and help you draw closer to Him. In Psalm 133:1 (NKJV), we're told, "Behold, how good and how pleasant it is for brethren to dwell together in unity!" And Hebrews 10:25 (NLT) says, "And let us not neglect our meeting together, as some people do, but encourage one another, especially now that the day of his return is drawing near." Oh, what a blessing it is to belong to the family of God!

Choose Happiness

Though you have not seen him, you love him. Though you do not now see him, you believe in him and rejoice with joy that is inexpressible and filled with glory.

1 Peter 1:8 (ESV)

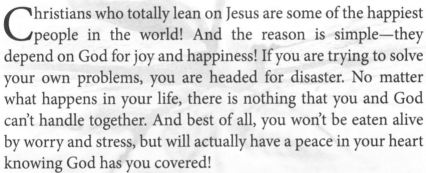

Christians who totally lean on Jesus are some of the happiest people in the world! And the reason is simple—they depend on God for joy and happiness! If you are trying to solve your own problems, you are headed for disaster. No matter what happens in your life, there is nothing that you and God can't handle together. And best of all, you won't be eaten alive by worry and stress, but will actually have a peace in your heart knowing God has you covered!

When you choose Jesus, you are choosing happiness! Why worry when you can be happy? The Bible says in Psalm 144:15 (NKJV), "Happy are the people whose God is the Lord." There is absolutely no reason to walk around sad, burdened, angry, or all stressed out, because, no matter what your circumstance, God can handle it. But you must release your grip and allow God to take control! In Psalm 34:17-19 (NIV), we're told, "The righteous cry out, and the Lord hears them; he delivers them from all their troubles. The Lord is close to the brokenhearted and saves those who are crushed in spirit. A righteous man may have many troubles, but the Lord delivers him from them all." Start each day by claiming this promise for your own, and then . . . *choose happiness!*

Check Your Focus

Thus says the LORD: "Stand in the ways and see, and ask
for the old paths, where the good way is, and walk in it;
then you will find rest for your souls."

Jeremiah 6:16 (NKJV)

People everywhere are stressed, overworked, overloaded, and trying to accomplish more than their ancestors could ever have believed possible. In fact, multitasking has grown to a whole new level, leaving many confused as to what their priorities are and what to do first. When you lose your focus of what's most important, you tend to just flit from one job to the next without really finishing anything. Not only is it impossible to do your best work, but you'll soon wear yourself out both physically and emotionally.

Instead of wandering aimlessly, give God complete control and prayerfully follow His plan for your life. When you're obeying His commands and following the path He leads, you'll no longer feel lost, wondering what to do or where to go. The Bible says in Psalm 25:4 (ESV), "Make me to know your ways, O LORD; teach me your paths." And best of all, when God's in charge of your life, you'll not only get a lot accomplished, but you'll have a lot less stress. When God's in charge, you don't have to worry—just trust God to take you where He wants you to go! Now is the time to check your focus and make sure you are giving your time, talents, and energy to what God wants for your life.

Share the Details

"Look at the birds of the air, for they neither sow nor reap nor gather into barns; yet your heavenly Father feeds them. Are you not of more value than they?"

Matthew 6:26 (NKJV)

―――◇―――

Many people don't talk to God about the insignificant things in their lives because, well, they feel they just don't want to *bother* God. But the truth is, there's nothing too small or too big that you can't share with God. In fact, He loves it every time you share your heart with Him. And yes, that includes the little details of your life. The Bible says in Luke 12:7 (NIV), "Indeed, the very hairs of your head are all numbered." Now, it doesn't get more insignificant than hairs on your head!

Do you get irritated when a friend shares the little things, like when their dog ran away, their boss was grumpy, or they couldn't find their keys? Of course not! If you really love your friend, you're interested in every aspect of their life.

So it is with God. The minute He hears your voice saying, "Dear Lord," He gets excited! He cares about what upsets you, as well as listening to your hopes and dreams. When you pray, just picture in your mind Jesus sitting on the edge of His seat, eyes intently focused on you, eager to hear your every word, and then He asks you this question found in Mark 10:36 (NKJV): "What do you want me to do for you?"

Look in the Mirror

*He who covers his sins will not prosper, but whoever
confesses and forsakes them will have mercy.*

Proverbs 28:13 (NKJV)

Some people have a hard time admitting they've made a mistake. Instead of owning up to their fault, they immediately go into *defensive mode* and try to justify their actions. But making excuses for your own blunders doesn't change what you did, nor does it make you look good in the eyes of others. Most of the time, people see right through your attempts to make yourself appear blameless, and you really haven't fooled anyone but yourself. More importantly, you can't fool God.

Self-preservation is a natural human response, but it can be a deceptive one. It's easier to see the faults in others than it is to see your own sin. But just take a good look in the mirror and you'll see what is wrong in your own life. You'll have a full-time job keeping yourself on the right path, with no need to point out the faults of others. The Bible says in Luke 6:41-42 (NKJV), "And why do you look at the speck in your brother's eye, but do not perceive the plank in your own eye?

In other words, don't be a hypocrite! No one is perfect—everyone is a sinner, so instead of focusing on everyone else's problems, work on your own! Ask God to help you see the sin in your own life more than you see the faults of others. And don't forget to ask Him for an extra measure of love for your fellow man. Before you're tempted to criticize someone else, stop and . . . look in the mirror!

Going to Heaven

"And he who overcomes, and keeps My works until the end, to him I will give power over the nations."

Revelation 2:26 (NKJV)

It's been said over and over again, "I'm a good person, and as long as I don't break any laws, I'm going to heaven." But that is not what the Bible says in Matthew 7:21 (NIV), where we're told, "Not everyone who says to me, 'Lord, Lord,' will enter the kingdom of heaven, but only the one who does the will of my Father who is in heaven."

You see, it's not about being a "good person" but rather loving God and believing in Him. The Bible even takes it one step further and says in John 14:15 (NKJV), "If you love Me, keep My commandments." God wants us to not only love and believe in Him, but to also *obey* Him by keeping His commandments.

There's a beautiful promise in this familiar scripture found in John 3:16 (KJV): "For God so loved the world, that He gave His only begotten son, that whosoever believeth in Him, shall not perish, but have everlasting life."

We need to stop fooling ourselves into thinking we can merrily go through life, just being a "good person," and not worrying about salvation—because if we do, we will miss out on eternity with our Lord and Savior! Make no mistake, not everyone will have eternal life. Only those who love and believe in the Lord Jesus Christ and keep His commandments get a ticket to heaven!

Pulling the Worry Wagon

Search me, O God, and know my heart;
try me, and know my anxieties.

Psalm 139:23 (NKJV)

———◆———

If there is one thing that will weigh heavy on your heart faster than you can sneeze at, it is . . . *worry*. It can distract you from even the simplest task, send you into a state of panic, and drive your blood pressure sky high. When you live in fear of bad news, you start pulling around the *worry wagon*, and it gets heavier and heavier with each fear that gets added in. Before you know it, your wagon is so loaded down that you can't push, pull, or nudge it anywhere! That is just not the way God wants us to live!

Instead of loading up the worry wagon every time you're tempted to stress, say a quick prayer! Give your worries to God and ask Him to help you trust Him more! Once you make this exercise a habit, it will change the way you react to all situations. God longs for you to love Him so much that you'll trust Him with your problems! And when you trade in your worries, He will replace them with His sweet peace!

In Psalm 112:7 (NIV), we're told, "They will have no fear of bad news; their hearts are steadfast, trusting in the LORD." What a precious promise to claim for your own! Start today and trade in that worry wagon for . . . God's perfect peace!

Seasons of Life

*You have taught me from my youth . . . Now also when I
am old and gray-headed, O God, do not forsake me.*

Psalm 71:17-18 (NKJV)

Our journey here on earth is like the seasons, representing the different phases of our lives. Spring represents birth and the innocence of everything new. Summer is filled with the vitality and naivety of youth, complete with hopes, dreams. and the pursuit of life at its fullest. Then it seems we quietly slip into autumn, with confidence from lessons learned, knowledge to approach challenges more realistically, and feeling a sense of urgency to accomplish our goals. Then, all too quickly, winter comes upon us.

Our hair reflects the fallen snow, we move a little slower, feel the aches and pains of aging, and still can't comprehend how quickly we've become the *older folks* we never thought we'd be. Our thoughts will take us to the things we are glad we did, things we wanted to do, and even regrets of things we did do. But all too soon winter will come to an end, and only what is done for Christ will last.

Now is the time to determine what mark you will leave on this earth—whatever you want to accomplish in life, do quickly. Don't put off until tomorrow what you can do today—for how you live today will determine whether or not you will live forever with Jesus. Choose to live a godly life, sowing seeds of kindness and sharing God's love in every season so that you'll be prepared for eternal life in heaven.

What Really Matters

Your ears shall hear a word behind you, saying,
"This is the way, walk in it," whenever you turn to the
right hand or whenever you turn to the left.

Isaiah 30:21 (NKJV)

If your days are spent running from one thing to the next, and it seems you fall into bed each night feeling like you have accomplished nothing, then it's time to talk with God about setting your priorities. With God in charge of your calendar, your life will be much more fulfilling and you'll spend your time doing things that are worthwhile and pleasing to Him instead of those that steal your time and energy.

You can also enjoy peace and calm knowing that you have nothing to fear, because God is leading and guiding each minute of your day. Allowing God to set your priorities also gives you the power to resist selfish impulses and useless distractions that the devil puts in your way. With Holy Spirit guidance, you can set goals and trust that they are the right ones. You can claim this promise in Psalm 32:8 (NKJV): "I will instruct you and teach you in the way you should go; I will guide you with My eye."

You never have to be afraid of making the wrong decision when you allow God to take charge of your life—He will give you divine direction as to where your time and attention is best directed. You just can't go wrong when heaven is your goal and your number-one focus is a closer walk with Jesus, because that is *what really matters.*

The Mate God Chooses

*Desire without knowledge is not good, and one who
moves too hurriedly misses the way.*

Proverbs 19:2 (NRSV)

Some say "love is blind," and that expression is probably referring to *new* love which usually only sees the good in each other. In the first few months of dating, each is on their *best* behavior, because naturally they want to make a good impression, as well as wanting the other person to like them. But the longer they date, the more *comfortable* they become, and that's when they start letting their guard down.

When that happens, you start to see the *real* person, not just who they want you to see. The best advice: never even date someone unless you have prayed about it first! There's nothing better than finding the mate that *God* chooses!

The most important questions to ask yourself in any relationship are . . . Is God present? They *say* they love Jesus, but do their actions show it? Is selfishness in their heart? Are they kind and loving toward others? Does their character reveal Christ in their lives?"

The Bible says in 1 Corinthians 13:4-5 (NKJV), "Love is patient." Remember that only God knows hearts, so when it comes to relationships, take your time and allow the Holy Spirit to lead and guide, so you will find the mate that God chooses. Because God's choice is the only one that will bring you true happiness.

April 4

Life of Flexibility

*Everywhere and in all things I have learned both to be
full and to be hungry, both to abound and to suffer need.*

Philippians 4:12 (NKJV)

Often times we can't understand why God *does what He does*! We question why we lost our job, why our house doesn't sell, why a loved one isn't healed, why a friendship ended, and on and on. What we don't do is maintain a joyful spirit when trouble strikes. And yet that is exactly what the Bible tells us to do in James 1:2-4 (RSV): "Count it all joy, my brethren, when you meet various trials, for you know that the testing of your faith produces steadfastness. And let steadfastness have its full effect, that you may be perfect and complete, lacking in nothing."

In other words, be flexible. Yes, live a life so flexible that you can be happy in any environment that God places you. If God wants you to remain in your current house, don't fret. Be flexible and know that God's plan is the *best* plan, and then be joyful! If He calls you to leave your comfortable home to work in a mission field across the ocean, that's okay too! Say, "Thank You, Jesus, that I can be part of Your plan. I trust You."

Learning to be flexible is only possible by being in the presence of God, learning from the Master! From Him you will gain wisdom, faith, and genuine trust—all valuable assets you'll need in making good decisions. God is using your trials to perfect your character and prepare you for heaven, and anytime you are choosing to be in God's will, that's the safest path to take, for He will never lead you astray!

For God's Eyes Only

Humble yourselves in the sight of the Lord,
and He will lift you up.

James 4:10 (NKJV)

Ministry is all about serving others. In fact, the name itself comes from the Greek word "diakoneo," meaning *to serve*, and is not meant to be a position of glory or prestige. This isn't a job for someone wanting to be noticed and held in high esteem, but rather requires a life of humility, quietly serving—not to impress others, but to be seen by God's eyes only!

However, there are some who think that ministry is only the work of pastors or traveling evangelists. But God has called us all to be *ministers*. The Bible says in Mark 16:15 (NKJV), "Go into all the world and preach the gospel to every creature."

In order to heed God's command, you must be fueled by Holy Spirit power! In 1 Peter 4:11 (NKJV), we're told, "If anyone ministers, let him do it as with the ability which God supplies, that in all things God may be glorified through Jesus Christ." The key words are "the ability which God supplies"! Make no mistake, God is calling *you* to minister for Him! But first, you must come before His throne with a humble heart and pray for an anointing of His Holy Spirit so that God can use you in a mighty way!

And don't forget to ask Him to strip away all pride and pretentiousness—giving you a servant's heart so that you won't be tempted to work for the applause of others, but to truly glorify your Lord and Savior!

Overcoming Temptation

For to be carnally minded is death, but to be spiritually minded is life and peace.

Romans 8:6 (NKJV)

Every day we face a variety of temptations. Some are trivial, such as seeing a piece of chocolate cake and salivating over the thought of devouring every delicious morsel! Other temptations have much more serious consequences, such as being tempted to lie, steal, commit adultery, or even kill someone! Temptation, however, is not a sin! It is when you succumb to the temptation that you're in trouble! Even Jesus was tempted in the wilderness, but He resisted temptation and didn't give in to the devil's evil plan!

One particular area that is talked about often is sexual temptation. There have been many godly men and women whose lives were destroyed by committing adultery, all because they did not resist their sexual desires. Even pastors and people in ministry have fallen, and although they asked forgiveness and were forgiven, their ministry was never the same as it would have been had they resisted the urge to sin.

There are numerous types of temptations, but the good news is that Jesus has promised that we *can* overcome! In 1 Corinthians 10:13 (NKJV), we're told, "But God is faithful, who will not allow you to be tempted beyond what you are able, but with the temptation will also make the way of escape, that you may be able to bear it." We can rejoice that God will give us the strength to resist temptation—all we need to do is lean on Him.

Pacing the Floor

But as we have been approved by God to be entrusted
with the gospel, even so we speak, not as pleasing men,
but God who tests our hearts.

1 Thessalonians 2:4 (NKJV)

There is really only one way to experience true inner peace, and that is to rely totally on God . . . for absolutely everything. You can avoid endless hours of worrying by simply putting your life in God's hands and trusting Him completely. Listen for the whispering of the Holy Spirit guiding you, and don't forget that God also speaks to you through His Holy Word! When you pray and follow God's divine direction, you skip hours of nail biting and pacing the floor in misery trying to figure out what to do and which way to go. That's because prayer takes the worry right out of the equation!

The Bible gives some good advice in Jeremiah 42:6 (NKJV): "Whether it is pleasing or displeasing, we will obey the voice of the LORD our God to whom we send you, that it may be well with us when we obey the voice of the LORD our God."

In other words, it doesn't matter whether or not you want to do what God asks you—just do it. Trust God's plan for you. Whatever decision or life choice you are struggling with, whatever annoying habit you can't give up, whatever heartache that is crushing your very soul, give it all to Jesus! Don't hold anything back. Give God all your worries, temptations, problems, and trials . . . and stop pacing the floor!

Powerful Words

Let the words of my mouth and the meditation of my
heart be acceptable in Your sight, O LORD,
my strength and my Redeemer.

Psalm 19:14 (NKJV)

It's far too easy to say the first thing that comes to mind without really thinking through the effect it might have on others. Careless words can cut right through the heart and cause deadly wounds that may never heal. Lifelong friendships have ended because of misspoken words, and even family members have ceased to talk for years, all because someone said something offensive.

The thing you need to remember is that once words come out of your mouth, you can never take them back! Just like throwing a glass of water onto the yard, you can never get that exact water back in your glass. It's gone forever. So it is with words. No matter how much you wish you could stuff them back in your mouth, you can't! The damage is done! Gossip, snide remarks, innuendos, and rude comments are powerful words that once spoken become lethal weapons.

Just as powerful are words spoken with kindness, giving encouragement and comfort. Words spoken in softness and love, melt hearts and bring incredible peace and joy! God wants us to use powerful words of love and encouragement to build others up, heal broken hearts, and give hope to the hopeless. In Ephesians 4:29 (NLT), we're told, "Let everything you say be good and helpful, so that your words will be an encouragement to those who hear them."

Never Give Up

*Why are you cast down, O my soul? And why are you
disquieted within me? Hope in God, for I shall yet praise
Him for the help of His countenance.*

Psalm 42:5 (NKJV)

There are ups and downs in this journey of life, and
unfortunately, some days are going to be better than others.
As Christians, we know that God never promised that all our
days would be bright and sunny, but He does promise that He
will be with us through every storm. So on those days when
you are discouraged and feeling like just *throwing in the towel*
and giving up, lean on Jesus! Go to God's Word for comfort and
assurance.

Think of Paul, who suffered unimaginable heartache and
pain, yet God sustained him through a shipwreck, beatings,
prison, and horrible persecution—through it all, Paul did
not give up! He said in 2 Timothy 1:12 (NLT), "But I am not
ashamed of it, for I know the one in whom I trust, and I am sure
that he is able to guard what I have entrusted to him until the
day of his return."

It was Paul's deep and unshakable love for his Lord and
Savior that gave him the courage to keep on going! And God
is still willing and able to do that for each of us today. No
matter what dark valley we are in, never give up. Lean on Jesus,
claiming Philippians 4:19 (KJV): "But my God shall supply all
your need according to his riches in glory by Christ Jesus."

God Expects Obedience

But He said, "More than that, blessed are those who hear the word of God and keep it!"

Luke 11:28 (NKJV)

———————

Some people think God just dreamed up a bunch of rules to make everyone miserable, but the real reason God gave the Ten Commandments is because He loves you and wants you to have a better life. But here's something you might not have thought about—did you know that there's a direct correlation between obedience and answered prayer?

The Bible says in 1 John 3:22 (NKJV), "And whatever we ask we receive from Him, because we keep His commandments and do those things that are pleasing in His sight." Pay special attention to the part that says, "because we keep His commandments." And in Psalm 84:11 (NKJV), we learn, "No good thing will He withhold from those who walk uprightly." God couldn't have made it more plain that His criteria for answered prayer is . . . obedience.

When you are praying and God doesn't seem to hear, ask yourself, *Am I obedient to God? Is there something in my life that goes against His law? Do I only pray when I want to use God to get what I want?* Before putting your requests before God, be obedient! You can start by praying the prayer David prayed in Psalm 51:10 (NKJV): "Create in me a clean heart, O God, and renew a steadfast spirit within me."

Informed Decisions

I have set the LORD always before me; because He is at my right hand I shall not be moved.

Psalm 16:8 (NKJV)

———◆———

There are times in life when you're faced with challenges that require some sort of action, and you're in a dilemma not knowing what to do. Perhaps you found out your boss is stealing from the company. Do you confront him—or pretend you don't know? Maybe you're spouse is abusive. Do you have the courage to leave the situation or do you continue to take the mistreatment? Or maybe a friend or family member is being unfairly treated. Do you stand up for the underdog or stay silent? Sometimes your silence contributes to someone else's pain. Other times, silence is the most Christian response. That's why divine guidance is essential to give you wisdom to know what to do.

Fortunately, you don't have to make decisions blindly, because you have access to the best Counselor and Guide. He is the only one who knows the future so there is no one better to seek advice from . . . than from God. He not only gives the best direction but He is your Friend and Ally. He loves you more than anyone else ever could and is your Protector, Champion, and Warrior who will fight for you. Only God can give you the courage to stand up for what is right. Determine today, in every situation, to seek Holy Spirit wisdom so you will always make informed decisions!

Watching the Clock

*Yet indeed I also count all things loss for the excellence of
the knowledge of Christ Jesus my Lord, for whom I
have suffered the loss of all things, and count them
as rubbish, that I may gain Christ.*

Philippians 3:8 (NKJV)

When we pray, it's important to have faith that God will answer according to what is best for us. We can always trust God's answer and have peace that the right thing is happening, even if God doesn't respond in the way that we want Him to. When we have a close relationship with our heavenly Father, we *want* what God wants, and whatever that may be is okay with us!

The more consistent our prayer life, the more we see real answers to prayer, which causes our faith to grow even stronger! Soon we will long for more time in His presence, and we won't be watching the clock to see if we have stayed an appropriate time on our knees! Our hearts become changed, and we won't want to be anywhere or do anything that separates us from our Lord and Savior!

If you're struggling to find the time for worship and to study God's Word, pray and ask God to give you an even deeper desire to be closer to Him. When you truly fall in love with Jesus, spending time with Him won't be a drudgery or something you feel you *have* to do to go to heaven—you'll look forward to every precious moment.

It's All Good

Now this is the confidence that we have in Him,
that if we ask anything according to His will, He hears us.
And if we know that He hears us, whatever we ask, we know
that we have the petitions that we have asked of Him.

1 John 5:14-15 (NKJV)

When bringing your requests before the throne room of God, it's important to remember that God's plan is always the best plan. But far too often, Christians approach God with their *to-do lists*, and even worse, tell Him *how* to answer their prayers! When spiritual stubbornness overtakes your faith in God, it's not long before you get irritated and blame Him when you don't get your way! But you will never experience real joy unless you allow God to have full control!

No matter how much you want God to work a miracle on your behalf, you need to give up your desires and expectations and trust Him to make the decision that is best for you. The Bible says in James 4:3 (NIV), "When you ask, you do not receive, because you ask with wrong motives."

When you don't get the job you wanted or you don't get the diagnosis you were hoping for, it doesn't mean that God doesn't love you or has abandoned you. God has good reasons why He does what He does! As long as you are following Jesus and His plan for your life, you have nothing to worry about—it's all good!

Choosing Friends

*He who walks with wise men will be wise, but the
companion of fools will be destroyed.*

Proverbs 13:20 (NKJV)

There are many types of friends in this world, some who are nurturing, uplifting, and encouraging, while others bring you down and influence you in negative ways. That's why it's so important to choose your friends wisely. There's an old expression that is so very true: "By beholding, we become." In other words, friends tend to mimic those whom they hang around with. Godly friends will lift you up, affirm you, and help make you a better person. They are there for you in the good times and the bad ones. Best of all, they will help strengthen your own walk with your best Friend, Jesus!

But if you choose friends who are selfish, critical, unkind, and like to walk on the dark side, they will bring you down! You can't possibly be the person God wants you to be and play on the devil's playground. The right friends will elevate and inspire you to be the best you can be and will share *heavenly goals*, so when choosing your closest friends, your number-one criteria should be that they love the Lord with all their hearts!

It's also important to remember that to have a friend, you must *be* a friend. In Proverbs 18:24 (NKJV), we're told, "A man who has friends must himself be friendly, but there is a friend who sticks closer than a brother." Be a friend who is kind, generous, understanding, comforting, and most of all, a strong spiritual witness. Evaluate your friendships and don't forget to ask yourself, *What kind of friend . . . am I?*

Dealing with Change

Jesus Christ is the same yesterday, today, and forever.
Hebrews 13:8 (NKJV)

———◆———

There is one sure thing you can count on in this world and that is *change*. Absolutely nothing stays the same. People deal with change differently—some eagerly anticipate what lies before, while others dread the mere thought of losing the comfort of what is familiar. There are those who would rather stay in a bad situation than to face change, even if that meant that they would suffer because of their choice.

Change can cause stress, anxiety, and tension, but there is one *constant* in our lives that *never* changes, and that is God's love for us. God affirms His love with His promise in Isaiah 54:10 (NRSV): "For the mountains may depart and the hills be removed, but my steadfast love shall not depart from you." And Malachi 3:6 (NIV) makes it clear: "I the LORD do not change." God's Word never changes either. We are told in 1 Peter 1:25 (ESV), "But the word of the Lord remains forever."

God is willing to help us through life's difficult twists and turns in our ever-changing world, for He alone knows the way. Whether the journey looks exciting or frightening, we can walk with confidence because God is with us and has promised in Hebrews 13:5 to never leave us or forsake us.

Oh, how comforting it is to know that God's love never changes! He loves us with an everlasting love and nothing will ever change that.

Humble or Be Humbled

Let another man praise you, and not your own mouth;
a stranger, and not your own lips.

Proverbs 27:2 (NKJV)

No one is better than anyone else! All men are created equal, and God loves all His children just the same—He doesn't play favorites! Unfortunately, we have all encountered someone who thinks they are better, smarter, more talented, and favored higher by God than anyone else, but they couldn't be more deceived! When someone is always bragging about their accomplishments, or "tooting their own horn" as some would say . . . it is never very impressive because whatever might have been noteworthy becomes annoying and just plain irritating in the minds of all those who have to listen to them! Eyes roll, and it's hard to even be polite as they go on and on . . . singing their own praises!

Well, guess what? Did you know that God doesn't care for bragging, either? In Luke 18:14 (NIV), we're told, "For all those who exalt themselves will be humbled, and those who humble themselves will be exalted." There is no room for pride in the heart of a Christian, period. All pride separates us from Jesus. The Bible says in James 4:6 (NIV), "God opposes the proud but shows favor to the humble." What is your choice—humble or be humbled?

Where Is Your Passion?

I press toward the goal for the prize of the
upward call of God in Christ Jesus.

Philippians 3:14 (NKJV)

The things we excel at are usually the things that we are most passionate about. Sometimes it starts when we are very young, such as a young boy who races to the front yard every time he hears an airplane, staring at the heavens for but a mere glimpse. The look on his face when he comes back through the door is sheer joy and exhilaration! And of course, he grows up to be a jet pilot, living out his dream! Most people are not so fortunate as to find their passion early in life. Many search and search and can't seem to get motivated about anything. In fact, most college freshman list their major as *undecided*. If this is your challenge as well, quit the search, for God has already mapped out His plan for your life, and there is no greater joy than following God's perfect plan!

The Bible says in Jeremiah 29:11 (NIV), "'For I know the plans I have for you,' declares the LORD, 'plans to prosper you and not to harm you, plans to give you hope and a future.'" You don't have to spend sleepless nights worrying about what you want to do because there is nothing you could possibly dream about that would be better than God's plan. Pray and ask God to show you what He wants you to do! And don't forget to ask Him to reveal your *passion*, because what *motivates* us, *moves* us! As you fully surrender your heart and life to Jesus, your wants and desires become lined up with God's, so there's no need to worry about what the future holds, because Jesus holds your future!

Grace and Mercy

Let each of you look out not only for his own interests,
but also for the interests of others.

Philippians 2:4 (NKJV)

When you are down-and-out and at the end of your rope, it is truly a humbling experience. No one likes being poor or being a beggar! It's not a good feeling to be so desperate that you have no other option than to ask for help. Usually, people approach their own family first, and if they can't help, then they go to friends, and the last resort is to ask any stranger that might have compassion.

Sometimes, folks can be judgmental and their willingness to help based on whether or not they think it's *your own fault* that you are in such a financial mess. Others just don't want to get involved! People pass by a homeless person on a sidewalk and turn their heads in the other direction in an attempt to avoid the pitiful sight, as if they can pretend they didn't just see a hopeless individual sitting in filth and squalor.

Acts 20:35 (NKJV) says, "It is more blessed to give than to receive." In other words, there is more joy in *giving* than being on the receiving end. And Jesus said in Matthew 25:40 (NKJV), "Assuredly, I say to you, inasmuch as you did it to one of the least of these My brethren, you did it to Me."

When we reach out to our fellow man in love and kindness, the Bible says it's like we did it to Jesus himself! If you are to make an error in judgment, always "err" on the side of grace and mercy!

Selfless Living

*And just as you want men to do to you, you also
do to them likewise.*

Luke 6:31 (NKJV)

Christians should always strive to be more like Jesus! He treated others with love, kindness, humility, and respect. If Jesus was on earth today, He wouldn't be yelling at the person who just took His parking space, gossiping about others, pushing Himself to the front of the line, or any other self-centered behavior. He was always thinking of His fellow man—not Himself. The best way to win hearts for Jesus is to follow His example. When someone is grumpy, show them kindness. When you're disrespected, let it go. When you are wronged, forgive. In all things, do as Jesus would do and return good for evil.

The Bible says in Romans 12:17 (NRSV), "Never pay back evil for evil to anyone. Respect what is right in the sight of all men." And in Proverbs 20:22 (NASB), we're told, "Do not say, 'I will repay evil'; Wait for the LORD, and He will save you." God makes it very clear how He expects His children to act in this verse found in Ephesians 4:32 (ESV): "Be kind to one another, tenderhearted, forgiving one another, as God in Christ forgave you." In other words, God wants us to love each other! There won't be any selfish people in heaven, so we need to be sure our hearts are tender toward our fellow man, thinking of others, being kind, compassionate, and respectful. Just imagine how much better this world would be if everyone followed this advice and practiced *selfless living*!

April 20

Tunnel Vision

The eyes of your understanding being enlightened;
that you may know what is the hope of His calling . . .
according to the working of His mighty power.

Ephesians 1:18-19 (NKJV)

————◆————

Sometimes there is so much focus on what *you* want to do that you don't stop and consider the bigger picture of what *God* wants. All you can think about is what's wrong in your life and what God should do to fix it. Your prayers quickly turn into a list of demands on just how you want God to answer. But prayer doesn't work that way. God didn't give you free access to Him just so that you can use Him to get everything you want. Simply put—you can't make plans for your life and expect God to bless them . . . just because you want Him to!

Jesus wants you to trust Him to make the best decisions. Present your needs and then have faith that God will respond according to what is best for you! And don't forget to thank Him for everything that He has already done. David thanked God for His blessings in Psalm 103:2-5 (NIV): "Praise the LORD, my soul, and forget not all His benefits . . . who satisfies your desires with good things so that your youth is renewed like the eagle's."

Sometimes you can be so focused on your troubles that you forget about all the blessings you've already received. The next time you find yourself afflicted with *tunnel vision*, thinking about all the things *you* want, instead, ask God what *He* wants. Pray for discernment, understanding, and wisdom . . . but most of all, pray, "God's will be done."

Do-Over

Therefore, if anyone is in Christ, he is a new creation;
old things have passed away; behold, all things
have become new.

2 Corinthians 5:17 (NKJV)

———◆———

There are not many times in life when you get a second chance or a *do-over*! For instance, when a loved one dies, it's too late to say, "I'm sorry," or restore your relationship. If you've spoken hateful words in anger, you can wish you didn't say them, but you can't take them back. Neither can you get back all the precious years you missed with your children because your work was more important.

However, there is redemption in Jesus Christ. You can't *fix* things, but God can! When you come to Him and ask for forgiveness, He forgives and wipes your slate clean. He gives you a do-over, allowing you to start your life over again, cleansed from all unrighteousness. The Bible says in 1 John 1:9 (NIV), "If we confess our sins, he is faithful and just and will forgive us our sins and purify us from all unrighteousness."

That word "purify" is especially reassuring! In Acts 3:19 (NIV), we're told, "Repent, then, and turn to God, so that your sins may be wiped out, that times of refreshing may come from the Lord." Yes, whatever mistakes you've made, *what's done is done*, but God can change your future, and He can even change the way you feel about your past.

With forgiveness, all guilt is removed, and that hopeless feeling is gone! It's not too late for God to give you a do-over. So why not start by asking Him today?

Declare Your Love

Seek the LORD and His strength; seek His face evermore!
1 Chronicles 16:11 (NKJV)

Whenever you make your mind up that you don't want to do something, you can usually find plenty of excuses to skip it. Sadly, many people find excuses when it comes to making God a priority in their lives. They are too tired to get up and go to church, justifying how hard they worked all week and they really need a break. They ease their conscience by telling themselves they'll go the next week—only next week never comes.

Others complain they don't go to church because of all the "hypocrites" and rationalize that they can just as easy worship at home—only it isn't long before they no longer worship God at all. Some attend church, but then go about their duties all week long without actually taking time for daily worship, much less even thinking about spiritual things.

Why is it that Christians can spend hours on their phones or computers, but can't manage to spare even five minutes to talk with their heavenly Father? When God is not a priority in your life, you will find yourself drifting further and further away from Him . . . one excuse at a time.

The Bible says in Jeremiah 29:13 (NIV), "You will seek me and find me when you seek me with all your heart." It's time to declare your love and commitment to God—no more excuses!

Train Up a Child

Correct your son, and he will give you rest;
yes, he will give delight to your soul.

Proverbs 29:17 (NKJV)

Children are a gift from God, but raising them is one of the most challenging jobs in the world. Once that little bundle is placed in your arms, you feel a tremendous amount of love and joy, but also a bit of fear knowing that you are 100% responsible for this helpless baby!

It takes constant prayer to know exactly what to do, especially in this sinful world we live in today. The Bible says in Proverbs 22:6 (NKJV), "Train up a child in the way he should go, and when he is old he will not depart from it." That is a wonderful promise that parents can claim!

It can be frustrating at times just trying to figure out what to do—whether to say *yes* or *no*. And then there's the whole issue of how to discipline. Scripture says in Ephesians 6:4 (NIV), "Fathers, do not exasperate your children; instead, bring them up in the training and instruction of the Lord."

Too many times parents lose patience, raising their voices and even strike in anger. But that's not God's way. It's important to discipline with *love* and pray for wisdom and patience, always striving to be like Jesus. Remember that God loves your child even more than you do, and the most important goals are to introduce them to Jesus and prepare them for their heavenly home.

God Is Never Boring

*For since the creation of the world God's invisible
qualities—his eternal power and divine nature—
have been clearly seen, being understood from what has
been made, so that people are without excuse.*

Romans 1:20 (NIV)

———◆———

Some people have a routine they do every day. They eat the
same thing for breakfast, take the same route to work, talk
to the same people at lunch, and continue doing the same old
things that they always do, for the simple reason because they
just *always* have and it's familiar and easy! There are even some
who eat the same food day after day! They can go to an ice
cream store with 33 flavors and only order vanilla—never once
even tasting all the other flavors.

For some people, it is fear that drives them to be creatures
of habit. Having to actually try new things is uncomfortable to
them. But if you never try new things, not only is it boring, but
you'll miss out on so many blessings that God has in store for
you. Unfortunately, many people lead a boring Christian life.
They go through the motions of living a godly life without really
being connected to God. Some repeat the same prayer over and
over, sit in the same pew each week, and arrive late and leave
early just so they don't have to actually talk to someone.

God is a very creative God and every day spent with Him is
a brand-new day! Allow God to move you out of your comfort
zone where you can begin truly trusting in Him! He will take
you places you've never been, and you can be sure that life with
Jesus . . . is never boring!

One Compromise Away

*For if we sin willfully after we have received the knowledge
of the truth, there no longer remains a sacrifice for sins.*

Hebrews 10:26 (NKJV)

The choices you make every day determine the person you are—including small decisions such as opening a door for someone, picking up fallen clothing from the store rack, or cleaning up a mess you didn't make. Of course, there are bigger tests of character, such as cheating on taxes, calling in sick, gossiping to friends, lying to the police about how fast you were driving, and so on.

The decisions you make are either influenced by selfish desires or the prompting of the Holy Spirit. Without God's guidance, you can easily be confused by the many dangerous paths to take. However, there is only one path that shines brightly, and on that path God provides His light to help you make the right choices. Without God's illumination, you'll head for disaster, left to fumble in a cloud of darkness and despair that leads to certain death. The devil is quite persuasive and quick to convince you to try *his* way . . . "just this once!" But make no mistake, *spiritual death is just one compromise away*!

Eve's one bad decision in the Garden of Eden not only cost her life, but the consequences of her actions are still impacting the world today! The Bible says in 1 John 1:7 (NKJV), "But if we walk in the light as He is in the light, we have fellowship with one another, and the blood of Jesus Christ His Son cleanses us from all sin." No matter how enticing sin is, nothing is worth missing out on eternity with Jesus—*absolutely nothing*!

Arms of Love

But You, O LORD, are a God full of compassion, and gracious,
longsuffering and abundant in mercy and truth.

Psalm 86:15 (NKJV)

Everyone needs love, especially when feeling sad, lonely or depressed. There's something quite comforting about being held in a warm embrace by someone you love and trust. Suddenly life doesn't seem so bad and you don't feel so helpless. So it is with God, for when you allow yourself to be wrapped in His arms of love, He will soothe your soul and give you a peace such as you have never known!

God understands you more than anyone else. He knows the very moment you feel too weak to even crawl, and tenderly He will pick you up and carry you. He will calm your fears, dry your eyes, and give you strength to go on. The Bible says in 1 John 4:16 (NIV), "And so we know and rely on the love God has for us. God is love. Whoever lives in love lives in God, and God in them." And in 1 John 3:1 (NIV), we're told, "See what great love the Father has lavished on us, that we should be called children of God!"

God loves us so much, He claims us as *His* children. We belong to Him. Truly, there is no better place to be than in the arms of Jesus! Reach out to Him today and dwell in His presence. As you feel His arms of love, be assured that you have nothing to fear—God will take care of your every need!

The more you get to know God as your personal Friend and Savior, the more you will trust yourself to His all-powerful, comforting arms of love.

A Clean Heart

*But we also glory in tribulations, knowing that
tribulation produces perseverance; and perseverance,
character; and character, hope. Now hope does not disappoint, because the love of God has been poured out in
our hearts by the Holy Spirit who was given to us.*

Romans 5:3-5 (NKJV)

As a Christian, you profess to love Jesus and to follow His example by being *like Him*. But all too often, you don't know the condition of your own heart. It is when you are put to the test that your real character is revealed. When someone gets angry and yells at you, what is your response? When a stranger cuts you off in traffic or lets the door slam in your face, how do you react? When your co-worker gets the promotion that was meant for you, how do you respond? It is during times like these that your true heart is revealed.

The Bible says in Mark 7:20 (NIV), "What comes out of a person is what defiles them." What you say and what you do tells people whether or not you belong to God. More importantly, if we want a home in heaven, our lives must reflect the character of Christ.

Ask God to perfect your character by praying David's prayer in Psalm 51:10 (NIV): "Create in me a pure heart, O God, and renew a steadfast spirit within me." When you have Christ's spirit living within you, your words and actions will reveal His love to everyone around you! Start each day by asking God to give you *a clean heart* so that you can truly shine for Him!

Surviving Failure

The LORD is good, a stronghold in the day of trouble;
and He knows those who trust in Him.

Nahum 1:7 (NKJV)

———◆———

When you have tried your very best and your *best* is still not *good enough*, it's human nature to feel like a *failure*. Then, when you start looking around at others who are successful, your feelings of inadequacy get even worse! Sometimes, it's in your job, personal relationships, or even marriage where you've failed. But no matter how low or how worthless you may feel, there is only one way to survive failure and that is to reach out to Jesus for comfort and healing.

He's not going to judge you or rub your nose in your mistakes. But He will give you unconditional love, support, and guidance. And He will be there for you 100% of the time! He will never forsake you or turn His back on you. He is not an "I told you so" God that gloats when you fail! Only God is perfect, so as long as you live on this earth, you *will* make mistakes—that's a fact!

The only *sure* thing in this world is God's presence, and no one else can promise you peace of mind or spiritual healing! Jesus can give you exactly what you need to pick yourself up and overcome all obstacles on the road to success! When you think about it, the only *real* failure . . . is to refuse God's help!

Lying Lips

It is better not to make a vow than to make one and not fulfill it.

Ecclesiastes 5:5 (NIV)

Making promises you don't intend to keep is not only wrong, but it's breaking the ninth commandment, found in Exodus 20:16 (NKJV): "You shall not bear false witness against your neighbor." One of the most common offenses is when someone says, "Please keep this in confidence," and then you turn around and tell someone else. No matter how you sugarcoat it, that is dishonest!

Justifying all the *honorable* reasons why you chose not to keep your word does not make it right. It is, in fact, a *sin*. Nor does it make it *okay* if you don't come out and actually tell, but *hint* enough for the person to figure it out! That is still a lie because you are not honoring your word.

Not only are you breaking God's commandments, your reputation will be damaged as well. You will be labeled *untrustworthy*, and worse, your integrity will be compromised. The Bible says in Jeremiah 17:10 (NIV), "I the Lord search the heart and examine the mind, to reward each person according to their conduct, according to what their deeds deserve."

If you are ever tempted to be dishonest, pray David's prayer in Psalm 120:2 (NIV): "Save me, Lord, from lying lips and from deceitful tongues." God wants you to honor Him by being honest, truthful, and dependable and to always keep your word.

Pure Thoughts

For the weapons of our warfare are not carnal but mighty in God for pulling down strongholds, casting down arguments and every high thing that exalts itself against the knowledge of God, bringing every thought into captivity to the obedience of Christ.

2 Corinthians 10:4-5 (NKJV)

As you go throughout your day, does your mind tend to wander? Do you find it hard to focus because your thoughts are a million miles away? If so, evaluate where your mind goes! Where do your thoughts travel during your most unguarded moments? What you think about is a strong indicator of what is most important to you. Are you thinking about your family, your job, or how you're going to pay the bills? How much time do you spend dwelling on spiritual things?

God doesn't want you to worry and fret about your problems! He wants you to trust Him with your trials, pain, and heartache, knowing He will see you through. He also wants you to have good thoughts, keeping your mind focused on Him. If you find yourself thinking about things that are pulling you away from God, then it's time to push the *reset button* by reading God's Holy Word and start filling your mind with things that are pure and true.

Prayer and Bible study are the best ways to get your thoughts focused in the right direction! The Bible says in Philippians 4:8 (NIV), "Whatever is pure, whatever is lovely, whatever is admirable—if anything is excellent or praiseworthy—think about such things."

Why Me?

Therefore, since Christ suffered for us in the flesh,
arm yourselves also with the same mind, for he who has
suffered in the flesh has ceased from sin.

1 Peter 4:1 (NKJV)

When everything's going smoothly in our lives, and then all of a sudden, something devastating happens, our first thought is, *Why me? How could God allow this to happen?*

It's hard to imagine why bad things happen to good people, but there are many different reasons. Sometimes, it's God's punishment. The Bible says in Hebrews 12:5-6 (NIV), "My son, do not make light of the Lord's discipline, and do not lose heart when he rebukes you, because the Lord disciplines the one he loves, and he chastens everyone he accepts as his son."

Other times, it is to perfect our characters or allow God's power and glory to be revealed through us. John 9:3 (NKJV) says, "Neither this man nor his parents sinned, but that the works of God should be revealed in him."

But not all trials are brought on by God. More often than not, it's the enemy at work trying hard to discourage and separate us from our best Friend, Jesus. Satan is good at pushing all our buttons, and he knows where we are weakest. There's nothing he won't do in order to accomplish his goal of getting us to turn on God. But don't allow the enemy one moment to gloat! Instead of being angry and asking, *Why me?* remain steadfast in your faith, for He will give you strength and comfort through every trial and tribulation.

Gift of Forgiveness

*In Him we have redemption through His blood, the
forgiveness of sins, according to the riches of His grace.*

Ephesians 1:7 (NKJV)

God's forgiveness is not for sale! You can't buy it, earn it,
or bargain for it. God forgives because of *who He is*, not
because of who we are or what we do. We don't have to be
perfect to receive God's forgiveness. That's great news because
no one is perfect and that would be an unobtainable goal! God's
grace and mercy is extended to all His children who love Him
and believe in Him.

We obey God to show Him how much we love and
appreciate Him, not to gain entry to paradise. Many people
don't understand just how loving our heavenly Father truly is.
They think He is looking down on us just waiting for us to mess
up so He can rain His wrath down upon us. But this is one of
Satan's lies and could not be further from the truth. Jesus loves
us so much that He died to save us! He doesn't desire for anyone
to perish but that each of us have eternal life!

Forgiveness is ours, just for the asking. The Bible says in
1 John 1:9 (NKJV) that all we need to do is "confess our sins,
and He is faithful and just to forgive us our sins and cleanse us
from all unrighteousness!" What an awesome God we serve!
Praise the Lord that forgiveness is not for sale, and neither is
God's love for us! Confess your sins to Jesus right now, this very
moment, and you'll receive His gift of forgiveness . . . with no
price to pay! Your bill was paid in full at Calvary.

Worshiping Idols

I hate those who cling to worthless idols;
as for me, I trust in the LORD.

Psalm 31:6 (NIV)

———◆———

God does not want His children worshiping idols. In fact, He feels so strongly about it that He wrote with His own finger on a tablet of stone, making it one of the Ten Commandments. It is recorded in Exodus 20:4-5 (NKJV): "You shall not make for yourself a carved image—any likeness of anything that is in heaven above, or that is in the earth beneath, or that is in the water under the earth; you shall not bow down to them or serve them. For I, the LORD your God, am a jealous God." And Leviticus 26:1 (ESV) says, "You shall not make idols for yourselves or erect an image or pillar, and you shall not set up a figured stone in your land to bow down to it, for I am the LORD your God."

You see, God wants you to love and obey Him and worship *only* Him. He doesn't want you to worship anything or anyone else. Some Christians worship idols without even realizing it, because anything that you love more than Jesus Christ . . . is an idol. It could be your fancy new car, a prestigious job, wealth, beauty, power, or countless other things—even people. If you love material things or your relationships more than you love God, then you are worshiping idols.

Whatever is standing in the way of your friendship with Jesus, move it or get rid of it. Nothing is more important than your relationship with God! Worship the King of the Universe . . . and only the King!

True Love

*My little children, let us not love in word or in
tongue, but in deed and in truth.*

1 John 3:18 (NKJV)

Very few people fully comprehend *true* love, yet of all the human emotions, it's the one most sought after! Many equate *love* with superficial things, such as diamonds, flowers, or candy. But the basis for true love comes from God. When we love as Jesus loves, there's no jealousy, anger, or walls of bitterness. Instead, we treat our loved one with respect and kindness, and place their needs and wants ahead of our own.

True love requires unselfishness, loyalty, and faithfulness, and is much more than simply giving gifts. It is God's love that gives us the ability to give our loved one the benefit of the doubt or overlook a slight grievance instead of letting it escalate into a war of unkind words.

You can never fully understand or comprehend *love* unless you are connected with our heavenly Father, because He is the giver of all love! The Bible says in 1 John 4:16 (NIV), "And so we know and rely on the love God has for us. God is love. Whoever lives in love lives in God, and God in them." And in Jeremiah 31:3 (NIV), we're told, "I have loved you with an everlasting love; I have drawn you with unfailing kindness."

There's no such thing as a *happy home* unless God lives there! Keep Jesus in your heart and you'll always know and experience *true love*—it truly is that simple!

Higher than the Ceiling

But without faith it is impossible to please Him, for he
who comes to God must believe that He is, and that He is
a rewarder of those who diligently seek Him.

Hebrews 11:6 (NKJV)

When approaching the throne room of God, it's important to have faith that God actually listens and answers your prayers, for prayer and faith go hand in hand! The Bible says in Matthew 21:21 (ESV), "Truly, I say to you, if you have faith and do not doubt, you will not only do what has been done to the fig tree, but even if you say to this mountain, 'Be taken up and thrown into the sea,' it will happen."

God certainly makes it very clear how important *believing in Him* is. Too often, prayers are prayed *hoping . . . hoping . . . hoping . . .* that God will hear, but not actually believing that He will. Yet, God says in Matthew 21:22 (KJV), "And all things, whatsoever ye shall ask in prayer, believing, ye shall receive." It's not enough to just *hope*—you must believe.

In 1 John 5:14 (NKJV), Jesus says, "Now this is the confidence that we have in Him, that if we ask anything according to His will, He hears us." You often hear people say, "I don't think my prayers go higher than the ceiling," and that's exactly what Satan wants you to think . . . but it's a lie! God hears not only your audible prayers, He hears your heart!

If your faith is weak, pray, "Lord, give me faith," and God will give you the trust you need to believe in Him! You can know without a doubt that your prayers go much higher than the ceiling . . . for they go straight to the throne room of God!

Deadly Disease

*The soul of a lazy man desires, and has nothing; but the
soul of the diligent shall be made rich.*

Proverbs 13:4 (NKJV)

One of the biggest reasons for *laziness* is lack of passion.
When there is nothing that excites or *motivates* our inner
self, we tend to just go through the motions of living. Co-
workers dislike laziness because they have to work extra hard
to make up for the one who is slacking! Family members get
frustrated too . . . for the same reason!

The Bible has quite a bit to say about how God feels about
laziness! In Ecclesiastes 9:10 (NKJV), we're told, "Whatever
your hand finds to do, do it with your might." God wants us to
work hard and do a good job!

Unfortunately, laziness carries over to our Christian lives
too! There are those who suffer with the deadly disease of
spiritual laziness. Fortunately, our heavenly Father has a cure!
All we need to do is pray and ask Him to take away all laziness
from within us!

Why not pray today, "Dear God, forgive me for the times
I have ignored the Holy Spirit's wake-up call. Remove this
deadly disease of laziness, and help me to get up early to spend
time with You. Fill me with energy so that You can use me in a
powerful way. I claim Your promise in Matthew 10:22 that 'he
who endures to the end will be saved.' O Lord, mold me and
make me into a worker who will endure to the end that I might
receive Your heavenly reward. In Jesus' precious name. Amen."

When Hope Seems Gone

And now, Lord, what do I wait for? My hope is in You.

Psalm 39:7 (NKJV)

‹——◆◇◆——›

There is nothing sadder than to look into the eyes of someone who has lost all hope! Without *hope,* there's really no reason to get up in the morning, to go about your daily duties, or even to function at all. People without hope go through the motions of living and are in constant misery. But, praise the Lord, there is no reason why anyone should live without hope, because Jesus *is* your hope! Because of Christ's sacrifice on Calvary, hope reigns eternal.

There's no need to live in darkness and despair, walking around with a dejected look on your face—Jesus is the answer! When you give your life over to Him, you can know beyond a shadow of a doubt that God has a bright future planned for you, living with Him in heaven for all eternity. It just doesn't get better than that! The Bible says in Isaiah 40:31 (NIV), "Those who hope in the Lord will renew their strength. They will soar on wings like eagles; they will run and not grow weary, they will walk and not be faint." And you can claim God's promise in Jeremiah 29:11 (NIV), "'For I know the plans I have for you,' declares the Lord, 'plans to prosper you and not to harm you, plans to give you hope and a future.'"

Romans 15:13 (NIV) shares God's promise: "May the God of hope fill you with all joy and peace as you trust in him, so that you may overflow with hope by the power of the Holy Spirit." Whenever you're discouraged and it seems all hope is gone, look up, for Jesus *is* your hope!

A Saintly Attitude

As each has received a gift, use it to serve one another, as good stewards of God's varied grace.

1 Peter 4:10 (ESV)

———◆———

Serving Jesus in any capacity is an honor and a privilege. However, many find it easier to surrender their lives in service to God if they are holding a job of importance. Speaking from a pulpit, holding a position of authority, or being highly regarded because of all your good works makes it a lot easier to say *yes* to God's call. But are you just as eager to serve God if you're called to do the *grunt* work, doing a job where there will be no *thank-yous* or deep appreciation for your labor? The Bible says in Philippians 4:12 (NKJV), "I know how to be abased, and I know how to abound. Everywhere and in all things I have learned both to be full and to be hungry, both to abound and to suffer need." And in Philippians 2:17 (NKJV), we're told, "If I am being poured out as a drink offering on the sacrifice and service of your faith, I am glad and rejoice with you all."

Ask yourself today, *Am I willing to be as insignificant as a mere drop in the bucket, being poured out until I have given all I have? Am I seeking to help others without wanting something in return? When doing a good deed, do I look around to see who is watching or pout if no one tells me how awesome I am?* A true test for a follower of Christ is humility! There are some, when called to do menial work for God, just can't muster up a saintly attitude, simply because of pride. Always remember to serve God for the right reasons and with a smile on your face.

Selfish Anger

The discretion of a man makes him slow to anger,
and his glory is to overlook a transgression.

Proverbs 19:11 (NKJV)

Of all human emotions, *anger* is without a doubt a *selfish* emotion! Just take a minute to consider where anger stems from: caring about *yourself,* how *you* are treated, and how situations affect *you* directly. Even if you are angry because someone treated your friend badly, it's still about *you* because it was *your* friend.

People watch the news and see terrible things reported all the time: murders, rapes, child abuse, theft, and a million other things, but most of the time, you don't get angry unless somehow, it affects you—a selfish reason for being angry. But whatever the reason, anger is downright destructive. It doesn't make you feel any better to get mad, and worst of all, it separates you from Jesus! You can't have God's love in your heart and harbor anger at the same time.

The Bible actually has a lot to say about being angry. Matthew 5:22 (NIV) says, "I tell you that anyone who is angry with a brother or sister will be subject to judgment." In other words, don't be angry, for you will be judged for that! And Ephesians 4:26 (NIV) tells us, " 'In your anger do not sin': Do not let the sun go down while you are still angry." Now that alone is the most important reason to let God handle the situations that tempt you to become angry. There is only one way to keep anger from consuming your life and that is by allowing Jesus to live in your heart . . . always!

Pray Without Ceasing

*Praying always with all prayer and supplication
in the Spirit.*

Ephesians 6:18 (NKJV)

Have you ever wondered what the Bible means in 1 Thessalonians 5:17 where we are instructed to "pray without ceasing"? Does that mean that we're supposed to stay on our knees 24/7 and pray? Of course not. The Bible is not describing a formal or noticeable act of prayer, but rather a way of life—an attitude of prayer, where we are comfortable talking with God anytime and anywhere! It is living life with a deep awareness of God at all times and allowing Him to guide our every thought, deed, and action. In other words, we should walk so close to Jesus that we consult Him about everything and acknowledge Him as our best Friend whom we want to share our life with.

When we are constantly in an attitude of prayer, it is life-changing, because every part of our day is influenced by God's presence. When something awesome happens, our first thought is to praise Him. When in the presence of evil, we send an SOS heavenward. And when tempted, we go to Jesus for strength to resist the temptation. Praying without ceasing allows us to live our lives with a continual ascending prayer where we consult God in every life circumstance. We need to pray with patience, pray believing and pray without ceasing!

Quitters Never Win

And David said to his son Solomon, "Be strong and of good courage, and do it; do not fear nor be dismayed, for the LORD God—my God—will be with you. He will not leave you nor forsake you, until you have finished all the work for the service of the house of the LORD.

1 Chronicles 28:20 (NKJV)

When you've said or done something you wished you wouldn't have, or even made a mistake at work that you're sure all your co-workers are talking about, it's not the time to quit and run! You might feel like the biggest loser in the world and be so embarrassed you want to hide under the closest rock, but that will never fix the problem or undo the damage that's already been done.

Running from your troubles is a cowardly thing to do and most certainly will not bring you peace, joy, or happiness for quitters never win and winners . . . never quit! Instead of running away, face the music! When you are humble and willing to admit mistakes, it is much easier for others to forgive you than if you try and hide it or defend your actions.

Ask for forgiveness and a chance to prove yourself, then go forward with Holy Spirit power, claiming Philippians 4:13 (NKJV): "I can do all things through Christ who strengthens me." Before long, no one will look at you and even remember the incident, because they will see a *winner*, not a *quitter*!

Directly to Your Heart

*This Book of the Law shall not depart from your
mouth, but you shall meditate in it day and night . . .
and then you will have good success.*

Joshua 1:8 (NKJV)

It's human nature to want as much information as possible
before making decisions. For instance, before accepting
a job, you want to know how much you'll be paid, what the
work environment is like, and if you like the people you'd be
working with. Before purchasing a house, you'll want to pay
for an inspection so you can know just what repairs might be
needed and how much they will cost, which allows you to make
an informed decision before signing on the dotted line.

Knowing the facts and being informed is not only prudent,
but wise. It's no different when it comes to spiritual things—
God wants you to *know* what you believe by studying His Holy
Word! It's dangerous to blindly accept what others say about
the Scriptures, including your pastor! God wants to speak to
you directly, so always listen to what He is telling you. The Bible
says in 2 Timothy 3:16-17 (ESV), "All Scripture is breathed out
by God and profitable for teaching, for reproof, for correction,
and for training in righteousness."

God wants you to search the Scriptures for yourself. Ask
God for wisdom, guidance, and understanding before reading
His Holy Word so you can hear God speaking directly to your
heart!

Resist the Devil

You are my hiding place; You shall preserve me from
trouble; You shall surround me with songs of deliverance.

Psalm 32:7 (NKJV)

———◆———

You may have every desire to obey God's voice and do the *right* thing, but when Satan puts temptation in your path, somehow you end up doing the very thing that you really didn't want to do. Afterwards, you're filled with guilt and disappointment because, once again, you sinned against God. The Bible says in Mark 14:38 (NIV), "Watch and pray so that you will not fall into temptation. The spirit is willing, but the flesh is weak."

It's important to stay close to Jesus so that you will not fall no matter what Satan throws at you! God will give you the strength to resist the devil, which is confirmed in Isaiah 40:29 (NIV): "He gives strength to the weary and increases the power of the weak."

And here's the good news: you can claim God's promise in 1 Corinthians 10:13 (NKJV), which says, "No temptation has overtaken you except such as is common to man; but God is faithful, who will not allow you to be tempted beyond what you are able, but with the temptation will also make the way of escape, that you may be able to bear it." It can't get much clearer than that! Being willing is not enough—you need God's Holy Spirit power to make the right choices. Stay close to Jesus and He will give you His strength to resist temptation and shine for Him!

Recipe for Disaster

Preserve my life, for I am holy; You are my God;
save Your servant who trusts in You!

Psalm 86:2 (NKJV)

Whenever you get lazy and start backing off of your time spent with God, it affects every aspect of your life! It is your constant connection with Him that gives you the wisdom, power, and strength to face each day, and without it, you are spiritually dead! It's like trying to drive a car without any fuel or energy source! Christians know that, but the devil is very cunning and is the expert deceiver. He knows when you are weak and is patient enough to wait until the very moment you are most vulnerable, and then he strikes. It may be when you are physically exhausted, your children have stomped on your last nerve, you can't pay the bills that are piling up, or an unreasonable boss has just crossed the line!

It's when you are at the breaking point that instead of turning to your best Friend, Jesus, you're tempted to pull away. But trying to solve your own problems is a recipe for disaster! Instead of skipping morning devotions because you just *don't feel like it* or you're too discouraged to open God's Word, drop to your knees and tell the Lord exactly how you feel. Open up and share your heart. Tell God you're discouraged and weak and let Him know how much you need Him! Jesus cares . . . He really cares! The most important part of your day is time spent with Jesus! He will give you the strength, power, and courage to face all the crisis moments in your life and the wisdom to make the right choices!

Complete Control

For all have sinned and fall short of the glory of God,
being justified freely by His grace through the redemption
that is in Christ Jesus.

Romans 3:23-24 (NKJV)

Sometimes it's quite difficult to navigate through all life's challenges, decisions and choices. Without God's instruction book, it's impossible not to make a real mess of our lives! Just one bad judgment call will send us spiraling down the slippery slope to disaster! The truth is, humans are not perfect and everyone makes mistakes, but praise the Lord, God never does! That's why it's important to give Him complete control over every aspect of your life. And what's really amazing: even when we mess up, He has the power to take the shattered pieces of our broken lives and turn them into something beautiful! It doesn't matter what you've done, there is nothing that God can't forgive. He's waiting with outstretched arms for you to run to Him, for He alone has the power to forgive.

The Bible says in 1 John 1:9 (NKJV), "If we confess our sins, He is faithful and just to forgive us our sins and to cleanse us from all unrighteousness." All we need to do is come to Jesus, confess our sins, and through faith, accept God's gift of forgiveness. It's that simple! Then just step back and watch what God can do! You don't have to worry, fret, or stay up all night worrying about what to do next! Just take a deep breath, relax, and enjoy the sweet peace of God's presence. It's awesome to see what happens when you give God complete control of your life!

No Room for Envy

Let us not become conceited, provoking one
another, envying one another.

Galatians 5:26 (NKJV)

———◆———

One of the biggest threats to *inner peace* is jealousy. One tiny seed planted in your heart soon grows out of control and its evil vines choke out every ounce of goodness. The Bible says in Proverbs 14:30 (NIV), "A heart at peace gives life to the body, but envy rots the bones." And in James 3:16 (NKJV), the warning is clear: "For where envy and self-seeking exist, confusion and every evil thing are there."

It's easy sometimes to look at what someone else has and want it for yourself. You may even think you deserve it more than they do and subconsciously begin to feel angry that you were not blessed in the same way—it could be material things, job status, financial value, or even a relationship. But harboring a deep desire for what someone else has will not bring you peace, joy, or contentment. The most important reason to get rid of all envy and jealousy is because it will prevent you from spending eternity with Jesus!

God says in Ephesians 5:5 (NKJV), "For this you know, that no fornicator, unclean person, nor covetous man, who is an idolater, has any inheritance in the kingdom of Christ and God." The best way to stomp out the weeds in a jealous heart is to embrace who God created you to be and be content with the gifts He gives you, for there is absolutely no room for envy in heaven!

Who Has Your Loyalty?

He who pursues righteousness and loyalty finds life,
righteousness and honor.

Proverbs 21:21 (NASB)

———◆———

One of the most important ingredients for any friendship is *loyalty*, for without it, the relationship is a meaningless. Far too often, people disregard loyalty, sometimes without even knowing it. Whenever someone comes to you and asks you to keep a secret from your friend, the minute you agree to keep their confidence, you have transferred your loyalty from your friend . . . to them. If truly loyal, your first response to such a request would be, "I won't keep secrets from my friend. If you still want to share your news with me, fine, but I won't promise to keep it secret." Taking that stand usually stops gossipers in their tracks, and more importantly, demonstrates your loyalty.

So it is with God—when we yield to Satan's temptations, listen to his lies, and follow his evil plans, we have transferred our loyalty from our only *true* friend, Jesus Christ, to the enemy. God wants us to be loyal to Him and loyal in our friendships here on earth, following biblical advice in Romans 12:10 (NIV): "Be devoted to one another in love. Honor one another above yourselves." God makes it very clear in John 15:13 (NASB) how we should value our friendships: "Greater love has no one than this, that one lay down his life for his friends." Jesus proved His loyalty and love toward each of us when He gave His life to die on a cross so that we can have eternal life with Him. There's no greater love than that!

Contract with the Devil

"What comes out of a man, that defiles a man. For from within, out of the heart of men, proceed evil thoughts, adulteries, fornications, murders, thefts, covetousness, wickedness, deceit, lewdness, an evil eye, blasphemy, pride, foolishness. All these evil things come from within and defile a man."

Mark 7:20-23 (NKJV)

———◇———

Satan wants you to think that indulging in His temptations is the only way to a *happy life*. But don't believe his lies for one moment. People who live self-centered lives couldn't be more miserable! When you spend the majority of your time living for *self* and partaking in worldly pleasures, your life is not only meaningless but it is a life without joy, hope, or the assurance of eternal life.

The Bible says in Galatians 5:19-21 (NIV), "The acts of the flesh are obvious: sexual immorality, impurity and debauchery; idolatry and witchcraft; hatred, discord, jealousy, fits of rage, selfish ambition, dissensions, factions and envy; drunkenness, orgies, and the like. I warn you, as I did before, that those who live like this will not inherit the kingdom of God." It doesn't get clearer than that! Bottom line, sin is a contract with the devil.

The moment you choose sin, your allegiance is to Satan. Instead of making all your decisions based on what *you* want, fix your mind on what God wants and enter into a contract with the only one who can save you, Jesus Christ.

Most Powerful Prayer

For God did not appoint us to wrath, but to obtain salvation through our Lord Jesus Christ.

1 Thessalonians 5:9 (NKJV)

———◅❖▻———

This world is filled with so much pain and heartache that Satan has a lot to smile about, and he really gets excited when people blame God for all their troubles! But it's not God's fault! Satan is the one who brought sin into this world and with it came misery, loss, and brokenness. There seems to be no end to heart-wrenching pain, such as domestic violence, world hunger, losing a loved one, terrorist attacks, and so much more.

But as painful as all these experiences are, they aren't the worst that can happen to you. The worst thing . . . is losing your relationship with God and missing out on eternal life with Him! Nothing is worse than that! No matter what trial you are going through, trust Jesus! Reach out to Him and He will help you! The same God that parted the Red Sea, fed the five thousand, and caused the walls of Jericho to fall down is still the lifesaving, all-powerful, miracle-making God today!

And the good news is, Satan doesn't have the power to separate you from God. Romans 8:38-39 (NIV) tells us, "For I am convinced that neither death nor life . . . nor anything else in all creation, will be able to separate us from the love of God that is in Christ Jesus our Lord." That's a promise we can claim for our own! The most powerful prayer you can pray is just these three words: "Jesus, save me!" It will bring tens of thousands of angels to your side in an instant!

Get Over Yourself

*For the Lord will be your confidence, and will keep
your foot from being caught.*

Proverbs 3:26 (NKJV)

People with poor self-esteem have a difficult time feeling *good enough* and can be their own worst enemy. They constantly look to others to see if they measure up and the first time they don't quite get it right, they immediately get down in the dumps thinking, *I'm always such a failure! I can't ever get anything right!* They don't take constructive criticism or suggestions well either, often moving to the defensive zone to ward off perceived attacks. But constantly putting yourself down and thinking negative thoughts about yourself is not how God wants you to be. Jesus loves you more than you could possibly know, and just because your talents are different than what He gave someone else, does not make you unworthy, second rate, or a total idiot!

Embrace the person God made you to be, and when you mess up, don't wallow in the "I blame me" game with thoughts like, *I'm such a screw-up, I don't know why anyone would want to be around me. I never get anything right*, and so on. Get over yourself! You are not so powerful that you can take credit for all the bad things that happen. Satan gets that blame! Above all, remember that God is your Creator and He *never* makes a mistake! So instead of self-loathing, praise God for creating you just the way you are, as David did in Psalm 139:14 (NRSV): "I praise you, for I am fearfully and wonderfully made. Wonderful are your works."

No Need to Stress

*Oh, fear the LORD, you His saints! There is no
want to those who fear Him. . . . those who seek the LORD
shall not lack any good thing.*

Psalm 34:9-10 (NKJV)

When you turn on the news and hear that the stock market is crashing and the world is in a financial crisis, it's enough to raise your blood pressure just thinking about it. The stress factor is elevated even more when faced with the mounds of bills piling up on your desk and not enough funds in your bank account to cover them. Even though everyone depends on money for day-to-day living, it's important to remember that God is your Provider. Your security is based on your relationship with Him, not on how much money you have. The Bible says in Matthew 6:24 (NIV), "You cannot serve both God and money." In other words, you need to focus on Jesus . . . and not be driven by the love of money.

This world's wealth will not bring lasting joy and peace! Whenever you're tempted to break out in a cold sweat about your finances, claim God's promise in Philippians 4:19 (KJV), "But my God shall supply all your need according to his riches in glory by Christ Jesus." You can trust God to take care of you, for He always keeps His promises. Notice, however, that He promised to provide your every *need*, not all your *wants*. Matthew 6:8 (NKJV) says, "For your Father knows the things you have need of before you ask Him." There's no need to stress when you allow God to take over every aspect of your life . . . including your finances.

Witnessing at Work

Repay no one evil for evil. Have regard for good things in the sight of all men. If it is possible, as much as depends on you, live peaceably with all men.

Romans 12:17-18 (NKJV)

In most work situations these days, it is not politically correct to talk about God while on the job. In fact, many companies have made it a policy not to do so, and sadly, people have even lost their jobs because of witnessing to their co-workers. But there are more effective ways of sharing your faith at work than actually *talking* about it, and that is by the way you act.

Whether you know it or not, people are watching you. They see you respond with kindness after a hurtful remark, your gentle spirit in the midst of a tense situation, or your self-control under fire. Actions speak louder than words and always showing a Christlike attitude is a powerful silent witness.

When you are known to be the one to *go the extra mile*, a hard worker who is willing to pull more than their fair share, and someone who always helping out, people will not only notice, but they'll want to find out your secret—what makes you so different than everyone else?

Others, when there is confrontation, would probably be angry, saying bad words, or stomping off impatiently. But when you are gracious, soft-spoken, and respectful of others, the light of Jesus shines through, and that is the most powerful witness you could ever be!

Greatest Stress Reliever

Anxiety in a man's heart weighs him down,
but a good word makes him glad.

Proverbs 12:25 (ESV)

When you feel like there are not enough hours in the day, expectations are too high, it's impossible to get everything done you need to do, and your life is spinning out of control, stop and ask yourself, *When was the last time I prayed? When was the last time I studied my Bible?* and *When was the last time I truly felt close to God?*

Quite often when you're stressed out and irritable and your anxiety level is sky-high, it's because you have neglected your quiet time with God. Somehow, the pressures of life and demands of others placed you on overload, and instead of making Jesus *first* in your life, He was relegated to the back burner. Whenever you neglect God, your life will spiral downward. You can't possibly be happy because Jesus *is* the joy of living! Yet, too often, when feeling burned-out and over-stressed, you reach for your smartphone to check all your social media accounts, which leaves you feeling even more anxious.

If you are truly seeking peace from the confusion and stress of this world, God's Word is the answer. Scripture confirms this in Psalm 62:1 (NIV): "Truly my soul finds rest in God; my salvation comes from him." Read His comforting words of love and allow the Holy Spirit to speak to your heart. Then, drop to your knees and ask for an extra measure of God's peace, the greatest stress reliever of all!

Willing but Weak

"And do not lead us into temptation, but deliver us from the evil one. For Yours is the kingdom and the power and the glory forever. Amen."

Matthew 6:13 (NKJV)

————◆————

As a Christian, you strive every day to be more like Jesus by being thoughtful, generous, kind, patient, and loving, but let's face it, no matter how hard you try, there are some days that walking that narrow path seems to be more difficult than others. You *want* to do the right thing, but your body is *weak*

The Bible says in Mark 14:38 (NIV), "Watch and pray so that you will not fall into temptation. The spirit is willing, but the flesh is weak." This was something that the apostle Paul struggled with as well. In Romans 7:15-17 (NIV), he expressed his frustration: "I do not understand what I do. For what I want to do I do not do, but what I hate I do. And if I do what I do not want to do, I agree that the law is good. As it is, it is no longer I myself who do it, but it is sin living in me."

Paul identifies the problem as sin living in him. So, the only answer to keep your heart pure and free from sin is to keep your focus on Jesus! If you don't keep your eyes on your Lord and Savior and stay in the safety of His arms, you will fall into temptation. Remember that when you are weak, Jesus is strong! When you feel like giving up and yielding to sinful desires, cling even closer to Jesus, for He is your strength, courage, hope, and power to fight the enemy! Claim Philippians 4:13 (NKJV): "I can do all things through Christ who strengthens me," and even in your weakness . . . God will give you the victory!

Secrets of Your Heart

And whatever you do in word or deed, do all
in the name of the Lord Jesus, giving thanks to
God the Father through Him.

Colossians 3:17 (NKJV)

Many Christians have the perception that if they want to go to heaven then they have to get their quota of *good deeds* done, as if they are earning their entrance fee to Paradise. But no one can *earn* or *buy* their way to heaven. Salvation is free to all who have surrendered their hearts to Jesus! But that doesn't mean we are off the hook when it comes to compassion toward our fellow man. Jesus set a wonderful example about how to treat others when He was here on earth. He was tender and kind with everyone, even those who were cruel and mistreated Him. He never spoke in anger or disgust to even those who lied, gossiped, or were mean to Him, but only spoke with love in His heart. It's impossible to *be like Jesus* and demonstrate His character if we have not surrendered our lives to Him.

The closer our relationship is to Christ, the more we become like Him. We will want to be kind and generous to others, not for *show* or to get compliments about how great we are, but rather because we truly love as Jesus loves! We need to be authentic and genuine in our actions. If we are just needing an *ego boost*, wanting recognition, and performing acts of kindness for the wrong reasons, not only will God know, but it will become obvious to others as well . . . because our actions betray the secrets of our hearts!

Burden of Unforgiveness

"For if you forgive men their trespasses, your heavenly Father will also forgive you."

Matthew 6:14 (NKJV)

People around the world are on an endless search for *real* happiness. Some search for contentment in all the wrong places, such as material things, sports, music, vacations, or finding their dream job. Then there are those who expect other people to *make* them happy and not understanding why it just doesn't work! Some have the perfect house, perfect job, and seemingly perfect life . . . but still are restless, discontent, and can't quite figure out just what is missing.

The truth is, no one can be truly happy without a close relationship with God. Many feel distant toward God because they are harboring bitterness, hatred, or unforgiveness in their hearts, not realizing it is standing between them and God's perfect peace. You can never experience God's gift of joy if your heart is filled with anger toward someone else. Even more important, when you study God's Word, it becomes clear that unforgiveness is *sin,* for it is direct disobedience to God.

When you think of all the things God has forgiven you for, it hardly seems unreasonable for God to expect you to forgive others! Forgiving is not a feeling, but an act of your will, because the reason to forgive is based on your love for your heavenly Father. When you forgive, your heavy burden will disappear and you'll experience real happiness and joy!

Releasing God's Power

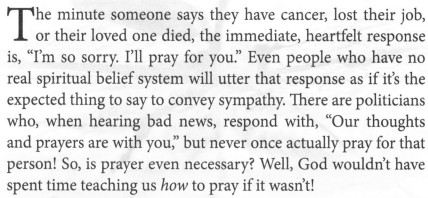

*"Ask, and it will be given to you; seek, and you will find;
knock, and it will be opened to you."*

Matthew 7:7 (NKJV)

The minute someone says they have cancer, lost their job, or their loved one died, the immediate, heartfelt response is, "I'm so sorry. I'll pray for you." Even people who have no real spiritual belief system will utter that response as if it's the expected thing to say to convey sympathy. There are politicians who, when hearing bad news, respond with, "Our thoughts and prayers are with you," but never once actually pray for that person! So, is prayer even necessary? Well, God wouldn't have spent time teaching us *how* to pray if it wasn't!

In Matthew 6:9-10 (NKJV), we're told, "In this manner, therefore, pray: Our Father in heaven, hallowed be your name. Your kingdom come. Your will be done on earth as it is in heaven." Throughout the entire Bible, we are told to pray . . . pray . . . pray . . . because prayer is absolutely necessary! If we want to be used by God to fulfill His work here on earth, we need constant communication with our heavenly Father.

Remember that prayer is a privilege that is *always* ours, but the *power* in prayer is always God's! When we pray, it releases God's power to carry out His will, not only in our lives, but also in the lives of those we pray for.

Truly Compassionate

*But whoever has this world's goods, and sees his brother
in need, and shuts up his heart from him, how does the
love of God abide in him?*

1 John 3:17 (NKJV)

When Jesus was here on earth, He showed us a wonderful example of someone who was truly compassionate. He spent day after day healing the sick, lifting up the downhearted, and ministering to the countless needs of others. The dictionary describes compassion as "a feeling of deep sympathy and sorrow for another who is stricken by misfortune, accompanied by a strong desire to alleviate the suffering." True tenderness starts with love in our hearts for mankind. When we see someone crying, hungry, sick or in pain, a compassionate heart longs to be able to *help*.

In some cases, helping is possible by giving food to the hungry, finding shelter for the homeless, or giving comfort to the grieving. Other times, it may be by donating funds or a placing a phone call of encouragement. One of the best ways to help is to pray an intercessory prayer for those who are hurting and in need. Instead of looking away when seeing someone who is down and out, take a moment to let them know you care and offer a prayer with them. Always strive to be like Jesus—kind, compassionate, and tenderhearted.

The Bible says in 1 Peter 3:8 (NIV), "Finally, all of you, be like-minded, be sympathetic, love one another, be compassionate and humble." Ask God to put more love in your heart for others, so that you may be truly compassionate like Him.

Lost the Vision

*Now therefore, if you will indeed obey My voice and keep
My covenant, then you shall be a special treasure to Me
above all people; for all the earth is Mine.*

Exodus 19:5 (NKJV)

———⋘⋙———

The Bible says in Proverbs 29:18 (KJV), "Where there is no vision, the people perish: but he that keepeth the law, happy is he." In other words, when people lose sight of God, they begin to sink as if in quicksand. They become reckless and lose their willpower over sin. Their prayer life fades away, and selfishness motivates even the smallest of life's choices and decisions. Some people consider themselves to have principles, but those consumed with idealistic principles rarely do anything to rise to a higher spiritual plane.

There's a big difference between holding on to a principle and having a vision of who God is and following His divine instruction. Losing sight of God's vision will not only put you in a very dark and lonely place, but you will *perish*. On the other hand, wherever there is *vision*, there is honesty, integrity, peace, and happiness because having a vision of God and doing *His will* is the only way to experience real joy on earth. It is also the only way to have eternal life with Jesus!

Take time today to examine your spiritual life. Have you lost the vision? Are you a person who has *principles*, but is just going through the motions of being a Christian? If so, reach out and grasp God's outstretched hand—hold tight and never lose sight of the *vision* to keep God's law . . . and you'll experience true happiness and joy.

Pain of Betrayal

I will bless those who bless you, and I will curse him who curses you; and in you all the families of the earth shall be blessed.

Genesis 12:3 (NKJV)

———◆———

When someone you love talks behind your back or shares your secrets with someone else, there's an immediate breakdown of trust. You can forgive, but forgiving doesn't mean that God expects you to bring them back into your *inner circle* and pick up where you left off. It takes wisdom from above to know God's plan and what you should do.

Betrayal hurts even more when a fiancée or spouse cheats. The feeling of rejection destroys confidence and shakes you to the core. If your fiancé will cheat *before* you're married, then the chances are pretty high that they'll cheat *after* marriage. Whether you are cheating through an emotional affair or a physical one—both are wrong in the eyes of God. There are many different forms of cheating, including hiding text messages or phone conversations that you don't want your spouse to see. Simply put—deception is destructive to marriage, period.

It takes Holy Spirit strength to forgive, as well as total dependence upon God for healing and restoration. However, if both parties are willing to work through their problems, leaning on God for wisdom, courage, and strength, healing *is* possible! Jesus experienced betrayal from not only His disciples, but from His own people who nailed Him to a cross! Lean on Jesus, the only one who can take away the pain of betrayal.

Cherished Sins

*"And you shall know the truth, and the
truth shall make you free."*

John 8:32 (NKJV)

In order to live a surrendered life with Christ, you must release your grip on the sinful pleasures that separate you from your Savior. If your hands are clasped tightly around Satan, you must let go in order to land safely in the arms of Jesus! God doesn't expect you to be perfect. Actually, it's quite the opposite! He is waiting for you to surrender all your sinful baggage that has weighed you down so that He can give you His sweet forgiveness. You'll experience joy and freedom such as you have never known.

As your new walk with God begins, the Holy Spirit will impress upon your conscience your transgressions and will give you the strength and power to let go of each cherished sin. That doesn't mean God gives you a list of all your sins and expects you to be transformed in an instant. Not at all! Instead, He is kind, loving, and patient and will equip you to do all that is required of you . . . in His perfect timing.

Slowly, God will open your eyes and allow you to see yourself through His eyes, and when you do, it's a humbling experience. It's not so much the shock of your own sins that will disturb you the most, but rather the pride in your heart. When you realize He sees the *real* you and yet loves you anyway, it's life-changing! Letting go of cherished sins and choosing Jesus is the best decision you could ever make!

Give Me Strength

Finally, my brethren, be strong in the Lord and in the
power of His might.

Ephesians 6:10 (NKJV)

———◆———

No matter where you turn, you simply can't escape the pain, suffering, and death in this sinful world. It can be so discouraging that your heart feels heavy and weary under the load. When you struggle with finding the words to even describe how you feel, turn to Isaiah 41:10 (NKJV), which says "Fear not, for I am with you; be not dismayed, for I am your God. I will strengthen you, yes, I will help you, I will uphold you with My righteous right hand." Discouragement is one of the devil's favorite tools to separate you from God. He knows which buttons to push and just the right amount of heartache needed to persuade you to *give up*.

But don't fall into the devil's trap! God has a special plan for your life, and sometimes He allows trials to strengthen your faith and keep you leaning on Him. If everything was always going great in your life, you would never know your need for a Savior. When life seems too heavy to bear, give your troubles to the greatest burden-bearer of all, Jesus Christ! Instead of plunging ahead, trying to fix your own problems, pray for strength and patience to wait upon the Lord. Claim God's promise in Isaiah 40:29 (NIV): "He gives strength to the weary and increases the power of the weak." Push away all negative thoughts and hold on to God's promise in Nehemiah 8:10 (NKJV): "Do not sorrow, for the joy of the LORD is your strength."

Live Life Now

*For I know the thoughts that I think toward you,
says the LORD, thoughts of peace and not of evil,
to give you a future and a hope.*

Jeremiah 29:11 (NKJV)

Some people live in the past, always looking back at what *used to be* or wishing they could relive past experiences, either to correct their mistakes or just re-experience wonderful memories. Then there are those who live in the future, deciding that when they get the perfect job, find a spouse, have a baby, buy a house, or make a million dollars, *then* . . . they will be happy!

Waiting for happiness based on some milestone you want to accomplish in the future, will only make you miss out on all the joy that surrounds you *today*. The best way to enjoy this journey here on earth is to live your life now, in the present, deciding to live each day for Jesus! Smell the roses, breathe in fresh air, take in the beauty all around you, and appreciate the many blessings God gives you every day! If you are constantly living in the past *or* the future, you'll miss out on everyday pleasures of life that only God can give.

God wants you to live as if each day was your last . . . but plan for the future! There's a big difference between *waiting* for the future and *planning* for the future. Live life . . . now, in the present, and live your life with Jesus as your example! When you focus on Jesus and never take your eyes off of Him, you are planning your future, which is eternity with Jesus Christ your Lord.

Hear with Your Heart

*A wise man will hear and increase learning, and a man
of understanding will attain wise counsel.*

Proverbs 1:5 (NKJV)

———◆———

One of the biggest challenges in any relationship is when
the person you're talking to . . . doesn't listen! It can be
downright aggravating when you try so hard to get the other
person to understand and their body language is screaming,
"I don't care what you have to say!"

Parents complain that their children never listen, teachers
get frustrated when students don't pay attention, and spouses
sometimes feel that their partner doesn't hear them. If you're
speaking to someone and it often feels as if you are talking to a
wall, it usually won't be long before that relationship begins to
crumble. Communication is of the utmost importance in any
healthy relationship, especially your relationship with God.

If your prayer life is one-sided, you'll have difficulty
discerning God's voice. To have a close relationship with Him,
you can't be the one doing all the talking. The Bible says in
Mark 7:14 (NASB), "After He called the crowd to Him again, He
began saying to them, 'Listen to Me, all of you, and understand.'"
God wants you to absorb all that He is saying to you. But in
order to listen for His voice, you need to *hear with your heart*.

Instead of opening your Bible and trying to make the
Scriptures say what you want them to say, listen intently for God's
interpretation. When communicating with God, remember to
hear with your heart.

Feeling the Pain

Indeed we call blessed those who showed endurance.
You have heard of the endurance of Job, and you have
seen the purpose of the Lord, how the Lord is
compassionate and merciful.

James 5:11 (NRSV)

When life seems unbearable and the pain so deep it feels you just can't breathe, what do you do? How do you handle the heartache? This is a sinful world and no matter how much you wish the sun would always shine, there is going to be times when thunderclouds rain on your parade. This world is full of disease, abuse, loneliness, rejection, divorce, and every other kind of agony that Satan uses to throw you into the depths of despair.

It is during the darkest days that Satan tempts you to believe life is not worth living and suicidal thoughts can dance across your mind. But don't give the devil one moment to gloat in victory! Jesus is the *only* Healer of hearts! He knows you better than you know yourself and stands ready to lift you from the pit of depression into His glorious light! God never promised that life would be perfect if you give your heart to Him, but He does promise to be with you through every trial and heartbreak!

You will never be able to *understand* every time pain rears its ugly head in your life, but no matter what is happening, just grab onto His outstretched hand. Suffering is a direct result of sin and will exist on this earth until Jesus comes. When you are feeling the pain, put your full faith and trust in Jesus and don't give up . . . God won't give up on you!

June 5

Limiting God

"Call to Me, and I will answer you, and show you great and mighty things, which you do not know."

Jeremiah 33:3 (NKJV)

Christians often put limits on what God can do. Instead of giving God full control and trusting Him to provide for their every need, they start doubting His power, forgetting that "with God, all things are possible." It's important to remember that it's never about what *you* can do, but rather what *God* can do through you!

For instance, if you feel God calling you to teach in a children's department at church, don't start thinking of a million reasons why you should say *no*. Rather than saying, "I can't do that. I don't even like kids, and I hate being up front," or "I'm too scared," your response should be, "I'll pray about it." Then, if you feel impressed by the Holy Spirit to take the position, go forward with confidence knowing that Jesus will be with you every step of the way. He will give you everything you need to accomplish His task—you have nothing to fear!

This is true in every situation. God will never call you to do a task for Him and then leave you in the lurch! He is trustworthy and loves you more than you could possibly know! Search your heart and think about what is getting in the way of a full commitment to Jesus! Then pray and ask God to create within you a clean heart and fill you to overflowing with His Holy Spirit. Stop putting limits on what God can do and make that giant step of faith . . . in whatever direction God leads.

Jesus Is Coming Soon!

"Watch therefore, for you know neither the day nor the
hour in which the Son of Man is coming."
Matthew 25:13 (NKJV)

———◆———

If we truly believed that Christ was coming soon, it is highly
doubtful that we would be living our lives in the same way.
We wouldn't be focused on getting rich or obtaining material
possessions, nor would we be striving for power or fame. We
would spend a lot more time loving our friends and family
instead of fighting over petty things and holding grudges.

If we really believed that it wouldn't be long until our Savior's
return, our heavenly goal would be our highest priority! But
sadly, we go through the motions of *believing*. As Christians, we
talk about Jesus' soon return and even sing about it: "Lift up the
trumpet and loud let it ring, Jesus is coming again!"But there
doesn't seem to be any sense of urgency.

The truth is, Jesus *is* coming again! The Bible says in John
14:3 (NKJV), "And if I go and prepare a place for you, I will
come again and receive you to Myself; that where I am, there
you may be also." And in 2 Peter 3:10 (NKJV), we're told, "But
the day of the Lord will come as a thief in the night, in which
the heavens will pass away with a great noise, and the elements
will melt with fervent heat; both the earth and the works that
are in it will be burned up."

There is no time to waste! We need to prepare our hearts and
lives *now* so we are ready to meet our Lord. Make no mistake
. . . Jesus *is* coming soon!

The Peacekeeper

The work of righteousness will be peace, and the effect of
righteousness, quietness and assurance forever.
Isaiah 32:17 (NKJV)

When tempers rise and accusations fly through the air, unless something is done to defuse the situation, it can easily escalate into something far worse than just *losing your temper*. Screaming, hollering, and getting angry really doesn't make things better. In fact, it makes them worse. Once words are spoken, you can never take them back, and more importantly, being mean and sarcastic is not Christlike behavior.

If your life feels like you are in the middle of a thunderstorm and you're being tossed around in a fierce wind, you need the ultimate *Peacekeeper*, Jesus Christ. You simply cannot live with that level of stress and experience the abundant life God wants you to have. The Bible has quite a bit to say about the importance of *peace*. In 1 Corinthians 14:23 (NKJV), we're told, "For God is not the author of confusion but of peace."

If you think that peace is not possible, think again, because God has given a wonderful promise in Psalm 29:11 (NKJV): "The Lord will give strength to His people; the Lord will bless His people with peace." Pray and ask God to come into your heart and life and give you His perfect peace today. He will! The next time your temper starts to rear its ugly head, call out to Jesus for help! Claim His promise in Isaiah 26:3 (NKJV): "You will keep him in perfect peace, whose mind is stayed on You, because he trusts in You." Allow Jesus to be your *Peacekeeper* today . . . and every day!

Surviving Divorce

And do not be conformed to this world,
but be transformed by the renewing of your mind, that
you may prove what is that good and acceptable
and perfect will of God.

Romans 12:2 (NKJV)

It's true that God does not like divorce, as He created the sanctity of marriage. He wanted a man and a woman to enjoy being together—to love each other, supporting each other through the hard times and sharing joy in the good times. But the reality is, you can't force someone to love you, and in this day and age, neither can you force someone to stay married to you.

If one in the relationship wants out, there is nothing you can do but pray and ask God to help you change the things you can change and accept the things beyond your control. Although divorce ends a marriage, it's important not to let it end your relationship with God! All too often, following a divorce, people blame God and turn away from their Lord and Savior. They allow bitterness and anger to dwell in their hearts, which snuffs out any chance of happiness. Don't allow resentment to separate you from God, not for one moment—not ever.

Losing your spouse is devastating, but nothing is worse than missing out on eternity with Jesus! Your relationship with Jesus is the most important relationship you can have. God alone holds the cure for a broken heart, and the only remedy for surviving divorce is to forgive, forget, and move on with Jesus!

Taking Directions

*"But this is what I commanded them, saying,
'Obey My voice, and I will be your God, and you shall
be My people. And walk in all the ways that I have
commanded you, that it may be well with you.'"*

Jeremiah 7:23 (NKJV)

Why is it that so many people have a problem with taking directions? At some time in our lives, most of us have probably used the phrase, "Don't tell me what to do!" because no one really enjoys being *bossed around*. But learning to take directions starts as as a toddler and the older we become, the more complicated or challenging those directions can be.

Children know that if they don't obey, there will be a consequence. Students soon learn that if they want to pass on to the next grade, they must listen to their teacher and follow instructions. Adults understand fully that if they don't do what their boss is asking, they'll lose their jobs. And patients can't expect to get well or have their health improve if they won't take the advice of their doctor. So it is with our spiritual life.

God has given us His Holy Word as an instruction manual to help us on our journey here on earth. When we follow what He tells us to do, we not only avoid the pain, heartache, and pitfalls along the way, but we also draw closer to our Lord and Savior! Learning to take directions is absolutely essential if we want to have a joy-filled life and extremely crucial if we want a rich spiritual life, enjoying a close relationship with our best Friend, Jesus.

Embracing Our Differences

Since you have purified your souls in obeying the truth through the Spirit in sincere love of the brethren, love one another fervently with a pure heart.

1 Peter 1:22 (NKJV)

Learning to love unconditionally is a lifelong process, however it is an essential lesson to learn if we are to enter the kingdom of heaven. If we want to be more like Jesus then we must be more tolerant of others. All throughout Scripture we are told to *love . . . love . . . love . . .* as Christ loves us. While here on earth, Jesus extended His love to everyone, even those who lied and gossiped about Him, mistreated Him, and judged Him wrongly. Everywhere He went, religious leaders sent spies to report back His every move, which was then exaggerated and used against Him. Yet, He bore it all in loving silence and showed only love to His enemies.

God wants us to do the same. When we are kind and loving to people that mistreat us, we are a silent witness for our Savior. We also need to be tolerant of others who are different than we are. God created us with our own unique physical characteristics, as well as personalities, intelligence, talents, and emotions. Instead of being irritated because others don't *think* the way we think, *look* the way we look, or *act* the way we act, we need to embrace each other's differences and love with God's unconditional love. God hates the sin but loves the sinner. As Christians, we sometimes get that message confused. When our hearts are filled up with God's love, we can't help but share His love with everyone we meet.

Words Speak Volumes

Death and life are in the power of the tongue, and those who love it will eat its fruit.

Proverbs 18:21 (NKJV)

How you talk says a lot about your character. If you are sarcastic, negative, or grumpy when you address others, it reflects on *who* you are, not just the mood you are in that day! Some people speak kindly to co-workers, friends, and even strangers, but once inside their own home, it's a whole different picture. They snap at their spouse, yell at their children, scold the dog, and basically treat their family without respect.

Using words with sarcasm and disgust no matter who they are addressed to doesn't reflect a heart surrendered to Jesus! Sharp words wound the soul, and once spoken, cannot be taken back. Instead of being negative, choose to be positive, kind, and loving. Let your words demonstrate to all those around you that you belong to Jesus! The Bible says in Colossians 4:6 (NIV), "Let your conversation be always full of grace, seasoned with salt, so that you may know how to answer everyone."

You may forget the words of kindness you spoke today, but those who received them may remember for a lifetime! Proverbs 16:24 (NRSV) says, "Pleasant words are like a honeycomb, sweetness to the soul and health to the body." Determine today to let your conversations reflect God's love—not just with those you want to impress, but to everyone, because your words speak volumes of not only who you *are*, but who you *belong to*!

Spiritual Food

I have taught you in the way of wisdom; I have led you in right paths. When you walk, your steps will not be hindered, and when you run, you will not stumble.

Proverbs 4:11-12 (NKJV)

Preparing our children for eternity is the most important job on earth! The Bible says in Proverbs 22:6 (KJV), "Train up a child in the way he should go: and when he is old, he will not depart from it." That's a beautiful promise for parents, as well as a great incentive to raise kids to love Jesus. A lot of prayer is needed to accomplish this task because this sinful world makes it even more challenging to keep kids' minds on spiritual things. We are warned in 1 Peter 5:8 (NIV): "Be alert and of sober mind. Your enemy the devil prowls around like a roaring lion looking for someone to devour." This world we live in gets more dangerous every day because Satan has mastered the art of disguising sin so that not only children, but parents as well, are fooled by his deceptions.

Some of the tools the devil uses are television, the Internet, video games, books, spiritualism, music, just to name a few. It's not always the tools that are wrong, it's how the kids are using them! That's why parents need to make sure they are spiritually feeding their kids. Before heading to the checkout counter with the latest book, toy, or video game, ask yourself, *Will this draw my children closer to Jesus?* If the answer is no, put them down and leave the store! Ask God to give you strength, courage, wisdom, and discernment to know the best spiritual food that will introduce your kids to Jesus!

June 13

Dangers of Impatience

Wait on the LORD; be of good courage, and He shall strengthen your heart; wait, I say, on the LORD!

Psalm 27:14 (NKJV)

———◄═►———

Sometimes it's hard to be patient, especially when you're feeling the pressure of not wanting to be late to a special event or talking to someone who just doesn't seem to comprehend what you are trying to tell them. It's especially frustrating when driving down the road and a car pulls out in front of you going ten miles an hour under the speed limit. But there are dangers that come with impatience. It may be just at the very second you pull out to pass that car that you see a huge truck coming straight at you! Or perhaps the person on the phone that you were irritated with turned out to be your boss's wife!

There are always consequences to your actions. Often your Christian influence, as well as your spiritual growth, is dampened by impatience. If you don't want to wait for God's answer and you get ahead of the Lord, there is almost always a bitter price to pay. Jesus wants you to follow Him, and although that may sound like a simple thing to do, it can prove quite challenging if you are not praying your way through every life situation.

When you make decisions on your own, jump to conclusions, or take matters into your own hands, you'll get in trouble every time! Determine today to stay so close to Jesus that you can hear His voice whispering words of comfort, direction, and guidance, and you will avoid the dangers of impatience!

Fight the Enemy

The Lord will guide you continually, and satisfy your
soul in drought, and strengthen your bones; you shall be
like a watered garden, and like a spring of water,
whose waters do not fail.

Isaiah 58:11 (NKJV)

The devil will give you a million reasons why you should *quit* and just give up. He wants to see you discouraged, down and out, and hopeless, because when you stop trusting in God, the devil wins! Make no mistake, the battle between good and evil is very real and Satan will not stop trying to deceive you as long as you're alive!

When you hear the enemy whispering, "You can't. You're not good enough. You're a failure. You're a disgrace. Nobody loves you," don't listen! Loudly declare, "Get thee behind me, Satan!" The Bible says in James 4:7 (NIV), "Submit yourselves, then, to God. Resist the devil, and he will flee from you."

If you feel you can't go on, claim Philippians 4:13 where God promises to give you strength. When you're too tired, claim Matthew 11:28-30 where God has promised to give you rest. When you're financially stressed, claim Philippians 4:19 (NIV): "And my God will meet all your needs." And when the future looks so dark you can't see through the haze, remember God's promise in Romans 8:28 (NIV): "And we know that in all things God works for the good of those who love him." Here is what you can count on: God's promises! The devil is a liar so don't listen to him for one moment—just keep your eyes on Jesus!

Whatever You Ask

*Then you will call upon Me and go and pray
to Me, and I will listen to you.*
Jeremiah 29:12 (NKJV)

Christians often get confused about what Jesus really meant when He said in Matthew 21:22 (NKJV), "And whatever things you ask in prayer, believing, you will receive." You could interpret this to mean that whatever you ask for, God will give it to you. If you want a million dollars, no problem, just pray and ask God for it! If you want a new car, a new job, fancy vacation, or even healing from a terminal illness, God will make it happen!

But here is what you need to know about prayer: when you pray, God answers according to what is best for you. He knows *everything* about you, especially what is good for you and what will make you happy. You can always pray and make your requests to God, but whatever you ask, don't forget to include, "Your will be done!" If you knew the end from the beginning, you would never want it any other way . . . than God's way!

Sometimes, you might be impatient and feel that God is ignoring you, but don't get discouraged, because God never ignores you! He always hears, always answers, and His timing is always perfect. The Bible says in 1 John 5:14-15 (NIV), "This is the confidence we have in approaching God: that if we ask anything according to his will, he hears us. And if we know that he hears us—whatever we ask—we know that we have what we asked of him."

Sting of Injustice

*"No weapon formed against you shall prosper,
and every tongue which rises against you in
judgment you shall condemn.*

Isaiah 54:17 (NKJV)

———◆———

Most people have felt the sting of injustice at some point in their life. Perhaps blamed for something they didn't do, their character tainted because of evil gossip, falsely accused of committing adultery, or maybe even sent to jail for a crime they didn't commit. It would be difficult to suffer injustice because of something you *did* do but just imagine how much harder it would be to suffer for something you *didn't* do!

But before you start feeling all sorry for yourself for all the times *you* were falsely accused, think of Jesus who suffered because of your sins, and He did so meekly and lovingly. He bore all the pain and heartache (which He did *not* deserve) willingly and without regret. He loves you so much that He gave His life for you so that you might live in heaven with Him for all eternity!

The Bible says in Isaiah 30:18 (NIV), "The LORD is a God of justice. Blessed are all who wait for Him!" So the next time you get discouraged, your life seems unfair, and you start to get a chip on your shoulder, stop and think of Jesus, your Savior. He took all the pain and injustice inflicted upon Him, without complaint, bitterness, or anger, but rather in loving silence. Never forget that God understands, cares, and is always there for you!

Darkness of Depression

*But You, O Lord, are a shield for me, my glory and
the One who lifts up my head.*

Psalm 3:3 (NKJV)

Many people for various reasons suffer from chronic depression. Causes could be genetics, finances, environmental influences, social circumstances, and many others. But whatever the cause, depression is an isolating and heartbreaking condition to live with.

Depression dates all the way back to Bible times. David and Jeremiah were spiritual, God-fearing men, and yet Scripture reveals that both men suffered from depression at various times in their lives. Pray for Holy Spirit power whenever depression threatens to rear it's ugly head, and with God's help, you'll win the battle, because through the blood of Jesus . . . there is *hope*! David cried out in Psalm 42:5 (NIV), "Why, my soul, are you downcast? Why so disturbed within me? Put your hope in God, for I will yet praise him, my Savior and my God."

If you are depressed, there's no shame in getting help from a trusted friend or professional counselor. But don't forget to reach out to your best Friend, Jesus! No matter how dismal your life may seem, Jesus will give you the strength to overcome every dark thought and feeling! Look, and you'll see *hope* all around you through the beauty of nature and by reading God's Holy Word. You can trust God to bring you out of the darkness of depression into His marvelous light!

Need a Refill

*For I consider that the sufferings of this present
time are not worthy to be compared with the glory
which shall be revealed in us.*

Romans 8:18 (NKJV)

There are peaks and valleys in this journey of life, and like it or not, some days will be better than others. One day, everything is going great and you're feeling *on top of the world*, and the next day it seems everything is going wrong! Your emotions are stretched to the limit trying to cope with life's challenges, such as struggling with insomnia, stress at work, a fight with a friend, a trip to the emergency room, a bitter divorce, a financial burden, or a hundred other reasons!

When stressed out, you often lose your temper, snap at your children, and become critical of everyone, including yourself! But God gives hope, for even during your most stressful day, you're not alone! God is right there pleading with you to let Him help! There is also reassurance that you will never be tested or tempted more than you can endure. The Bible says in 1 Corinthians 10:13 (NIV), "And God is faithful; he will not let you be tempted beyond what you can bear." Here is even more reason to calm your fears, for the last line of verse 13 says, "But when you are tempted, he will also provide a way out so that you can endure it." What a fantastic promise!

Our God has promised to be our *Deliverer*! When you're stressed to the max and your spiritual cup is running dry, ask God for a refill of His Holy Spirit and receive His power and strength to see you through each and every day!

Send the Devil Running

Blessed is the man who endures temptation; for when he has been approved, he will receive the crown of life which the Lord has promised to those who love Him.

James 1:12 (NKJV)

When we are at our lowest, weakest, and most vulnerable time in our lives, the devil will tempt us the most! He knows when we are weak, and he loves to trip us up any way he can. He also knows that God has something awesome planned for us, so the enemy would love nothing better than for us to fall and give it all up for a few moments of earthly pleasure! But there is *nothing* on this earth that is worth missing out on eternity with Jesus!

When faced with that *right-or-wrong* decision, send up an SOS prayer and God will send angels to your rescue! But better yet, pray *before* you are tempted. The Bible teaches us to pray in Matthew 6:13 (ESV), "Lead us not into temptation, but deliver us from evil." The most powerful weapon you can use against Satan is prayer, for the mere mention of *Jesus' name* sends the devil running!

Never think for a moment that you will be spared from temptation, because the devil knows his time is short, and he is working hard to separate you from God. But fear not, because you do have Holy Spirit power at your disposal to resist. Hebrews 2:18 (NKJV) tells us, "For in that He Himself has suffered, being tempted, He is able to aid those who are tempted." Keep grasping God's hand and you'll have nothing to fear.

Pray for Blessings

And God is able to make all grace abound toward you,
that you, always having all sufficiency in all things,
may have an abundance for every good work.

2 Corinthians 9:8 (NKJV)

God loves to give good gifts to His children. The Bible says in James 1:17 (NIV), "Every good and perfect gift is from above." So, if we know that all good and perfect gifts come from God, why are we so reluctant to ask God for them? We know that He loves to give his children gifts, for in Psalm 37:4 (NKJV), we're told, "Delight yourself also in the Lord, and He shall give you the desires of your heart." That is a promise that we can claim, and all we have to do is ask! It really is that simple! Matthew 7:7 (NKJV) says, "Ask, and it will be given to you; seek, and you will find; knock, and it will be opened to you."

God wants us to come to Him with our requests, and He gets great joy upon bestowing blessings in answer to our prayers. In fact, Jesus said in Matthew 7:11 (NKJV), "If you then, being evil, know how to give good gifts to your children, how much more will your Father who is in heaven give good things to those who ask Him." There is only one reason that we fail to receive God's blessings and that answer is found in James 4:2 (NASB): "You do not have because you do not ask."

You can trust God to always keep His word! Prepare to pray for blessings by approaching God's throne with holy boldness, claiming His promises, putting selfishness away, and asking for only God's will to be done!

Understanding God's Will

I will instruct you and teach you in the way you should go; I will guide you with My eye.

Psalm 32:8 (NKJV)

———◆———

It's not always easy to discern what God's will is for our lives. Of course, as Christians, we want to know *His plan* and can be quite upset with God if He doesn't send us in the direction we want to go. . . or in the time-frame we have in mind. But God wants us to trust Him and lean on Him fully. And that means *patiently* waiting upon the Lord. The Bible says in Psalm 37:7 (NKJV), "Rest in the LORD, and wait patiently for Him." Sometimes we find answers as He speaks to us through His Holy Word, while other times the answers come in the unfolding of events, the words of a godly friend, or directly from Holy Spirit guidance.

One thing we know for sure . . . is that God wants what is best for us and it is always His will for us to stay close to Him. We're told in John 16:13 (NIV), "But when he, the Spirit of truth, comes, he will guide you into all the truth." You don't have to *understand* God's will; you just need to listen to His still small voice gently leading and guiding, and then be obedient. The good news is that when you lean fully on Jesus, you just can't mess up! And don't forget that Jesus is trustworthy. He never fails and He won't take you down a path you should not go! Don't worry about *understanding* God's will or where He's taking you—just keep holding God's hand and everything will be just fine.

Forgive Yourself

As far as the east is from the west, so far has He removed our transgressions from us.

Psalm 103:12 (NKJV)

As Christians, we know and trust that God has the power to forgive. When we've made a mistake and ask God for forgiveness, our discretion is not only forgiven but forgotten as well. The Bible says in Micah 7:19 (NIV) that He will "hurl all our iniquities into the depths of the sea." So why is it then, that although God has forgiven us, we cannot forgive ourselves?

When we've made even the smallest mistake, we're quick to wallow in self-condemnation and suffer with self-loathing. Even though we know God has forgiven us, somehow we just don't *feel it* in our hearts. Perhaps that's the reason so many people keep asking God to forgive the same sin over and over again—there's no need because when God forgives, He forgives completely! No need to keep begging and asking Him to forgive the same sin, for He hurled it into the depths of the sea the very *first* time we asked!

As long as we keep punishing ourselves with guilt-ridden hearts, we can't experience the real joy God wants us to have. Nor can we have a relationship with God that is built on faith and trust. Start a new relationship with God today by believing His promise in 1 John 1:9 (NIV), "If we confess our sins, he is faithful and just and will forgive us our sins and purify us from all unrighteousness." God has forgiven you . . . now forgive yourself!

Prescription for Joy

*"I, even I, am He who blots out your transgressions for
My own sake; and I will not remember your sins."*

Isaiah 43:25 (NKJV)

Too often, people hold onto hurt, pain, and anger as if
that was somehow going to make them feel better. They
tell the first person who will stop long enough to listen, and
they endlessly share all the intimate details of how they were
mistreated. The bad thing about that is, every time they talk
about it, the pain just gets deeper and the hurt more bitter! As
long as you are carrying around an anchor of pain, you cannot
possibly be happy! And even worse—unless you forgive, God
won't forgive you!

The Bible says in Matthew 6:15 (NIV), "But if you do not
forgive others their sins, your Father will not forgive your sins."
Missing out on eternity is a pretty hefty price to pay for holding
on to pain! Even those who *think* they have forgiven, sometimes
fall into the *poor-me trap* and keep dredging up the pain, but
as long as you insist on regurgitating all the bad things that
have happened to you, you will not heal! It's like having surgery
and then ripping out your stitches over and over again—all the
while clueless as to why you can't seem to get well!

The prescription for joy is this: forgive, forget, and move on
with Jesus! It really is that simple! Write that prescription down
and put it on your refrigerator, in your Bible, on a sticky note
stuck to the dash of your car, etc. and keep it there until it finally
sinks in—Jesus is the *only* Healer of hearts!

Just Be Real

*If we say that we have fellowship with Him, and walk in
darkness, we lie and do not practice the truth.*

1 John 1:6 (NKJV)

———◆———

You might be surprised to know that God loves *you*! Yes,
the same *you* that makes mistakes, is filled with flaws, and
has real struggles—He loves *you* just the way you are. He's not
waiting for you to be *perfect* before He extends His love to you,
nor is He wanting you to pretend to have it all together for His
benefit! Just be real with God . . . without pretense. Talk to Him
heart-to-heart in your own down to earth voice.

God's not wanting a polished, proper, flowery prayer, but
rather honest *real talk*, friend-to-friend. There's nothing worse
than being fake, and just like most people can see right through
the pretense, so can God. Being *real* with your heavenly Father
allows your heart to be open so that God can not only speak to
you but transform you!

There are plenty of religious fakes in the world who don't
have a clue who God really is. The truth is, being dishonest or
misrepresenting truth is a sin, for the Bible says in Proverbs
12:22 (NRSV), "Lying lips are an abomination to the LORD, but
those who act faithfully are his delight."

Make Jesus your best Friend by having an open, honest
relationship with Him—in other words, be yourself, and *just
be real*!

Pray for Courage

Be of good courage, and He shall strengthen your heart,
all you who hope in the Lord.

Psalm 31:24 (NKJV)

———————⟨◆◆◆⟩———————

Everyone, even the seemingly most self-confident person, needs courage to face each day. Some days require more courage than others, especially if you're shy and timid. Most people think of the need for courage only when facing a dangerous situation, but there are endless circumstances that require courage, such as trying to break a bad habit, discipling a child, asking for a promotion, giving a speech, being alone, asking for forgiveness, or or any other challenge that is out of your comfort zone.

If you are ever tempted to run away from your troubles, let Jesus help you stay and fight the battle. Ask God for an extra measure of courage to help you face whatever trials are before you. The Bible says in Psalm 138:3 (NIV), "When I called, you answered me; you greatly emboldened me." Moses said in Deuteronomy 31:6 (NIV), "Be strong and courageous. Do not be afraid or terrified . . . for the Lord your God goes with you; he will never leave you nor forsake you."

That's a pretty powerful promise you can claim every day! Always remember that in every situation, lean on Jesus. Pray for courage and God will replace all feelings of intimidation and fear with Holy Spirit boldness, allowing you to truly shine for Him and accomplish all that He has planned for you.

Trusting His Perfect Plan

*Evening and morning and at noon I will pray, and cry
aloud, and He shall hear my voice.*

Psalm 55:17 (NKJV)

Christians talk a lot about wanting *God's will* to be done, but there's no possible way to know God's will unless we have open communication and talk with Him about every detail of our lives. It is through prayer and the study of God's Word that we will find the guidance and wisdom that we need. The Bible says in Psalm 119:105 (NIV), "Your word is a lamp for my feet, a light on my path." And in James 1:5 (NIV), we're told, "If any of you lacks wisdom, you should ask God, who gives generously to all without finding fault, and it will be given to you."

When we experience a close relationship with Jesus, it affects every part of our day! Unexpected problems won't cause us to panic because we are trusting in God's divine wisdom and guidance, knowing His strength will carry us through. And if things don't turn out the way we hoped, we won't blame God for punishing us. Instead, our difficulties are viewed as *blessings* in disguise.

Sometimes we forget that God knows best, and we want Him to answer our prayers the way *we* want Him to. However, if we knew the end from the beginning, we would never want it any other way . . . than God's way! Make Jesus your best Friend, sharing your heart with Him and trusting in His perfect plan. And don't forget to end every prayer request with, "Lord, Thy will be done!"

No Comparison Policy

How precious also are Your thoughts to me, O God!
How great is the sum of them!

Psalm 139:17 (NKJV)

People spend a lot of time worrying about what others are thinking of them. They even make decisions about what they will or will not do based on what others *might* think. But if you had the superhuman ability to hear people's thoughts, you might be surprised to learn that no one is thinking bad thoughts about you. In fact, they are probably not thinking about you at all! They haven't zoned in on your squeaky voice, how big your nose is, or how terrible your hair looks. However, what you might overhear in their thoughts is them worrying about what *you* think! So this begs the question, why allow your fears of what others *may* think to prevent you from living a fun-filled, happy life?

Instead of worrying about what others think, concern yourself with what God thinks, for His opinion of you is all that matters! God created you to be exactly the way you are and there is no need for self-loathing! Can you imagine how boring this world would be if everyone looked exactly the same, and had the same talents and abilities?

God knew what He was doing when He created each of His children uniquely different. Practice a *no comparison policy*, and, instead of being despondent or jealous because you don't look like someone else or have their talents, thank God for creating you just the way you are. And don't forget to praise Him for being such an awesome Creator God!

Perfection Is Attainable

*Being confident of this very thing, that He
who has begun a good work in you will complete it
until the day of Jesus Christ.*

Philippians 1:6 (NKJV)

Most people have an awareness of the person they want to be, but many times a person's sense of who they are is quite different from how others see them. It's easy to become blind to your daily actions, which portray your true character to others. When you have the love of Jesus in your heart, He shines out in everything you do. This includes being a patient and courteous driver, even if you're late for an important meeting, being kind to the person who is rude in the checkout line, or giving a warm smile to that person who is annoying instead of wishing they would just go away.

Human nature pulls us in the opposite direction, but as Christians, we strive to be the person God wants us to be: a true ambassador for Him. But when you fail, instead of becoming discouraged and slipping into the pool of despair, reach out to Jesus. Ask for forgiveness and don't forget to pray for an extra measure of strength, courage, and more love for your fellow man. Above all, remember that the only *perfect* person that has ever lived on this earth . . . is Jesus! He set an example of how we should live through His daily acts of kindness and mercy.

No one is perfect, and God doesn't wish for you to be despondent because you cannot meet your own expectations of perfection. Perfection is attainable, but *only* through Christ.

Starting Over

*"I will heal their backsliding, I will love them freely, for
My anger has turned away from him."*

Hosea 14:4 (NKJV)

Looking back over your life, have you made decisions that you regret? Are you suffering the consequences, frustrated that you've been so foolish? Wouldn't it be wonderful if you could start your life over, knowing *then* what you know *now*? That way you could avoid the bad choices you made that have made you so miserable! Here's the good news: you *can* start over! Surrender your heart to Jesus and ask Him to forgive your past mistakes! God is full of grace and mercy and will wipe away your transgressions, as if they never happened! Of course, there are consequences for sin, so forgiveness doesn't mean that He will erase the memories from your mind.

Remembering helps prevent you from making the same mistakes all over again. God wants you to learn from your sins, but He doesn't throw them in your face to remind you of what a loser you are! God is a God of love and He will replace your guilt with new understanding and turn whatever mess you made of your life . . . into something beautiful! He can transform every mistake and ugly part of your life into something wonderful to glorify Him. Jesus longs to set you free from the bondage of a painful past. Ask him for a *do-over*, for He can rewrite your life's story beginning right now, this very moment. Why not change your life today by surrendering your heart to God and *starting over*.

Risk-Free Decision

*Now faith is the substance of things hoped for,
the evidence of things not seen.*

Hebrews 11:1 (NKJV)

———◆———

Why is it that some people have such a difficult time trusting others? Usually, it's because of the pain of past experience, which makes it difficult for anyone to get over their *protective wall*. Sometimes that wall is justified and needed, particularly in a dysfunctional relationship. But if your guard is always up, you'll never experience the real joy of friendship.

Any close relationship is based on trust and loyalty, and without that, it's just superficial and meaningless. Unfortunately, many people treat God in the same manner. They don't fully trust Him. They don't share their life with Him or ask for wisdom and guidance. Neither do they go to Him to solve their problems, choosing instead to fix things on their own. It's not until they've made a complete mess of their lives that they turn to God for help. Oh, how much easier it would to give God full control of your life in the first place!

It's mind-boggling why Christians have such a hard time trusting God when He loves each of us so much that He gave His Son to save us. Who better to trust your life to? He has definitely earned your trust. The good news is that there is absolutely no risks when giving God your problems. Put your full faith in God and you'll experience a purposeful, joyful, and meaningful life enjoying the sweet assurance that Jesus is a loyal friend, and the best part is . . . it's a risk-free decision!

Little Things Matter

For God is not unjust to forget your work and labor of love which you have shown toward His name, in that you have ministered to the saints, and do minister.

Hebrews 6:10 (NKJV)

Often in life, people focus on achieving greatness, and while there's nothing wrong with setting high goals, it's important not to lose sight of the little things that matter. Little acts of kindness say a lot about your character, such as allowing a driver to have that choice parking space you had your eye on, paying the toll for the random driver behind you at the toll booth, letting someone go ahead of you at the checkout line, holding the door open for someone, or mowing your elderly neighbor's lawn. And let's not forget the power of a smile or simple compliment that can do wonders to brighten someone's day. All these seemingly small acts carry eternal significance.

The Bible says in Luke 6:35 (NASB), "But love your enemies, and do good, and lend, expecting nothing in return; and your reward will be great, and you will be sons of the Most High; for He Himself is kind to ungrateful and evil men." You see, when you do kind things for others, you are actually doing them for God, and He is immensely pleased! In fact Jesus said in Matthew 25:40 (KJV), "Inasmuch as ye have done it unto one of the least of these my brethren, ye have done it unto me." Take time each day for what might seem like *little things*, for even if no one else notices, God does!

Jesus Is All You Need

Truly my soul silently waits for God; from Him comes my salvation. He only is my rock and my salvation; He is my defense; I shall not be greatly moved.

Psalm 62:1-2 (NKJV)

Don't be deceived into thinking the *things* of this world will make you happy. It's not wealth or fame that bring peace and contentment. Far from it! Look around and you'll see evidence of plenty of rich and famous people who are absolutely miserable! Without God, you will never achieve real joy and happiness! Jesus is all you need!

When you are too tired and feel like giving up, God has promised in Exodus 33:14 (NKJV), "My Presence will go with you, and I will give you rest." When you feel like a failure and the mountains seem impossible to climb, Jesus reassures you in Matthew 19:26 (NKJV), "With God all things are possible." When you are thirsty, Jesus promises in John 7:38 (NKJV), "He who believes in Me, as the Scripture has said, out of his heart will flow rivers of living water."

And when you are discouraged, brokenhearted, and too weak to take another step, Jesus will carry you . . . yes, carry you! These comforting words found in Isaiah 46:4 (NIV) say it all: "Even to your old age and gray hairs I am he, I am he who will sustain you. I have made you and I will carry you; I will sustain you and I will rescue you."

The more time you spend in His presence, the more your heart will truly know that . . . Jesus is all you need!

Talk Is Cheap

Therefore be imitators of God as dear children.
And walk in love, as Christ also has loved us and
given Himself for us, an offering and a sacrifice to
God for a sweet-smelling aroma.

Ephesians 5:1-2 (NKJV)

The old expression, "actions speak louder than words," has been passed down from generation to generation, but the meaning is the same. It is much easier to tell someone you care about them, but it means so much more to actually *show* them how much you care. When you tell your friend, "You mean so much to me, I truly value your friendship," it really doesn't feel like *love* when you're screaming at them the next day because they did something you didn't like!

Real love is demonstrated by your actions, not just your words. It is the same in your relationship with Christ. You can tell God you love Him every day, but when you choose to break His commandments, it doesn't *show* Him your love. Talk is cheap, but *doing* what you say is worth so much more!

Determine to show your love by reflecting God's character in everything you do and say! He loves to hear your praises as well as *see* you demonstrate your love for Him. Remember that God wants you to love Him so much that it shows in your actions, not just in what you say!

Praise Party

*Let my mouth be filled with Your praise and
with Your glory all the day.*

Psalm 71:8 (NKJV)

Whenever you feel discouraged or depressed, instead of racing to your *pity* party, have a *praise* party. No matter how bad the problem is you are facing, someone else has it worse than you do! There are all kinds of people who suffer hardships—some are homeless, don't have friends or family, battered and beaten, unjustly thrown in prison, and even suffering for lack of food or shelter, who, in spite of their dismal circumstances, joyfully praise Jesus!

Praising Jesus is the very best cure for depression! Start your *praise* party by counting your blessings, beginning with the best blessing of all: having a Lord and Savior who died so that you might live with Him in heaven for all eternity! The Bible says in 2 Samuel 22:4 (NIV), "I called to the LORD, who is worthy of praise, and have been saved from my enemies."

Once you begin praising Jesus, it won't be long before all those dark, discouraged thoughts fade away and your heart will sing. Psalm 30:11 (NKJV) says, "You have turned for me my mourning into dancing; You have put off my sackcloth and clothed me with gladness."

Cancel your pity party—it's time for a *praise* party to thank Jesus for His many blessings! And don't forget to praise Him for being such an awesome God!

Paid in Full

*He saved us, not because of any works of righteousness
that we had done, but according to his mercy, through
the water of rebirth and renewal by the Holy Spirit.*

Titus 3:5 (NRSV)

Heaven is not for sale. We can't buy it, earn it, or steal it. There's only one way to spend eternity with Jesus and that is to give our hearts to Him. He alone has the tickets to heaven, and each one is stamped in His own blood, *Paid in Full*! Jesus paid the highest price He could pay . . . dying on a cross, so that we could live! He loves us so much that He can't imagine heaven without us, and He longs to set us free from the bondage of sin. Oh, what amazing love! We have nothing to fear when we give our hearts to Jesus—not even death, because when we claim Jesus as our Savior, death means life . . . eternal life!

The Bible says in John 3:36 (NIV), "Whoever believes in the Son has eternal life," and in Romans 6:23 (NIV), we're told, "The gift of God is eternal life in Christ Jesus our Lord." There's an important lesson in the biblical story of Naaman, who, when asked to do something as simple as dip in the Jordan River seven times, didn't want to do it . . . because it was too easy! Now, if God had asked him to do something difficult, he would have done so with great determination, but something *little* felt too insulting. We can be a bit like that at times—thinking that salvation just couldn't possibly be so easily obtained by something as simple as a surrendered heart. But it is! All we need to do is give our hearts to Jesus and eternity is ours!

Avoiding Time with God

Draw near to God and He will draw near to you.

James 4:8 (NKJV)

As Christians, we know that spending time in prayer and Bible study is important if we want to experience a vibrant spiritual life. So why is it that so many people avoid spending time with God—someone they claim to love, honor and worship? The biggest excuse we tell ourselves is, "I don't have time." But if we're really honest, we have the time, we just choose to do other things!

Everyone has the same number of hours in a day, but we choose to spend our time doing all the things that are most important to us! Trying to balance all the demands of our busy lives can be exhausting, but, oh, how sad that almost everything else takes precedence over spending time with our Creator, King of the Universe! We tell ourselves that *tomorrow* we'll make time, but tomorrow never comes!

Whenever we lose sight of *who* God is and what He has done for us, we lose our desire and motivation to spend time with Him. When someone is *really* important to us, we *make* time for them, and so it is with God! The more we love Him, the deeper our desire to be close to Him, and reading the Bible and praying becomes precious time that we guard fiercely. When we truly fall in love with Jesus, spending time with Him won't be something we feel we *have* to do, but rather something that we look forward to and count as a privilege to communicate directly with our Lord and Savior!

Valley of Decision

A man's heart plans his way, but the LORD directs his steps.
Proverbs 16:9 (NKJV)

E very day we are forced to make decisions. From the moment we open our eyes in the morning, our decision-making process starts. *Should I get out of bed or hit the snooze button for ten more minutes of sleep? Do I wear the red shirt or the blue one? Should I eat breakfast or skip it?*

Or course, there are more serious decisions that we have to make, and with every choice we are faced with, we must keep in mind that for every *action*, there is a *reaction*. If we make wrong choices, we will suffer the consequences. Just one decision can alter the course of our lives, and that's why it's important to ask God to be part of all the decisions we make! With God in charge, we never have to ask ourselves, *Am I doing the right thing?* We can move forward with confidence knowing that God is leading and guiding each step of the way!

Talk to Jesus about the little things *and* the big things! Whether it is as small as what to eat for dinner or as critical as changing a career path, God wants us to lean on Him fully and completely! When you are in the valley of decision and don't know where to turn, go to Jesus first! He is a great listener and He is truly interested in all you have to say! In Psalm 16:2 (MSG), we're told, "I say to God, 'Be my Lord!' Without You, nothing makes sense.'"

This Is War

*For our light affliction, which is but for a
moment, is working for us a far more exceeding and
eternal weight of glory.*

2 Corinthians 4:17 (NKJV)

Now more than ever before, God's people are fighting the biggest battle they could ever face, and that is the battle between good and evil. Make no mistake . . . this is war! And Satan is pulling out all the stops, for he has every intention of winning. The devil knows his time is short, and he is using every weapon in his arsenal to destroy you. The Bible says in 1 Peter 5:8 (NKJV), "Be sober, be vigilant; because your adversary the devil walks about like a roaring lion, seeking whom he may devour."

The enemy knows where you are weak and most vulnerable. He will attack your marriage, your children, your friends, your family, your job, and wherever else he thinks he can get to you. He has intimate knowledge about you that could take you down with accurate precision. There is only one way to win the war against Satan and that is to put on the whole armor of God. You *cannot* and *will not* win on your own power!

Don't wait any longer! Make Jesus Lord of your life and He will not only fight your battles but He will reward you with eternal life.

A Cheerful Giver

For if the willingness is there,
the gift is acceptable according to what one has,
not according to what one does not have.

2 Corinthians 8:12 (NIV)

Many people today don't really know what it means to *sacrifice*. They think they have sacrificed if they put a couple of dollars in the offering plate each week at church or donated a stained and torn piece of clothing to the "poor." The dictionary describes sacrifice as "a loss or something you give up, usually for the sake of a better cause." *Real* sacrifice is motivated by love, and so the amount we are willing to give up is so much greater when given out of love. Parents who love their children sacrifice their time, not to mention countless hours of lost sleep. We sacrifice our time by helping someone in need. When our hearts are filled with God's love, our desire to sacrifice for others grows, as does our desire to sacrifice our offerings for the Lord's work!

Sacrifice isn't just giving what you can afford—it's *giving up something* so you can give more to God! And when you give, do so joyfully. The Bible says in 2 Corinthians 9:7 (NKJV), "For God loves a cheerful giver." And in Malachi 3:10-11, God promises, " 'Bring the whole tithe into the storehouse . . . Test me in this,' says the Lord Almighty, 'and see if I will not throw open the floodgates of heaven and pour out so much blessing that there will not be room enough to store it.' " Put God to the test today and you will find, the more we give, the more God blesses!

Really Listen

So then, my beloved brethren, let every man be swift to hear, slow to speak, slow to wrath.

James 1:19 (NKJV)

Have you ever talked with a friend who cuts you off while you are speaking and tries to finish your sentence? They assume they already know what you are going to say before you say it and try to just get to the point. Some zone out all together, letting their mind wander off to other things, while you are still talking. It's not a very satisfying conversation when someone isn't really listening to you. Their mind is already made up about what you are going to say and you can see on their face that they haven't heard a word you've said.

People who don't listen to all the facts make poor decisions, simply because they think they know it all. Neither do they have close friendships because having a friend who doesn't care enough to listen as you share your life isn't a very loving friend! Jesus is a loving Friend and He is your best Friend who will always listen to you! But He also wants you to listen to Him! The Bible says in Luke 8:18 (NLT), "Pay attention to how you hear. To those who listen to My teaching more understanding will be given. But for those who are not listening, even what they think they understand will be taken away from them."

When you read God's Word, really listen as He speaks to you! Don't skim the pages thinking you know everything. Listen . . . really listen, and you will hear God's voice!

Negative Nonsense

A merry heart does good, like medicine, but a
broken spirit dries the bones.

Proverbs 17:22 (NKJV)

The world is made up of two different kinds of people—those who see the glass *half-empty* and those who see it *half-full*. It comes as no surprise that the half-full viewers are the happiest! Filling your mind with negative nonsense is not only bad for your personality, but it doesn't make you very endearing to others, and more importantly . . . separates you from God! It's impossible to be negative and have a Christlike attitude.

The Bible says in Proverbs 15:13 (NASB), "A joyful heart makes a cheerful face, but when the heart is sad, the spirit is broken." And Psalm 68:3 (NASB) says, "But let the righteous be glad; let them exult before God; yes, let them rejoice with gladness." Wow! It doesn't get clearer than that. God wants His children to be glad! No matter what crisis you are going through or disappointing event that threatens to ruin your day, give it to Jesus and go forward with a positive attitude, knowing God is in full control and He has you covered.

God has the answer for you in James 5:13 (NASB): "Is anyone cheerful? He is to sing praises." There's no way you can be grumpy if you're singing praises to Jesus! When you find yourself having a bad day and you're struggling to find the joy, ask God for an attitude adjustment and then start singing and praising Jesus!

Honoring God at Work

Let the favor of the Lord our God be upon us,
and prosper for us the work of our hands—O prosper
the work of our hands!

Psalm 90:17 (NRSV)

———◆———

Most Christians would never dream of being a thief, yet many steal every day and don't even realize it. When they go to work, instead of being conscious that their employer is paying for their time, they visit at the watercooler, sharing personal stories about their lives, then chit-chat on the phone with a friend or family member, and if they meet someone in the hall, they'll stop to tell a joke or share how they spent their vacation. All those minutes spent talking about personal things takes your time from accomplishing the job you're being paid to do. Not only are you robbing your company of time they are paying for, but you're also causing other people to do the same.

The Bible says in Colossians 3:23 (NRSV), "Whatever your task, put yourselves into it, as done for the Lord and not for your masters." And in Proverbs 10:4-5 (NKJV), we're told, "He who has a slack hand becomes poor, but the hand of the diligent makes rich. He who gathers in summer is a wise son; he who sleeps in harvest is a son who causes shame."

God does not condone laziness or dishonesty, so determine today to honor God at work by having an honest work ethic. Use your talents and energy to do the best job you can do, letting your employer and co-workers see Jesus in you!

Save Our Children

All your children shall be taught by the LORD, and great shall be the peace of your children.
Isaiah 54:13 (NKJV)

Wouldn't it be wonderful if more people had a burden for introducing children to their best Friend, Jesus! What a different world this would be if kids grew up knowing how much God loves them. Sadly, we are living in a time where parents view religion as a social event, going to church on weekends, but then going about their business the rest of the week, as if God was not even present in their lives.

It's amazing how many people claim to be followers of Christ, yet don't even know how to pray to God in an intimate way. Others have no faith that God really hears *their* prayers . . . or answers. It's no wonder why young people stop attending church as soon as they are old enough to refuse! If parents don't have a close relationship with God, then how can they expect their children to? Parents need to first recommit their lives to God and then pray for wisdom and guidance in raising their little ones.

The Bible says in Proverbs 22:6 (NKJV), "Train up a child in the way he should go; even when he is old he will not depart from it." God will honor our prayers to save our children, so pray passionately for their salvation and experience this truth in 3 John 1:4 (NKJV): "I have no greater joy than to hear that my children are walking in the truth."

Learning to Forgive

*"Judge not, and you will not be judged; condemn not,
and you will not be condemned; forgive, and
you will be forgiven"*

Luke 6:37 (NKJV)

The Bible is very clear about how God feels about *forgiveness.* In Matthew 6:15 (NIV), we're told, "But if you do not forgive others their sins, your Father will not forgive your sins." Many times we *think* we have forgiven, but we really haven't. We are harboring bitterness that we don't even realize is there. Unless we get rid of all unforgiveness in our hearts, we can never have a close relationship with our heavenly Father, nor will God be able to carry out His perfect plan for our lives. But even worse, we will miss out on eternity with Jesus, because, without God's forgiveness for our sins, we won't be going to heaven!

We need to ask God to reveal any unforgiveness in our hearts and help us not to hold grudges against family members, friends, or strangers who have *done us wrong.* God's requirement to forgive is not dependent upon the person asking for forgiveness or whether or not the mistreatment was justified. We are to follow Jesus' advice in Matthew 18:21-22 (NKJV): "'Lord, how often shall my brother sin against me, and I forgive him? Up to seven times?' Jesus said to him, 'I do not say to you, up to seven times, but up to seventy times seven.'" Learning to forgive is something we all need to do. Our salvation depends on it!

I'll Do It Myself

Do you see a man wise in his own eyes? There is more hope for a fool than for him.

Proverbs 26:12 (NKJV)

Pride has a way of creeping into your heart without even realizing it. Sometimes it's in the very way you protect your image, not wanting anyone to think you are helpless or incapable. It may be as simple as driving around for hours rather than stopping to ask for directions, or using all your might to move a piece of heavy furniture instead of asking the neighbor to assist you. It can feel rather humbling to *ask for help*, but there's no shame in seeking assistance. In fact, the person you're asking is probably more than happy to help! When you lend a hand to someone in need, there is a great blessing to be gained.

The Bible says in Acts 20:35 (NKJV), "It is more blessed to give than to receive," and in James 4:6 (NRSV), we're told, "God opposes the proud, but gives grace to the humble." Lending a helping hand is a way to say, "I care about you, you matter to me." So it is with God, for He cares about every detail of your life, and He loves for you to come to Him for help, no matter how little or big the request.

The next time you're tempted to say, "I'll do it myself," reconsider allowing someone the blessing of helping you. And don't forget to ask your best Friend, Jesus, for His help . . . first!

God's Name Is Holy

That at the name of Jesus every knee should bow . . .
and that every tongue should confess that Jesus Christ is
Lord, to the glory of God the Father.

Philippians 2:10-11 (NKJV)

Although there is only one true God, He has many different names, and every name tells something about His character. Some of the most common names that immediately come to mind are Father, Lord, Savior, King of Kings, Counselor, Protector, Deliverer, Healer, and Friend. But, there is one name that becomes even more endearing when you understand the meaning of what happened at Calvary . . . and that name is Jesus! Just knowing the sacrifice Jesus made to pay the price for your sins is more than enough reason to love Him and treat Him with the highest regard.

And yet there are some Christians who have no idea how important it is to speak God's name with reverence, no matter which name you use. They say the name of Jesus in an aggravated tone when they stub their toe or their favorite sports team lost the game. But the Bible says in Exodus 20:7 (NKJV), "You shall not take the name of the Lord your God in vain, for the Lord will not hold him guiltless who takes His name in vain."

Whenever you use the name of God as a *swear word* or even in a casual manner, it is not only a sin but will bring a curse upon you because it breaks one of God's commandments! Whatever name you use when speaking about God, always remember . . . God's name is holy!

Thy Servant Heareth

*"My sheep hear My voice, and I know them,
and they follow Me."*

John 10:27 (NKJV)

God doesn't speak in complicated ways but rather in a manner that is easy to understand. Why is it then that some still question if they are really hearing God's voice? Perhaps answers to prayer are seen as *coincidences* instead of discerning His power at work? Sometimes God allows things to happen to get your attention and bring you to the point where you are ready to listen to Him and respond with, "Speak Lord, for Thy servant heareth."

If you do all the talking when praying and fail to listen, you miss the guidance of your heavenly Father. Instead of telling God all your troubles and then telling Him how to solve them, try listening for His answers. You can be sure God's solution is far better than what you were asking for. God knows the end from the beginning, and He alone knows what is best for you.

The Bible says in Luke 11:13 (NKJV), "If you then, being evil, know how to give good gifts to your children, how much more will your heavenly Father give the Holy Spirit to those who ask Him!" Never ask someone else's advice before asking God first, for what God thinks is far more important than what your friends think!

Determine today to be a good listener when communicating with God. Instead of demanding that your prayers be answered *your* way, remember to say, "Speak Lord, for Thy servant heareth," and then wait for His answer.

Too Blessed to Be Stressed

*For I have satiated the weary soul, and I have
replenished every sorrowful soul.*

Jeremiah 31:25 (NKJV)

Most people feel stressed trying to meet the demands in this fast-paced world. They have too many things to do in too short of time and their minds are racing a hundred miles an hour! It's no wonder why there's so many who are zoned out on anti-anxiety pills and suffering from depression! But life doesn't have to be this way! God wants you to have life and have it more abundantly! Claim God's promise in Psalm 55:22 (NIV): "Cast your cares on the Lord and he will sustain you; he will never let the righteous be shaken." You can also claim Isaiah 26:3 (NIV): "You will keep in perfect peace those whose minds are steadfast, because they trust in you."

Oh, what a loving and faithful God who provides and takes care of His children. When you're at your wit's end and everyone is standing on your last nerve, stop, take a deep breath and reflect on all the blessings in your life! Especially think back on the hard times—those times that you thought life was so bleak you couldn't possibly imagine living another day, yet God pulled you through! During every struggle in your life, you have not been alone, for your best Friend, Jesus, has been with you every step of the way, and He's not going to fail you now!

Pray and ask God to organize your calendar. Only say *yes* to what He wants you to do, and say *no* to everything that isn't on *God's list*! You'll soon realize that you're *too blessed to be stressed*!

Seeking Wisdom

Blessed is the one who finds wisdom, and the one who gets understanding.

Proverbs 3:13 (ESV)

When praying for wisdom, some people expect an answer to come almost like a bolt of lightning, giving them just the right insight to solve their problem. Others believe all they have to do is pray and they'll receive supernatural knowledge at just the right moment. Although God does and has provided wisdom in these manners, there are many ways that He imparts wisdom. Sometimes, it's by revealing a weakness in your own character that helps you grow in your relationship with God and with your fellow man.

The Bible says in James 1:5 (NKJV), "If any of you lacks wisdom, let him ask of God, who gives to all liberally and without reproach, and it will be given to him." When God asked Solomon in 1 Kings 3:5 (NKJV), "Ask! What shall I give you?" He was so pleased with Solomon's request for wisdom that He blessed him abundantly with knowledge—so much so that he was known far and wide as the wisest king who had ever lived. God gave King Solomon a kind heart, compassion, and a genuine love for others.

It's good to remember that the best reason to seek wisdom is not to win the lottery or to be smarter than everyone else, but rather to enrich your relationship with God, your family, your friends, and all those around you.

Jesus Paid It All

I have been crucified with Christ; it is no longer I
who live, but Christ lives in me; and the life which I now
live in the flesh I live by faith in the Son of God,
who loved me and gave Himself for me.

Galatians 2:20 (NKJV)

No matter what trials you have faced in the past or are currently going through, nothing compares to the suffering that Christ went through . . . for you! So, before you start complaining and blaming God, stop and think about just how much Jesus loves you and what He has done for you. No one deserves His love, yet because He loves you so much and couldn't possibly imagine heaven without you, He came to this earth to pay the price for your sins so that you might spend eternity with Him in heaven!

The Bible says in John 3:16 (NIV), "For God so loved the world that he gave his one and only Son, that whoever believes in him shall not perish but have eternal life." Love just doesn't get any stronger than that. Jesus paid it all! So, if God loves you enough to send His only Son to die on a cross just for you, don't you think He loves you enough to see you through every heartache, pain, and sorrow?

The apostle Paul writes about why we should rejoice in our trials in Romans 5:3-5 (ESV), "We rejoice in our sufferings, knowing that suffering produces endurance, and endurance produces character, and character produces hope, and hope does not put us to shame, because God's love has been poured into our hearts through the Holy Spirit who has been given to us."

Walking on Eggshells

The Lord is not slack concerning His promise, as some count
slackness, but is longsuffering toward us, not willing that any
should perish but that all should come to repentance.

2 Peter 3:9 (NKJV)

Being around people whose mood changes from one moment to the next can be quite stressful. Having to worry about saying or doing the wrong thing is not a peaceful way to live. When you break out in a sweat worrying that someone will yell, scream, or act out in anger when you say something, it is not good for your peace of mind or your health. You shouldn't have to approach people you love, friends, or even acquaintances, with fear and trepidation. People like this are unpredictable and toxic and doing the *eggshell walk* gets old really quick!

You can't have a close, loving relationship with anyone if it is based on fear. Sometimes the only way to resolve a relationship like this is to forgive and walk away. How wonderful to know that God is a loving God, and you'll never have to worry about what kind of mood He is in. In fact, the Bible says in Hebrews 13:8 (NKJV), "Jesus Christ is the same yesterday and today and forever."

Don't forget that God loves it when you talk to Him about anything and everything. Nothing you say is stupid, silly, or ridiculous, no matter how trivial it may seem to others! You can tell Him how you really feel and not worry about an angry reaction, because God loves you . . . *really* loves you. Praise the Lord that there is no such thing as *walking on eggshells* when it comes to talking to your best Friend, Jesus!

Between You and the Lord

First of all, then, I urge that supplications, prayers,
intercessions, and thanksgivings be made for everyone

1 Timothy 2:1 (NRSV)

One of the best things you can do for someone you love is pray for them—not just a casual mention of their names, but really pray . . . passionately! When you are praying for those you love, not only does it benefit those you are praying for, but it also gives you more patience, tenderness, and love in your heart for them as well. You become more sensitive to their needs and desires, and when differences of opinions arise, you are much more equipped to handle them in a Christlike way.

The Bible says in Philippians 2:3-4 (NASB), "Do nothing from selfishness or empty conceit, but with humility of mind regard one another as more important than yourselves; do not merely look out for your own personal interests, but also for the interests of others." It's selfish to pray only for your own needs. God wants you to think of others and prayerfully uplift their needs as well. However, it's important to pray with a humble spirit. No one wants to hear a self-righteous person announce they are praying for them. Telling a weaker brother or sister that you are praying for them could easily send them running away from God instead of drawing them closer.

Remember that you are no better than anyone else, including the person you are praying for. Romans 3:23 (NKJV) says, "For all have sinned and fall short of the glory of God." Sometimes, it's better to keep your prayers just between you and the Lord!

The Three "D's"

He who dwells in the secret place of the Most High shall abide under the shadow of the Almighty.

Psalm 91:1 (NKJV)

You love God, go to church, and even pray every day, but have you learned the real joy of dwelling in God's presence? Do you desire to spend time alone with your Creator? Or when push comes to shove, you simply have no time to give God?

If you want a vibrant life with Jesus, put God first, starting with the three "D's":

1. *Decide* daily to begin your day with personal devotions (praise and worship to your Lord and Savior).

2. *Determine* in your heart to make this special time with God your highest priority.

3. *Discipline* yourself to be persistent and diligent, letting nothing interfere or distract you from this alone time with your heavenly Father.

The Bible says in James 4:8 (NKJV), "Draw near to God and He will draw near to you." The more time you spend with God, the more time you'll want to be with Him, and soon you'll find that the ten minutes you set aside . . . is just not long enough! You'll be surprised at how much better your day will be when you start the day with Jesus. Decide right now to make God your highest priority and spend quality time with Him not only today . . . but every day!

One Step at a Time

We are hard pressed on every side, but not crushed;
perplexed, but not in despair; persecuted, but not
abandoned; struck down, but not destroyed.

2 Corinthians 4:8-9 (NIV)

When you feel like everything is going wrong in your life and no matter what you do you just can't seem to get a break, instead of giving up in despair . . . turn to Jesus! Don't be afraid to tell Him how you really feel: "God, I just can't take this anymore!" He hears your cries, and He responds to your prayers! The Bible says in Psalm 34:17 (NKJV), "The righteous cry out, and the LORD hears, and delivers them out of all their troubles."

Even when things look dark and you are at the end of your rope, with God your life is not hopeless. You can look back in history and see that never once did God desert His people . . . and He won't desert you either! Jesus loves you more than you could possibly know and no matter how discouraged or broken you feel, Jesus is there to lift you up and comfort you in His arms of love! He *is* your hope! You can claim God's promise in Isaiah 41:10 (NKJV), "Fear not, for I am with you; be not dismayed, for I am your God. I will strengthen you . . . I will uphold you with my righteous right hand."

When you are tempted to give up, pray for strength and claim Joshua 1:9 (NIV), "Have I not commanded you? Be strong and courageous. Do not be afraid; do not be discouraged, for the LORD your God will be with you wherever you go." Hold God's hand and go forward with faith that He will lead you safely where you should go . . . one step at a time!

Living in Harmony

*But may the God of all grace, who called us to His
eternal glory by Christ Jesus, after you have suffered a
while, perfect, establish, strengthen, and settle you.*

1 Peter 5:10 (NKJV)

When a terrible injustice has been done to you or someone you love, sometimes it's hard to just let it go. All-consuming hurt and anger keeps the painful memories churning over and over again in your mind. But dwelling on the pain will never bring peace of mind and will keep you covered in a cloud of darkness. There is only one way to escape and that is to give it all to Jesus! He knows what you have gone through and understands your suffering. He also knows why He permitted it to happen. But instead of blaming God or even demanding to know *why* . . . you need to just trust Him!

When someone has done you wrong, of course you will hurt, because God didn't create you with a heart of stone. He doesn't expect you to not feel the pain, but He does expect you to forgive. Once you release all your bitterness and anger to Him, He will take away the gloom, and the light of His presence will take all darkness away. The Bible says in John 16:33 (NLT), "Here on earth you will have many trials and sorrows. But take heart, because I have overcome the world."

When we get to heaven, there will be no more hostility, jealousy, or hatred, but only the amazing, transforming love of Jesus, which will be in the hearts and souls of everyone there. Oh, what a glorious day that will be when we meet our Savior face-to-face and live in harmony for all eternity.

Don't Be a Doormat

*Humble yourselves under the mighty hand of God,
that He may exalt you in due time, casting all your care
upon Him, for He cares for you.*

1 Peter 5:6-7 (NKJV)

There's a difference between surrendering to *God* and surrendering to *man*. In order for our will to become God's will, we must surrender to Him! But sometimes the devil causes confusion regarding just whom to surrender to! One sure way you can always distinguish between God and Satan is this: God will never ask you to do something that violates His Holy Word or goes against what the Holy Spirit is impressing upon your conscience.

You can trust God to give you wisdom and discernment. There are some who struggle with surrender because they have been battered and abused. Once they escape the violence and begin their journey of healing, it's quite difficult to submit to anyone, including God, because of the emotional trauma. But God understands and cares deeply! He will give power to the weak and strength to the broken so that trust in Him will be restored.

Make no mistake, it is not God's will that anyone be abused! Nor does He want His children to lay down and be a doormat! There are those who submitted to their abuser and lost their lives because of it! That's not God's plan! Surrender to Jesus *first*, resting in His arms of love, and you can trust Him to take care of everything else!

The Devil's Lies

The Lord is my rock and my fortress and my deliverer;
my God, my strength, in whom I will trust; my shield
and the horn of my salvation, my stronghold.

Psalm 18:2 (NKJV)

It's much easier to trust Jesus when everything is going smoothly in your life. But when things turn sour and you're overwhelmed with the drama of your own heartache, it's not quite as easy! However, real faith is exercised not only in the good times but in the tough times too. It is when you are going through your darkest hour that you need to cling to Jesus the most! You can be sure that Satan will take advantage of your weakness—he knows all the buttons to push. If you're not careful, you'll start believing all Satan's negative thoughts, such as *God doesn't love me, God's trying to punish me,* or *I'm a failure.* But don't believe the devil's lies for even one moment! You can fight the enemy with God's sword of truth, so never forget that Jesus is there for you.

Don't underestimate the power of God. The Bible says in Psalm 91:14-15 (NIV), we're told, "'Because he loves me,' says the LORD, 'I will rescue him; I will protect him, for he acknowledges my name. He will call on me, and I will answer him; I will be with him in trouble, I will deliver him and honor him.'" It just doesn't get better than that! Belonging to Christ puts you in position of strength, so give your burdens, troubles, and heartache to Jesus. He is the only one who has the power to save you!

Choose the Narrow Path

*In the way of righteousness is life, and in its
pathway there is no death.*

Proverbs 12:28 (NKJV)

———◆———

There are many people in this world who prefer to take the *easy way out* rather than do what it takes to accomplish the task. If something looks like it's *too much work* or *too demeaning a task*, they just walk away. Perhaps someone has always dreamed of being a doctor and is smart enough to pass all the exams and be accepted in medical school, but when they got there and realized what it would take—the many hours *on duty* at the hospital, sleepless nights, and endless hours of studying—they say, "No way! That takes too much work!"

So, instead of realizing their dream, they end up in a dead-end job they hate, all because they wanted the easy way and refused to walk the narrow path to success! The Bible gives very clear instructions in Matthew 7:13 (NIV), "Enter through the narrow gate. For wide is the gate and broad is the road that leads to destruction, and many enter through it."

Don't be like everyone else! Instead of following the crowd, thinking it's *not cool* to follow Jesus, choose the narrow path and stand up for what is right. Allow Christ to shine through you! It's not always easy being a follower of Christ, but you can count on the Holy Spirit to protect, teach, and guide you in every step you take. So when you think about that, the narrow path is actually the *easiest* path after all, because you are holding God's hand. And when clasping the hand of your Savior, you just can't go wrong!

Behind Your Back

A perverse man sows strife, and a whisperer
separates the best of friends.

Proverbs 16:28 (NKJV)

When you hear the expression "behind your back," you know immediately that it means someone is talking about you to other people. Usually it's not intended for you to hear because it's very hurtful when people say mean things about you. But . . . what if people were saying good things about you instead of whispering hurtful gossip? Just imagine how much better this world would be if people only shared things they liked about someone and gave only positive comments!

Now think about how awesome it would be if you talked about God "behind His back," telling everyone you met just how wonderful He is. And everywhere you went, you bragged on God's goodness! But, of course, it's impossible to talk *behind God's back* because He sees and hears everything!

But have you considered how God feels when He hears you take His name in vain or hears someone telling off-color jokes? He certainly doesn't rejoice when He hears unkind things said about Him. He also doesn't like to hear you talk bad about any of His children. He loves each one and doesn't appreciate gossip and slander. In fact, God calls it sin! In Ephesians 4:29 (NIV), we're told, "Do not let any unwholesome talk come out of your mouths, but only what is helpful for building others up according to their needs, that it may benefit those who listen." Remember, when you talk behind God's back . . . He's listening!

Heavenly Time Schedule

*I will bless the LORD at all times; His praise shall
continually be in my mouth.*

Psalm 34:1 (NKJV)

An enormous amount of time is spent just *waiting*! Waiting
in this life is inevitable, whether you are waiting in line at
the car wash, waiting for your dinner to arrive at a restaurant,
or waiting for test results which will determine whether you live
or die. But how you choose to spend your time while waiting
is up to you! You can waste that time doing something useless,
spend it worrying and pacing the floor, or you can trust that
God will do what is best for you . . . and then praise Him!

God understands and cares when you suffer. He knows
waiting for a job and worrying about how you will feed your
family, buy medicine, or pay your rent takes real faith. Living
in *limbo* is stressful if you're not walking with Jesus, because
not knowing what the future holds can be quite a nail-biting
experience. But sometimes God allows us to have cloudy vision,
where we can't see where our next step is, in order to bring us
to a place where we are totally leaning on Him.

Remember that *God's timing* is different than ours. The
Bible says in 2 Peter 3:8 (NIV), "With the Lord a day is like
a thousand years, and a thousand years are like a day." God is
on His eternal, heavenly time schedule, which is quite different
from our temporary, earthly one. He sees the big picture that
we can't see, so it's better to wait on God's perfect plan and
His perfect timing. In the meantime, spend the *waiting game*
trusting and praising your Lord and Savior!

In the Midst of Trials

*In this you greatly rejoice . . . you have been grieved
by various trials, that the genuineness of your faith . . .
though it is tested by fire, may be found to praise, honor,
and glory at the revelation of Jesus Christ.*

1 Peter 1:6-7 (NKJV)

There's a verse in the Bible that has some people scratching their heads and wondering what in the world God meant. It's found in James 1:2 (NIV): "Consider it pure joy, my brothers and sisters, whenever you face trials of many kinds." Now one might say, "Just wait one minute! Does God actually want me to enjoy my heartache?" Well, of course not! Keep on reading verse three: "Because you know that the testing of your faith produces perseverance." And verse four: "Let perseverance finish its work so that you may be mature and complete, not lacking anything."

God is perfecting our characters in order to prepare us for heaven, and we must persevere to stay strong, fight the good fight, and finish the race! There's a reason God allows us to experience trials, although it doesn't mean every time we go through heartache that it's God's fault. Sometimes life just happens as the result of sin! But how we respond to our hard times is what's important!

Instead of blaming God, lean on Him! Ask for strength, courage, and comfort, and you'll find that working through each trial grows a perseverance that is faith-building. Then, even in the midst of the trial, you'll find reasons to sing for joy and praise God!

Never in a Hurry

"If you ask anything in My name, I will do it."
John 14:14 (NKJV)

Have you ever been angry with God for not answering your prayers the way *you* wanted Him to? Or perhaps you felt He never answered at all? There are times that people pray for healing, and when their loved one dies, they think that God didn't answer. Or if their prayers to conceive a child doesn't result in pregnancy, then it's assumed God doesn't love them. And when the *dream job* doesn't become a reality, all of a sudden, it's *God's fault* because He didn't care. But the truth is, God *always* answers prayer. It may not be in the time frame you want or the way you want, but He always answers!

The Bible says in Matthew 7:7 (NIV), "Ask and it will be given to you; seek and you will find; knock and the door will be opened to you." And in Matthew 21:22 (NKJV), "And whatever things you ask in prayer, believing, you will receive." Many interpret these scriptures as meaning they can get whatever they want, as long as they pray for it! But it's important to remember to pray, "God's will be done." You don't know the end from the beginning, but God does, and He alone knows what is best for you! Many times, had God given you what you asked for, it would have ended in disaster, and you would've wished you had never prayed for it! You just can't go wrong when you are praying for God's will! Remember that God never gets in a hurry . . . but He always gets there on time!

Choose Your Attitude

Do all things without murmuring and arguing.
Philippians 2:14 (NRSV)

Attitude is a choice—you can either choose to allow God to shine through you in every situation or you can choose to have a sour attitude when things don't go your way. No one can *make* you angry, mad, or even sarcastic, because it is *you* who holds the power over your emotions. But once you let the actions of someone else or a dismal situation dictate your mood or behavior, you are no longer in control, and that's a dangerous place to be.

Wallowing in self-pity and bitterness, harboring negative thoughts, complaining and criticizing is not God's way. The Bible says in Philippians 2:5 (NLT), "You must have the same attitude that Christ Jesus had." And in Philippians 4:11 (NIV), we're told, "I am not saying this because I am in need, for I have learned to be content whatever the circumstances." Don't dwell on the ugly things in life—choose the attitude of Christ.

It's not humanly possible to always be content and happy, but with God all things are possible. It is Christ Jesus who gives you the strength to be like Him each day. Every morning before heading out the door, spend time in prayer and ask God to give you the power to be like Him. Choose a Christlike attitude and don't forget to claim Philippians 4:13 (NKJV): "I can do all things through Christ who strengthens me."

What We Don't Deserve

Let us therefore come boldly to the throne of grace, that we may obtain mercy and find grace to help in time of need.

Hebrews 4:16 (NKJV)

Someone once said, "Grace is when God gives us what we don't deserve and mercy is when God doesn't give us what we do deserve." Oh, how true this is! Without God's grace and mercy, everyone would be lost! David called for God's mercy quite often. He prayed in Psalm 69:16 (NIV), "Answer me, LORD, out of the goodness of your love; in your great mercy turn to me."

Of course, everyone desires God's grace and mercy and eagerly request it, but how many actually extend God's compassion to those who are not deserving? When we make a decision that affects someone else, do we hold them up to a higher standard? Do we demand justice? If God demanded *justice*, that would require each of us to pay for our own sins, and everyone would be cast out of heaven for all eternity! Jesus forgave us for our sins and made a way for our salvation through His death on Calvary, even though we didn't deserve it.

In Ephesians 4:7 (NIV), we're told, "But to each one of us grace has been given as Christ apportioned it." One thing that God asks us to do is to love each other and to treat each other as we would want to be treated. Now, that doesn't mean He wants us to lie down and be a rug that everyone walks over, but it does mean that we should demonstrate His love, grace, and mercy toward others.

The Blame Game

*For if our heart condemns us, God is greater than
our heart, and knows all things.*

1 John 3:20 (NKJV)

Whenever things don't turn out the way you want them to, it's easy to blame yourself. You tell yourself that if only you had been the perfect parent, then your kids would have turned out better; if you had been a better person, then your spouse wouldn't have cheated; or if you hadn't said the wrong thing, you wouldn't have a black eye. The truth is, not everything that goes wrong in life is your fault.

First of all, this is not a perfect world. Humans make mistakes. And even if you were the best parent in the world, it still comes down to your children reaching the age where they reap the consequences for their own choices. A spouse's lack of character made them cheat, not you. And no one ever deserves to be battered, no matter what was said. When you play the "blame game," and take responsibility for all that goes wrong, the only one who wins is Satan! He loves to see you upset, feeling guilty, disheartened, and depressed!

Instead of riding the *guilt train*, get on the *praise train*! Praise God for all the things that are going *right* in your life and start counting your blessings. If you've done something wrong, then ask God to forgive you, believe in His forgiveness, and move on with joy in your heart. Leave the things you cannot change to God and let Him take care of it while you are comforted by His warm embrace.

World Without Hate

Whoever hates his brother is a murderer, and you know that no murderer has eternal life abiding in him.

1 John 3:15 (NKJV)

Imagine for a moment what a beautiful world this would be if *hatred* did not exist. People would actually be kind to one another, judgment and biases would be abolished, and everyone would love each other. But sadly, because of sin, *hate* is not only existent but prevalent in the world today. One of the worst forms of hatred is judging people because of the color of their skin. It's mind-boggling to think that you could actually hate another human being whom God created based solely on their genetic makeup or country they happened to be born in!

Just imagine how this makes God feel. He created man to be equal. No one is better than anyone else and that includes whatever skin color they have. Generations of people have experienced unfair suffering and persecution from people filled with hatred towards them . . . all because of skin color! The Bible says in 1 John 4:20 (ESV), "If anyone says, "I love God," and hates his brother, he is a liar; for he who does not love his brother whom he has seen cannot love God whom he has not seen."

The bottom line is, God wants everyone to love each other as He loves us! This popular children's song says it all: "Jesus loves the little children, all the children of the world. Red and yellow, black and white, all are precious in His sight." Ask God to fill your heart with more love for your fellow man, regardless of skin color, and live a life without hate!

If God Seems Distant

*"I will betroth you to Me forever; yes, I will
betroth you to Me in righteousness and justice, in
lovingkindness and mercy."*

Hosea 2:19 (NKJV)

———◆———

Christians who rarely go to church, neglect daily devotions, and hardly ever pray need to reexamine their view of God. Because when you see God as this stern *being* way up in the heavens somewhere, keeping track of all your sins, it doesn't make you long to be close with Him. In fact, it becomes easier and easier to hit the snooze button rather than spend time in worship and praise.

The truth is, when you lose sight of who God really is, your desire to spend time with Him diminishes greatly and you actually start running from Him. But when you truly understand what an awesome, loving, generous God He is (who loves you so much that He can't imagine heaven without you), it changes everything! You not only make time, but you crave even more time in His presence. Knowing God as a loving heavenly Father, who is honest, trustworthy, and has your back 100% of the time makes all the difference in your relationship with Him.

So, if God seems distant, examine just *who* He is. You won't be able to resist falling in love with Him. It will change your relationship from serving out of obligation to worshiping Him with a deep desire to draw even closer to your Lord and Savior!

He Always Answers

*"Therefore I say to you, whatever things you ask
when you pray, believe that you receive them,
and you will have them."*

Mark 11:24 (NKJV)

———— ◆◆◆ ————

One of the wonderful rewards of being a believer in Jesus Christ is never having to worry about anything! When you put your full trust in your Lord and Savior, you will experience peace such as you have never known, because God has your best interest in mind . . . always! And best of all, when you pray, He *always* answers! You just need to relax and put your full faith and trust in Him, because He has it all under control.

Sometimes His answer may be instantaneous, while other times you may have to wait days, weeks or even years for your answer. But if you knew the end from the beginning, you wouldn't want it any other way . . . than God's way! The first time you experience a direct answer to your prayer, you might be tempted to think, *Hmm, that's probably just a coincidence.* The second time you have more confidence to know something intentional is happening. But soon you realize that it is God responding, and He is forever faithful to those who seek Him.

The Bible says in Matthew 6:8 (NIV), "Your Father knows what you need before you ask him." The next time something rocks your world and you're tempted to panic, take a deep breath and say, "Thank you, Lord, for always having my back. I'm not gonna worry, You already have it covered."

We Always Have Hope

This I recall to my mind, therefore I have hope.
Through the LORD's mercies we are not consumed,
because His compassions fail not. They are new every
morning; great is Your faithfulness.

Lamentations 3:21-23 (NKJV)

The expression, "I hope so," is often said in response to someone trying to reassure us that everything is going to turn out fine. But as Christians, we know that our *hope* is backed up with the power of God's promises and there is nothing *iffy* about that! God is a *sure thing*, and we can always count on Him to keep His Word! Sadly, there are people who put their hope in all the wrong places and end up despondent and disillusioned. They learn the hard way that there is only one place to put our hope and that is in Jesus Christ.

Because of His sacrifice on Calvary, we have *hope*! God is faithful and trustworthy, and He will do what He says He will do! We can count on Him 100% of the time to comfort, strengthen, guide, heal, and forgive.

The Bible says in Isaiah 40:31 (NIV), "Those who hope in the LORD will renew their strength. They will soar on wings like eagles; they will run and not grow weary, they will walk and not be faint." No matter what trial or struggle we are going through, with God, we always have *hope*!

Examine Your Motives

But for those who are self-seeking and who reject the truth and follow evil, there will be wrath and anger.

Romans 2:8 (NIV)

God wants us to love everyone, even our enemies, and when we do something kind for someone, we are putting into practice God's message in Matthew 25:40 (KJV): "Inasmuch as ye have done it unto one of the least of these my brethren, ye have done it unto me." But have you ever stopped to examine your motives for doing something nice for someone?

When you opened that door for a lady in the wheelchair, were you expecting a *thank-you*, and if you didn't receive it, did you feel a bit slighted? When you offered to give a ride to a co-worker whose car broke down, were you motivated by a genuine desire to help or were you secretly wanting him to feel indebted to you or perhaps even tell your boss what a great person you are? When you sat next to a sister in church who always sat alone each week, did you do so to show genuine love to her or was your desire to impress your church family and to appear "holier" in their eyes?

Many times people don't really see the pride in their hearts and may not even realize their selfish agenda. It's important to ask God to open your eyes so that you can examine your motives, and should any selfishness exist, to remove it and fill you to overflowing with His love so that you may share with others . . . for the right motives!

Best Is Yet to Come

And now, O LORD GOD, You are God, and Your words are true, and You have promised this goodness to Your servant.

2 Samuel 7:28 (NKJV)

Wouldn't it be wonderful if everyone was trustworthy, honest, and kind? Just think how awesome it would be to do business and not worry you're getting a bad deal? And wouldn't it be reassuring if you could confide in someone and trust that you won't see it the next day all over social media? And how amazing it would be if you could walk down the street anytime day or night and feel safe?

But the truth is, there will not be equality, complete honesty, or safety as long as we live on this sinful earth. This world is not fair and it never will be until Jesus comes again! But there is hope while on this life's journey because there is someone you *can* trust with all your heart and that person is Jesus! He will never let you down, deceive you, or hurt you in any way! And the good news is, He loves you so much that He's coming soon to take you home to heaven to live with Him for all eternity!

Soon, the things of this earth will pass away and you will never feel sad, discouraged, angry, or lonely ever again! You will be happier than you could ever dream possible. No matter how bleak life looks today, stay faithful and keep holding God's hand . . . the best is yet to come!

Bridging the Gap

Let all that you do be done with love.
1 Corinthians 16:14 (NKJV)

The enemy would like nothing better than to drive a wedge between family members. He knows which buttons to push that will cause you to lose your patience or your temper, become irritated, or give a snide remark. Whenever you start acting in a unchristlike way, the devil wins! When you let go of God's hand for even a moment, Satan is quick to rush in, and that is when you'll fall.

Hard feelings have a way of creating walls that soon seem too high to climb. Many times, family feuds have gone on for years where neither side can remember what started the fight in the first place, yet they hold on to all that anger! The only way to find your way back to each other is to allow God to *bridge the gap*. He alone can heal hearts and melt away the anger.

Determine today to love as God loves and rid your heart of all jealousy and foolish pride. If we can't love our own family, then God tells us that we can't possibly love Him. It's clear in 1 John 4:20 (NIV): "If someone says, I love God," and hates his brother, he is a liar; for he who does not love his brother whom he has seen, how can he love God whom he has not seen?" Whatever is standing in the way of family unity, open the door with the key of forgiveness. There's nothing that is worth missing out on eternity in heaven. Allow God to be first in your life and *love* as He loves . . . starting in your own home!

The Battle Is Won

*God is our refuge and strength, a very present
help in trouble. Therefore we will not fear, even though
the earth be removed, and though the mountains be
carried into the midst of the sea.*

Psalm 46:1-2 (NKJV)

The world today is faced with wars, terrorist attacks, natural disasters, human tragedies, and financial collapse. It seems no matter which way you turn, there are dangers on every side, which can easily keep you in a state of panic. And if you throw politics in the mix, it seems this world is going downhill fast!

All the scary things going on today prove just how much you need a Savior. When you feel afraid, give your uneasy feelings, your fears, and your anxiety to God. Ask Him to hold your hand and never let go! He will calm your fears and take away that queasy feeling in the pit of your stomach. No matter what is happening in the world, you can depend on Jesus, for He will never let you down!

In these uncertain times, choose to focus your mind on what the Bible tells us in Isaiah 41:10 (NIV): "So do not fear, for I am with you; do not be dismayed, for I am your God. I will strengthen you and help you; I will uphold you with my righteous right hand." You might not be in control, but you can trust the one who is—and that is God, the King of the Universe. Even when life seems dismal and bleak, remember there's no need to be afraid, because the battle is already won!

Praise God!

Listening to God's Voice

*My son, give me your heart, and let your
eyes observe my ways.*

Proverbs 23:26 (NKJV)

———◆———

There are times we hear the pleadings of the Holy Spirit, but we second-guess what God is telling us and disregard His voice because we don't want to do what He asks. We miss many *divine appointments* as well as *divine direction* as to what we should do, where we should go, or what plan He has for us.

Ignoring God's voice is a dangerous thing to do! When God speaks, listen! We can't expect to do all the talking when we pray—God wants us to listen to what He has to say too! And He also wants us to *obey*. Obedience to God is something we all struggle with! It comes down to our own selfish desires versus God's desires.

Our biggest battle here on earth is with *self*! We want what we want . . . when we want it! But in order to have the abundant life here on earth that God wants us to have, we must surrender our will to His will! The more we fall in love with Jesus, the more we want to be like Him and the more *our will* becomes *His will*. The Bible says in Luke 11:28 (NKJV), "Blessed are those who hear the word of God and keep it!" Choose today to listen to God's voice, and then go one step further by praying, "Lord, make me *instant* to Your will."

How God Views Success

*Then you will prosper, if you take care to fulfill
the statutes and judgments with which the LORD charged
Moses concerning Israel. Be strong and of good courage;
do not fear nor be dismayed.*

1 Chronicles 22:13 (NKJV)

One of the most sought after goals in life . . . is success! But everyone has a different view of just what *success* really means. To some, it is based on financial gain, power, or fame, while others think they have achieved success if they have the lifestyle of their dreams—wonderful spouse, perfect children, beautiful house, and lavish vacations. But God views success much differently because He measures success in terms of your personal relationship with Him. Are you obedient in accomplishing His purposes and goals? Are you faithful in your tithes and offerings? Do you cherish your *alone time* with Him? Are you kind and loving? Do you share His love with others?

There are many Bible characters who were considered failures by their friends and acquaintances but were highly successful in God's eyes. For instance, Jeremiah was poor, homeless, and thrown in prison, and although he was God's messenger for forty years, no one listened when he spoke. People thought he was a complete failure, but in God's eyes he was a huge success because he was faithful in all that God asked of him. Strive to achieve success in *God's eyes* and you'll not only enjoy a more meaningful and joy-filled life here on earth, but in heaven for all eternity as well.

Choose Your Canoe

For the mind that is set on the flesh is hostile to God, for
it does not submit to God's law; indeed, it cannot.

Romans 8:7 (ESV)

It's impossible to *walk with Jesus* and *hold hands with the devil*! You cannot possibly be a follower of Christ simply by attending church, then doing whatever you want the rest of the week: drinking, gambling, cheating, gossiping, or any other sin against God. The Bible says in Joshua 24:15 (KJV), "Choose you this day whom ye will serve." God says that we must make a choice! We are either *for* Him or *against* Him. We can't be wishy-washy or straddle two canoes! We must decide—are we serving God or Satan! There is no in between.

The Bible warns us about how God feels toward *lukewarm* people. In Revelation 3:16 (KJV), we're told, "So then because thou art lukewarm, and neither cold nor hot, I will spue thee out of my mouth." It doesn't get much clearer than that! Jesus is coming soon, and there is no time to go out and sample worldly pleasures, then just in the nick of time before Jesus comes, decide you'll serve God! It just doesn't work that way!

The main reason we should want to go to heaven isn't because we don't want to go to hell! Not at all! Our reason should be that we love Jesus with all our hearts and we want to spend eternity with our Lord and Savior! Don't wait any longer. Choose today whom you will serve. *Praise God !!!*

August 16

Loving Our Enemies

No one has seen God at any time. If we love one another,
God abides in us, and His love has been perfected in us.

1 John 4:12 (NKJV)

All throughout Scripture, God pleads with us to love one another! He urges us to especially care for the children, sick, elderly, and less fortunate. The Bible says in Matthew 25:40 (KJV), "Verily I say unto you, inasmuch as ye have done it unto one of the least of these my brethren, ye have done it unto me." It is very clear how God wants us to show our love for our fellow man. However, He's not just talking about our family, friends, or people who are nice to us—it includes our enemies too.

There's nothing in the Bible that tells us it's okay to be mean to our enemies! In fact, it is just the opposite. Jesus wants us to love those who are mean and hateful. In Proverbs 24:17 (KJV), He counsels us, "Rejoice not when thine enemy falleth, and let not thine heart be glad when he stumbleth."

God doesn't want us to experience one tiny moment of pleasure when we see our enemies fall! Not even when a boss has fired us unfairly, a family member has cast us out, or a church member has spread gossip and lies. Matthew 5:44 (NIV) says, "But I tell you, love your enemies and pray for those who persecute you." And Luke 6:28 (NIV) instructs us, "Bless those who curse you, pray for those who mistreat you." Bottom line—we are to love each other as God loves us and share His unconditional love with everyone we meet!

Ask for Help

*My help comes from the LORD, who
made heaven and earth.*

Psalm 121:2 (NKJV)

Sometimes it is foolish pride that gets people in trouble. It's easy to have the *I'll-do-it-myself* attitude. But stubbornness can lead to serious consequences! Asking for help loading your own moving truck could not only save you from an aching back or a ruptured disc but could actually make what would have been a dreaded chore . . . a fun day with friends! Calling for assistance is nothing to be ashamed of. Neither will people think more highly of you just because you have a reputation of being a *one-man band*!

When you have experienced the benefit of someone helping you, there's a willingness in your heart to reach out and help someone else. Proverbs 3:27 (NIV) tells us, "Do not withhold good from those to whom it is due, when it is in your power to act." People helping people creates memories and lasting friendships. It's much easier to walk this life's journey surrounded by friends than it is to be alone. And let's not forget the one you can count on the most—Jesus Christ our Lord. He stands willing to help anytime day or night—all you need to do is ask! He loves you and will act on your behalf, so whatever problems you have, never be afraid, ashamed, or too shy to *ask for help*!

The New You

But be doers of the word, and not hearers
only, deceiving yourselves.

James 1:22 (NKJV)

When you surrender your life to Christ and accept Him as your Lord and Savior, it is as if you've been born again! However, spiritual rebirth requires change as old habits are done away with and new healthy ones emerge. The Bible says in Matthew 5:48 (NKJV), "Therefore you shall be perfect, just as your Father in heaven is perfect." Now this doesn't mean that you *on your own* instantly have the strength to resist all temptations to sin and now live a perfect life. No, not at all! It is your connection with Christ and Christ alone that gives you the courage, power, and strength to overcome the enemy.

As your family, friends, and those you work with notice the change in you, make no mistake, not all will be supportive of the *new* you. Some will mock you and question you: "What's so wrong with doing that?" "You're just no fun anymore." "Come on, just this once won't matter!" No doubt your newfound faith will be put to the test. But it is far more important what God thinks of you than what others think of you!

If your friends are trying to separate you from your Savior, then it's time to find new friends. Choose those who will encourage you, for there is absolutely nothing that is worth missing out on heaven! Confidently shine for Jesus and let everyone see the *new you*!

Spiritual Death

For we must all appear before the judgment seat of Christ,
that each one may receive the things done in the body,
according to what he has done, whether good or bad.

2 Corinthians 5:10 (NKJV)

Someone once said that "spiritual death is only one compromise away," and that is so true, because the moment you choose not to live up to what you believe, you are lost! It's so easy to make excuses and justify in your mind that it's okay to compromise. But, the truth is, you can rationalize yourself right into hell! It starts off with little things, such as stretching the truth on a resume to make it seem like you are more qualified than you really are or calling in *sick* when you really wanted a day with your friends. Soon, the compromises get easier and easier, until it feels so natural you no longer feel the guilt—and the devil wins!

The Bible encourages us in Ephesians 6:14 (NIV): "Stand firm then, with the belt of truth buckled around your waist, with the breastplate of righteousness in place." And Isaiah 33:15-16 (NIV) says, "Those who walk righteously and speak what is right . . . they are the ones who will dwell on the heights." God makes it very clear how He values honesty, purity and faithfulness, so stand firm for the right! When you have the character of Jesus, you will be a person of integrity. Remember there is no such thing as *little white lies*. Guard your thoughts and mind, because what you *think* determines your actions. Avoid *spiritual death* by staying faithful to God's Holy Word— never yielding to compromise!

Most Popular Book

*For the word of God is living and powerful, and sharper
than any two-edged sword, piercing even to the division
of soul and spirit, and of joints and marrow, and is a
discerner of the thoughts and intents of the heart.*

Hebrews 4:12 (NKJV)

There are more Bibles sold in the world than any other book,
yet it's the most misunderstood, misquoted, and ignored
book. Instead of having a place of honor in our homes, it sits
dusty on a shelf, table, or out-of-the-way place. Few people
truly understand what a privilege it is to have direct access to
God's Holy Word, for He speaks to us directly through each
precious page, impressing our minds through the Holy Spirit as
we prayerfully read His words.

The more we study and pray, the closer our relationship with
Him grows, and soon we know God as our personal Friend who
we go to for guidance, wisdom, and comfort. His will becomes
our will and running to Jesus becomes our *first* resort, not our
last. We can listen for God's voice as we study the Bible . . .
and hear Him speaking. Oh, what an amazing God we serve,
who loves us so much that He wants to communicate with His
children directly!

If the Bible is in the attic or sitting in a box in your garage,
why not dust it off and begin reading God's Word. Allow Him
speak to your heart and start your new life today . . . getting to
know your Savior!

A Servant's Heart

*Serve wholeheartedly, as if you were serving
the Lord, not people, because you know that the Lord
will reward each one for whatever good they do,
whether they are slave or free.*

Ephesians 6:7-8 (NIV)

When we are helpful, kind, and loving to others, we are serving Jesus by embracing His principles. His light shines through us and brightens the lives of those we come in contact with. Our hearts become changed and people we once looked at as irritating and annoying, we now see through God's eyes and view them with tenderness. God's love changes even the hardest of hearts!

In 1 Corinthians 12:5 (NIV), we're told, "There are different kinds of service, but the same Lord." God doesn't call all of us to do the same thing. He has a special plan for each of us. No matter what our profession, whether we are educated or not, rich or poor, the only criteria for serving Jesus is to surrender our hearts and lives to Him and allow Him to use us however He sees fit.

The Holy Spirit will guide, gently nudging us throughout our day, giving us the wisdom and direction to carry out His will. Having a *servant's heart* comes from knowing and loving our Master, and the reward is experiencing God's sweet peace and genuine joy! When we fall in love with Jesus, we can't help but want to share His love with the world around us, and that includes loving people to Jesus . . . with a *servant's heart*.

Claim the Victory

*He who sins is of the devil, for the devil has sinned from
the beginning. For this purpose the Son of God was
manifested, that He might destroy the works of the devil.*

1 John 3:8 (NKJV)

Our salvation has been purchased by the blood of Jesus,
but that doesn't mean that Satan has given up trying to
separate us from the only one who can save us! In fact, the devil
knows his time on earth is short, and he is trying harder than
ever to tempt us to sin. He is clever and oh so cunning at making
worldly pleasure seem enticing. He's an expert at disguising the
evils of this world, making them seem *not so bad*. He makes it
easier and easier to say, "Well, just this once," or "I'll enjoy the
pleasures of this world, and then I'll give my heart to Jesus."

But if we yield to temptation, before we know it, we are
weighed down with the guilt of our sin and sink deeper and
deeper into the devil's trap! Don't be deceived into thinking the
enemy is not a threat and definitely don't underestimate his evil
power. There's no doubt about it, Satan is dangerous! We are
cautioned in 1 Peter 5:8 (KJV), "Be sober, be vigilant; because
your adversary the devil, as a roaring lion, walketh about,
seeking whom he may devour." But the good news is this: God
is much more powerful than Satan, and all we need to do is
stay close to Jesus. With Christ by our side, we can resist the
deceptions of the enemy and . . . claim the victory!

Thank God for Friendship

Two are better than one, because they have a good reward for their labor. For if they fall, one will lift up his companion. But woe to him who is alone when he falls, for he has no one to help him up.

Ecclesiastes 4:9-10 (NKJV)

There are people in our lives that seldom receive the praise and thanks that they deserve. Unfortunately, those people are often the very ones who we are closest to—who love, support, and defend us. They are so much a part of our lives that sometimes they can be taken for granted! Some of us have lots of friends, while others may only have one or two, but each friend deserves to know just how much they mean to you.

There are many ways to show your love and appreciation. It may be a simple gesture of sending flowers, a handmade card, an email, or text to express your sentiments. But the best way you can show your appreciation to God for bringing your special friends into your life . . . is to lift them up in prayer! Not only thank God for their friendship, but ask Him to bless them and to provide His care and protection over them. Praying for someone is one of the most amazing gifts you could ever give!

Why not reach out today to the friends in your life and let them know how much you love them. And start with your best Friend, Jesus! He especially wants to hear how much He means to you.

Welcome Mat for Trouble

*For waywardness kills the simple, and the
complacency of fools destroys them.*

Proverbs 1:32 (NRSV)

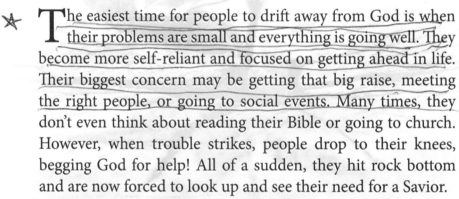

The easiest time for people to drift away from God is when their problems are small and everything is going well. They become more self-reliant and focused on getting ahead in life. Their biggest concern may be getting that big raise, meeting the right people, or going to social events. Many times, they don't even think about reading their Bible or going to church. However, when trouble strikes, people drop to their knees, begging God for help! All of a sudden, they hit rock bottom and are now forced to look up and see their need for a Savior.

There are many stories in the Bible where God allowed trials to turn people's hearts heavenward. For instance, the prodigal son was on top of the world when he had lots of money; there was no shortage of friends or parties to go to. But when his money dried up and he was in the middle of a pig pen, he saw his need for a Savior, repented, and begged God's forgiveness.

No one likes to experience difficult times, but when it accomplishes the goal of drawing us closer to Jesus, then it's time to throw out the welcome mat for trouble! When things are going well, we tend to lean on self, but when things get tough, we lean on Jesus! We can thank God for the trials that bring us into a oneness with our Lord and Savior.

Center of Your Home

But if anyone does not provide for his own, and especially for those of his household, he has denied the faith and is worse than an unbeliever.

1 Timothy 5:8 (NKJV)

Pastors often preach about the importance of loving your fellow man and treating others with respect, but sadly, in many cases, this doesn't carry over to families. It doesn't seem right when people strive to make the world see them in the very best light, but once in the privacy of their own home, it's a whole different story.

The tone of their voice changes. There's screaming, yelling, or just the opposite—the silent treatment. This definitely doesn't show love or respect! When there is love at home, it affects everything about your life. And it not only changes the person you are, it changes everyone around you! With love in your home, there is beauty, peace, and tranquility. There is also joy in heaven as God loves to see homes that reflect His character.

If you really want a home filled with love, God must be in the center. Since God *is* love, real love is just not possible without Him! Make God first and foremost in your life and enjoy the abundant life that He wants to give you as promised in John 10:10 (NRSV): "I came that they may have life, and have it abundantly."

Celebrate Friends

*Faithful are the wounds of a friend, but the kisses
of an enemy are deceitful.*

Proverbs 27:6 (NKJV)

From the very beginning of time, God gave us the gift of friendship. He made us to be *social* people with a need for relationships. That's why He created Eve to be a companion for Adam. It's more meaningful to share a beautiful sunset or a special occasion with someone who cares about you. And you wouldn't laugh nearly as loud at a funny story if you were by yourself! It's easier to endure heartaches if we have someone to share our burdens with.

The Bible says in Galatians 6:2 (NIV), "Carry each other's burdens, and in this way you will fulfill the law of Christ." Even those special moments in our lives are more joyous if shared with friends! When a couple decides to get married, they start planning their wedding based on how many friends can attend. Real, genuine friends are loyal, supportive, and loving . . . in the good times and the bad! Proverbs 17:17 (NKJV) says, "A friend loves at all times."

Friendships need to be nourished, cherished, and treasured. But remember, to have a friend, you must first . . . *be* a friend!" Follow Jesus' example by being kind, unselfish, and loving and you'll have more friends than you can imagine. Celebrate your friends today by doing something special for them, and most importantly, don't forget your best Friend of all . . . Jesus!

Get Some Sleep

It is vain for you to rise up early, to sit up late, to eat the bread of sorrows; for so He gives His beloved sleep.

Psalm 127:2 (NKJV)

If you are tossing and turning and sleep won't come because you just can't quit thinking about the mess you're in, stop worrying—God has you covered. No matter what problem you are facing, God already has it figured out! The Bible says in 1 Peter 5:7 (NLT), "Give all your worries and cares to God, for He cares about you." And in Philippians 4:5-7 (NIV), we're told, "The Lord is near. Do not be anxious about anything, but in every situation, by prayer and petition, with thanksgiving, present your requests to God. And the peace of God, which transcends all understanding, will guard your hearts and your minds in Christ Jesus."

It's easy to trust God when everything is going great, but the minute the tables are turned and tragedy strikes . . . that is when your faith is really put to the test. It doesn't matter whether you are facing financial ruin, the love of your life just left you, or you just received a death sentence, God has your back! You can trust Him to do the right thing for you because He always has your best interest at heart. Claim Romans 8:28 (NKJV): "And we know that all things work together for good to those who love God, to those who are the called according to His purpose." Once you give your troubles to God, roll over and get some sleep!

Jesus Loves Me

Whom have I in heaven but You? And there is none upon
earth that I desire besides You. My flesh and my heart fail;
but God is the strength of my heart and my portion forever.

Psalm 73:25-26 (NKJV)

There is a popular song that is sung by children all over the world that has a special message for adults as well. The words go like this: "Jesus loves me this I know, for the Bible tells me so. Little ones to him belong, they are weak but He is strong." Even in this simple song, the message is clear that people are weak . . . but Jesus is strong! And the really good news is that "Jesus *loves* you," and you can always depend on His strength to take care of you.

On the days you feel anxious and nervous, unable to muster up the confidence you need to face the challenges ahead, lean on Jesus! When you feel the peer pressure of having to measure up and go forward with confidence, yet inside your heart is trembling with fear, lean on Jesus! Instead of feeling worthless or guilty for not meeting your own expectations, consider this: God doesn't expect you to be strong every moment of your life! If that were so, you would never need Jesus!

Learn to reach out to Jesus, the only one who loves you more than anyone else possibly could! His strength far surpasses anything you could possibly do on your own, and God's strength is all you ever need!

Leaving a Legacy

When a man's ways please the LORD, He makes even his enemies to be at peace with him.

Proverbs 16:7 (NKJV)

If you found out that you only had one year to live, how would you spend your time? Would you sell everything you own to go on that dream vacation? Or perhaps buy that sports car you always wanted? Most people are more concerned about leaving loved ones behind and wanting their life to mean something. When Jesus was here on earth, He knew that He didn't have long to live and that He was going to die. He made every moment count preparing for the day He would leave this earth, and right up to His last breath, He left a legacy of love for each one of us.

He treated everyone with kindness, respect, and genuine concern. No matter how badly people treated Him, His response was always loving, meek, and gentle. Jesus lived a sinless life here on earth and the way He loved His fellow man will be remembered and passed on from generation to generation!

Have you thought about how you would like to be remembered? What kind of legacy do you want to leave? Ask yourself in every difficult situation, *What would Jesus do?* Reevaluate your life and ask God to open your eyes so you can see what He sees. Determine today to be more like Jesus . . . and start creating a legacy of love.

Mountain-Moving Faith

So then faith comes by hearing, and
hearing by the word of God.

Romans 10:17 (NKJV)

Imagine what a different world this would be if we had more faith in God! If we truly put our faith and trust in Him, then there would be no more worrying, fear, or anxiety. Why, it would eliminate stress completely! The Bible tells us in Matthew 17:20 (NKJV), "If you have faith as a mustard seed, you will say to this mountain, 'Move from here to there,' and it will move; and nothing will be impossible for you." There hasn't been any news flashes of someone moving a mountain, so it's safe to say, we could all use more faith!

Thankfully, God honors even the tiniest amount of faith. And the more we exercise the faith we do have, the more it grows! Sometimes God allows us to go through trials and tribulations to strengthen our faith in Him. You can also increase your faith by studying God's Holy Word and claiming His promises!

Faith is critical to our spiritual growth, for we will never know God's amazing plans He has for us unless we blindly step out in faith and follow His leading. Ask God to remove all doubt from your heart and replace it with an extra measure of His *mountain-moving faith*!

Learning to Be Content

The fear of the LORD leads to life; then one rests content, untouched by trouble.

Proverbs 19:23 (NIV)

If God gave you everything that you *think* you want, in most cases, it probably wouldn't make you very happy. Too often the things that you think you just *have* to have aren't good for you at all. And if you were to see the end from the beginning, you wouldn't want it anyway! Having what you want and wanting what you have are two very different things!

Instead of always wanting more in life, it's good to take stock of what you do have and take time to appreciate God's blessings. There's a wonderful feeling of freedom when you are not always chasing after something bigger and better than what you have. Trying to keep up with what our neighbors have or what they are doing is not very satisfying. Don't be envious of others—just thank God for all that He has done for *you*! Take time to *smell the roses* and appreciate the amazing gifts that He has already given you.

The Bible says in Philippians 4:11 (NRSV), "I have learned to be content with whatever I have." Learning to be content is a really good lesson for everyone, and when you experience contentment, then you can truly love and appreciate God's amazing gifts!

Justified Gossip

*Keep your tongue from evil, and your
lips from speaking deceit.*

Psalm 34:13 (NKJV)

Christians know how God feels about gossip because the Bible makes it very plain how much He despises a lying tongue. In fact, He rates it right alongside murder, stealing, and wickedness, for in 1 Peter 4:15 (NKJV), we're told, "But let none of you suffer as a murderer, a thief, an evildoer, or as a busybody in other people's matters." Plain and simple—there will be no gossipers in heaven! Jesus Himself said in Matthew 12:36 (KJV), "But I say unto you, that every idle word that men shall speak, they shall give account thereof in the day of judgment."

Why is it then that so many Christians practice *justified gossip*? This is the art of spreading rumors as long as the gossip begins with, "I am only telling you this so you can pray for them." Most of the time, gossip perpetrators have no idea what they are talking about. They heard the juicy news from someone . . . who heard it from someone . . . who heard it from someone else, and so on, but no one ever contacted the actual person being talked about to see if the rumor was even true! Many have never even met the person who is under attack.

Character assassination is actually a form of *murder* using a powerful weapon called *words*. When you struggle with the urge to gossip, stop and pray the prayer of David in Psalm 141. There's no such thing as *justified gossip*, and God has no tolerance for slander of any kind!

God's Transformation

*If we confess our sins, He is faithful and just to forgive us
our sins and to cleanse us from all unrighteousness.*

1 John 1:9 (NKJV)

All too often you hear of Christians who were raised as children to love Jesus, but in their teen years, drifted away. Some strayed because of *rebellion*, others because of hard feelings toward other church members, some stopped praying and reading their Bibles, and some . . . for a million other reasons. Whatever it was, once they quit going to church, it became harder and harder to find their way back. Many times people have to hit *rock bottom* to look up and see their need for a Savior!

You often hear of an adult losing a mother or father who was praying for them and it shook them to the core, bringing them back to the Lord. Sometimes it takes losing every earthly possession and having nowhere else to turn before they turn to Jesus! Everyone needs the Lord, for He is our only hope of salvation and eternal life. Without Him, we are lost!

Ask yourself today: *How healthy is my spiritual life? Do I put God first above everything else? Am I spending time with God each day, through prayer and Bible study? What does Jesus really mean to me?* Invite God to search your heart and open your eyes to areas that are lacking in your spiritual life, and then allow Him to change you. If you have distanced yourself from your Lord and Savior, don't wait any longer . . . run into His waiting arms today and experience God's transformation!

Light of His Presence

*The angel of the LORD encamps all around those who
fear Him, and delivers them.*

Psalm 34:7 (NKJV)

It's easy to be frightened when we watch the news highlighting all the wicked events happening in our world. It's filled with stories of murder, kidnapping, robbery, floods, fires, and the list goes on and on. The criteria for making it on the news seems to be *if it bleeds, it leads*! It's no wonder why so many people live in fear carrying guns and dead-bolting their houses at night. But God has promised to protect us. In Psalm 97:10 (NKJV), we're told, "You who love the LORD, hate evil! He preserves the souls of His saints; He delivers them out of the hand of the wicked."

We need not worry when our lives are surrendered to God. We can thank Him for His love and goodness and claim His promise to hide and protect us from trouble (Psalm 121:7-8). We need to remember that God is our safe place to run to, and He is ever looking out for us. Just think what it will be like when we get to heaven and learn about all the times our guardian angels stepped in to save us! We are in serious danger if we are trying to *go it alone* without praying for divine guidance. It is a dark and dangerous world out there, but when we stay close to Jesus, we are shielded by the light of His presence . . . and there's no safer place to be!

Your Blessing List

*In everything give thanks; for this is the will of God
in Christ Jesus for you.*

1 Thessalonians 5:18 (NKJV)

***

No matter what trials you are going through, there are people somewhere in the world who are experiencing something much worse. You can complain you don't make enough money to provide all the fresh fruits and vegetables for your family, yet there are people who are literally starving because they have *no* food! Not even scavenging through the garbage provides enough substance to silence the hungry cries of their children.

You grumble about a friend who betrayed you, a job you hate, your gray hair and wrinkles, your car that needs repaired, not once considering the homeless man on the street that has no friends, the people who can't get a job, those who are mourning the loss of loved one, or the family that can't even afford a car. Instead of concentrating on what you *don't* have, be thankful for what you *do* have—God's amazing love! 1 Thessalonians 5:18 (NIV) advises us to "give thanks in all circumstances."

God loves you so much, and He wants you to be happy. He gives you blessings every day—starting with just waking up in the morning and enjoying another day of life! You may not even realize all the things you have to be thankful for, so before you complain about how your life is so miserable, stop and make a *blessing list.* When you're done, you'll be thanking God for all the wonderful things He has done for you.

The Happiness Express

Teach me to do Your will, for You are my God; Your
Spirit is good. Lead me in the land of uprightness.

Psalm 143:10 (NKJV)

Some people decide to be Christians because they want to make sure their ticket to heaven is secure. They know they don't want to go to hell, so they board the "Happiness Express" headed for heaven. But Christianity is not about choosing God out of fear, but rather because you love Him. When you truly realize just how much Jesus loves you, you can't help but want to give your heart completely to Him!

Only a life surrendered to Christ will give you the true joy God wants you to have. And it is with Holy Spirit guidance that you can successfully navigate through the trials and struggles in this sinful world. Without God, your life will be a disaster! God wants you to choose your destiny based on *love*, not *fear*!

In other words, choose Jesus because you love Him with all your heart, not because you are afraid of burning in hell! Very simply, it's all about love and surrender to God. When you belong to Christ, your ticket is paid in full and you can board the "Happiness Express" bound for heaven! Time is running out and the train is about to leave the station, so don't delay! Make sure you get your ticket today!

Everlasting Arms

The LORD also will be a refuge for the oppressed,
a refuge in times of trouble.

Psalm 9:9 (NKJV)

No one *likes* to go through hard times, nor do they wish for a *bad day*, but it is through life's toughest battles that you'll receive some of your biggest blessings. Without the hard times, you would never know your need for a Savior. When everything is going smoothly, you're focused on the great time you're having, celebrating with friends and living *the good life*. But when trouble knocks on your door, it sends you crying for help to the only one who has the power to help you!

It is while on your knees that you are humbled and realize just how much you need God in your life. Through all the heartache and pain you'll draw closer to God. You'll find yourself listening for His voice, sharing your sorrow, and learning to trust Him fully, knowing He will help you and will do what's best for you. The Bible says in Psalm 34:19 (NIV), "The righteous person may have many troubles, but the Lord delivers him from them all."

Learning real life, character-changing lessons doesn't come from having a boatload of money, lots of friends, or fame. It is when the rent is due, the baby is sick, you lost your job, or your friend betrayed you that you'll lean on God the most! Leaning on the everlasting arms of Jesus is a great place to be!

Salvation Is Free

*The kindness and the love of God our Savior toward
man appeared, not by works of righteousness
which we have done, but according to His mercy
He saved us, through the washing of regeneration and
renewing of the Holy Spirit.*

Titus 3:4-5 (NKJV)

———◆———

There are Christians who, although they believe in Christ, have not fully grasped the full meaning of *salvation*. They believe that if they work hard enough for the Lord, then they will be worthy of saving. And so they work tirelessly at church, in the community, and in missions, all the while *hoping* it will be enough—as if all their work will be rewarded with a guaranteed ticket to heaven! But they are sadly mistaken.

No one can *work* their way to heaven. The price for salvation was paid in full at Calvary when Christ died on the cross. The Bible says in Ephesians 2:9 (NLT), "Salvation is not a reward for the good things we have done, so none of us can boast about it." Only through the blood of Jesus Christ can we be saved. Acts 4:12 (KJV) confirms this: "Neither is there salvation in any other: for there is none other name under heaven given among men, whereby we must be saved."

God's promise in John 3:16 (NIV) was given for everyone: "For God so loved the world that he gave his one and only Son, that whoever believes in him shall not perish but have eternal life." When you accept Jesus as your Lord and Savior, there is nothing more, or less, that you can do to be saved. Jesus paid the price on Calvary—salvation is free!

Practice Honesty

He who works deceit shall not dwell within my house;
he who tells lies shall not continue in my presence.

Psalm 101:7 (NKJV)

It's hard to decipher nowadays whether or not the truth is the truth! People have become so accustomed to telling a story and slanting the facts that you don't know what to believe. And each time the story is told, the details keep changing. After a while, the person exaggerating loses all credibility and you train yourself to listen to that person knowing you are not hearing the whole truth.

Sadly, a person who exaggerates the truth not only tarnishes their reputation, but they do not have integrity! Even more important, *stretching the truth* is the same thing as lying in God's eyes, and lying is a sin! The Bible says in Proverbs 12:22 (NIV), "The LORD detests lying lips, but he delights in people who are trustworthy. And in Leviticus 19:11 (NKJV), God commands, "You shall not steal, nor deal falsely, nor lie to one another."

Being honest, trustworthy, and a person of integrity is critically important to God, and it should be critically important to you too because your salvation depends on it. Remember that you will take you character to heaven with you. If your goal is to be like Jesus so that you can spend eternity with Him, then you must not *stretch the truth* or tell *little white lies*, but rather practice honesty in all that you do and say!

Prison with No Bars

For God has not given us a spirit of fear, but of power
and of love and of a sound mind.

2 Timothy 1:7 (NKJV)

Many people live in a prison that has no bars, locks, or guards, because they are held captive by the prison of fear! It keeps them locked up, afraid of their own shadow. The list of things people are afraid of is endless: heights, snakes, needles, the dark, dying, being alone, etc. There are even those who live in fear of what others think of them—never wanting to speak up or be noticed for fear of embarrassment. But it is not God's plan that we live in fear!

The Bible says in Isaiah 41:10 (NKJV), "Fear not, for I am with you; be not dismayed, for I am your God. I will strengthen you, yes, I will help you, I will uphold you with My righteous right hand." With Jesus by our side, we have no reason to fear! In Psalm 27:1 (NKJV), we're told, "The LORD is my light and my salvation; whom shall I fear? The LORD is my strength of my life; of whom shall I be afraid."

God alone has the key to release you from the darkness of fear. You don't have to miss out on life's opportunities because of being afraid. All you have to do is pray and ask God to give you holy boldness so that you may become the person He wants you to be, living each day without fear!

Cloud of Pain

*"Come to Me, all you who labor and are heavy
laden, and I will give you rest."*

Matthew 11:28 (NKJV)

There are times when life can be so painful that it may feel
as if the burden is just too heavy to bear. The shroud of
darkness is so thick that it's hard to see through the cloud of
pain. Everything seems dark, and even though your head knows
better, your heart tells you that no one cares. Maybe you've
been struggling with a longtime illness that doctors can't seem
to find the cure for and you are just plain tired from the sheer
fight to stay alive. Perhaps you are in a loveless marriage that
your friends think is perfect, but you alone know what goes on
behind closed doors and you are so emotionally drained from
living the lie that you don't know how to do it anymore.

It may feel like you are alone and no one loves you, but God
is there and *He* loves you! You may even feel that you are not
worthy of anyone's love, but God makes you worthy! The Bible
says in Psalm 34:17-19 (ESV), "When the righteous cry for help,
the LORD hears and delivers them out of all their troubles. The
LORD is near to the brokenhearted and saves the crushed in spirit. Many are the afflictions of the righteous, but the LORD delivers
him out of them all." So when life seems too heavy to bear and
you have no strength to go on . . . lean on Jesus, and He will give
you strength and courage to escape the cloud of pain.

Inspired by Love

*Owe no one anything except to love one another, for he
who loves another has fulfilled the law.*

Romans 13:8 (NKJV)

The greatest gift God has given to us is His love, which is the greatest love of all, but He also put the *ability* to love each other in our hearts. From the first moment a baby is born, their development is based on whether or not they receive love. Scientists discovered long ago that babies who were not held, cuddled, kissed and loved developed slower and did not thrive the same way as babies who were *loved* did.

Everyone needs to feel loved and appreciated. Love actually inspires us to be better people. When someone expresses love toward us, it makes us want to be our best so that we don't disappoint them. Whether it is a family member or friend, just knowing someone believes in you, thinks you are wonderful, and loves you unconditionally motivates you to be the best that you can be! Love is so important in our lives that God actually *commanded* us to love each other. Jesus said in John 15:12 (NIV), "My command is this: Love each other as I have loved you." And in 1 Thessalonians 3:12 (NIV), we're told, "May the Lord make your love increase and overflow for each other and for everyone else, just as ours does for you." Start your day by thanking God for the people in your life who love you, and don't forget to thank Jesus too . . . because He loves you most of all!

Don't Go Alone

Trust in the LORD forever, for in YAH, the LORD,
is everlasting strength.

Isaiah 26:4 (NKJV)

———◄═◆═►———

There are some people in this world who never want to ask for help. They would rather spend four hours struggling to do something by themselves then ask for assistance, getting the job done in half the time. Whether it is pride, lack of confidence, a case of extreme shyness, or whatever, they simply choose to go it alone—even if it means failure.

The truth is *everyone* needs *someone* at some point in their life, and there is no shame in asking a friend to help. Trying to move a refrigerator down a flight of stairs can be quite challenging for one person, but two can make the job so much easier and faster. Sometimes you might not want to ask for help because you don't want to be beholding to the person helping. Perhaps they might have ulterior motives for wanting to help, or you know they will want you to do something for them in return.

There is one Friend that you can always count on for help, and He is your best Friend—Jesus. Instead of struggling through life's challenges alone, lean on Jesus for support. He will give you His strength, courage, wisdom, and when you are depending on God for directions, you can't go wrong! No matter where you are going, don't go alone . . . take your best Friend, Jesus.

Highest Priority

"You shall have no other gods before Me."
Exodus 20:3 (NKJV)

———◆———

When deciding what needs to be accomplished each day, you first start by mentally prioritizing your *to-do* list. Some things are as trivial: Do you stop at the dry cleaners on the way to work, or is getting to that meeting on time more important? Do you work through lunch, or call a friend to meet you? Do you work overtime to earn some extra cash, or skip it to spend time with your family? There are countless other scenarios (many with more serious consequences), but the choice of how you spend your day is up to you.

Your highest priority should always be to make God first in your life. Nothing is more important! The Bible says in Matthew 22:37-38 (NIV), "Love the Lord your God with all your heart and with all your soul and with all your mind. This is the first and greatest commandment." God's made it very simple: come to Him and He will help you accomplish all the things He wants you to. You'll never have to worry about prioritizing your calendar!

If you start every morning with prayer, praise, and worship, you're bound to have a better day. Making God your *highest priority* is the best decision you could ever make!

Deadly Words

*Fathers, do not embitter your children, or they
will become discouraged*

Colossians 3:21 (NIV)

———◄—►———

Parents, be careful what you say to your children because *what* you say and *how* you say it can leave scars that will last forever . . . for your words will become their inner voice. For instance, if you talk to your kids in a disgusted tone, it tells them that they are worthless and not worthy of your respect. Comments such as "You're so stupid!" "Go away! Can't you see I'm busy?" "You're such an idiot" "Shut up—just stop talking" "Go outside and leave me alone" "Your room is mess! You're such a pig!" "Can't you do anything right?" or a hundred other demeaning remarks are downright deadly.

Deadly words can scar your children so badly that they will live their entire lives reliving your hurtful remarks over and over again! As adults, they'll struggle with insecurity and self-loathing, which will affect their relationships (both personal and professional) and they may not even know why! As Christians, we know that we are all striving to be like Jesus. He loved children and treated them with tender kindness and doesn't want children to be mistreated. In fact, the Bible says in Luke 17:2 (NIV), "It would be better for them to be thrown into the sea with a millstone tied around their neck than to cause one of these little ones to stumble." Children of all ages deserve to be treated with respect and love. Parents, guard your tongues, and instead of using deadly words . . . speak in tones of love.

Holding on to Hatred

"And forgive us our debts, as we forgive our debtors."
Matthew 6:12 (NKJV)

———◆◆◆———

Some people think that forgiveness only benefits the perpetrator of the crime, but the truth is, forgiveness is a win-win for everyone! When you forgive the person who hurt you, it's quite empowering! You can feel the weight of all that pent-up anger just roll away! As long as you hold on to bitterness, you will never experience the true freedom of forgiveness. It's not wrong to feel *anger,* as that is one of the emotions God created, but it's definitely not okay to stay angry! In fact, God feels so strongly about unforgiveness that He says in Matthew 6:15 (NIV), "But if you do not forgive others their sins, your Father will not forgive your sins." That's very serious, since your salvation depends on forgiving others.

God's requirement for forgiveness does not mean, however, that you must maintain a relationship with the offender. In some cases, you'll need to cut off all contact because it's not safe to be around the person who has hurt you, even if it is a family member. There may be someone who is no longer alive but you've held a grudge against them for years—give it to Jesus and ask Him to put forgiveness in your heart. Holding on to hatred is not worth missing out on heaven. Just forgive, forget, and move on with Jesus. To reap the full *benefits of forgiveness,* love your enemies with God's love, giving your hard feelings and anger over to Him. He will replace all your hurt and pain with joy such as you have never known!

Quicksand of Grief

*And God will wipe away every tear from their eyes; there
shall be no more death, nor sorrow, nor crying. There shall
be no more pain, for the former things have passed away.*

Revelation 21:4 (NKJV)

When you lose someone you love, it's only natural that
you mourn their loss although sometimes people don't
know when it's time to move on. Everyone expresses their
feelings differently. Some hide their sorrow, stuffing the pain
deep within, pretending they are fine when they're not. There's
no shame in expressing grief. Even the Bible says in John 11:35
(NKJV), "Jesus wept."

Our Lord is no stranger to grief, and He empathizes with
His children whose hearts are burdened with pain. The Bible
says in Matthew 5:4 (KJV), "Blessed are they that mourn: for
they shall be comforted." However, God doesn't want you to get
stuck in the quicksand of grief. When you focus only on your
loss, you forget to *live*. Crying a bucket of tears or even an ocean
full won't bring back your loved one. Nor is it healthy for you
as you sink lower and lower into the pit of depression. Anyone
who really loved you would not want you to grieve for them
forever, and neither does God.

There comes a point when you need to move on and
experience the life God has planned for you. There is life after
grief. Give your burden of loss to Jesus today and start living
the abundant life God wants to give you.

It's Your Choice

For none of us lives to himself, and no one dies to himself.
For if we live, we live to the Lord; and if we die, we die to the
Lord. Therefore, whether we live or die, we are the Lord's.

Romans 14:7-8 (NKJV)

There are many people today who live alone—some by choice and others because they simply haven't found that *perfect mate*! The Bible says in Genesis 2:18 (NKJV), "It is not good that man should be alone," which is why He created Eve to be with Adam. So, it is safe to say that *marriage* was God's idea. But when you read 1 Corinthians, chapter 7, it is clear that God wants each of His children to be happy and allows them to choose for themselves whether or not they want to marry. But if they choose to stay single, it is good, because it is easier to stay focused on spiritual things.

Now those two texts might sound contradictory, but they really are not. God is merely giving His children the ability to decide what makes them happy. There's no shame in being single or in being married. God has blessed both choices! Some people desire close companionship and would feel lonely without a spouse. Others may be independent, love their privacy and alone time, and feel like they could better serve God being single. Either way is pleasing to our Savior. Please know this: you are never really alone because God is always with you and loves you more than anyone else possibly could. You can even thank God for the blessing of loneliness as this might be the perfect lifeline to draw you even closer to Him.

Responsibility of Power

But indeed for this purpose I have raised you up,
that I may show My power in you, and that My name
may be declared in all the earth.

Exodus 9:16 (NKJV)

There will always be those who *have* the power and those who don't. Of course, the ones who don't are at the mercy of those who do. For instance, there are teachers who are really great teachers because they love to teach, but then there are those who just love having the power to fail their students! There are husbands who, just because they are taller, bigger, or stronger, use their power to beat their wives. And there are also people who have high positions in their jobs who use their status of authority for evil purposes.

On the other side, people are applauded when they use their influence for good: helping the homeless, protecting the helpless, and reaching out to the hurting. There's a huge responsibility that comes with having *power*, for *how* you use it determines your character. If you have an opportunity to help someone else, use your power for good. Pray and ask God to give you opportunities to help a struggling brother or sister have a closer walk with Jesus. Pray and God will give you Holy Spirit power to know exactly how He wants you to witness for Him. Power is a blessing if used wisely. Thankfully, there is someone you can count on who will never misuse His power, and that's our loving God! He rules supremely with love, kindness, ultimate fairness, and matchless power. God uses His magnificent power to seek and save the lost!

Can-Do Attitude

For we dare not class ourselves or compare ourselves with those who commend themselves. But they, measuring themselves by themselves, and comparing themselves among themselves, are not wise.

2 Corinthians 10:12 (NKJV)

One of the best traits you can have is *self-confidence*. It makes all the difference in the world as you face difficult challenges along this journey of life because it's hard to accomplish anything if you constantly feel like a failure. And if you tell yourself that you're worthless long enough, pretty soon you'll start to believe it and you won't live the abundant, joyful life God wants you to have. When you don't believe you're good enough, smart enough, talented enough, or even worthy to be in this world, you will surely have a miserable life! And this same *can't-do attitude* carries over to your spiritual life as well.

When you tell yourself what a failure you are and that you can't imagine how anyone could love you, including God, you become despondent, distant, and instead of reaching out to Him for help, you tend to pull away. But instead of running away from God, give Him a chance. He is a most loving, compassionate, and forgiving God, and no one loves you more than He does! If you're filled with self-doubt, self-loathing, or just feeling discouraged because you think no one cares, remember Jesus loves you! Ask God to give you a *can-do* attitude and claim His promise in Philippians 4:13 (NKJV): "I can do all things through Christ who strengthens me!"

Easily Offended

Be completely humble and gentle; be patient, bearing with one another in love. Make every effort to keep the unity of the Spirit through the bond of peace.

Ephesians 4:2-3 (NIV)

How you treat others would be totally different if you could see inside their hearts. You might not have given the person who took their time getting off the elevator that dirty look if you knew that just moments before they learned their only child was killed and they were paralyzed with grief. And you might have had more patience with the grumpy sales clerk if you knew she was a single mom and working three jobs.

It's easy to make judgment calls about people based on what you see, but what God sees is far more accurate and gives the real picture of what is going on. That's why it's important to spread the love, share a smile, and forgive quickly. When someone is unkind to you, unless you know you did something to deserve it, don't take it personally! Don't be easily offended and have unkind thoughts toward others. Chances are, it had nothing to do with you but rather what that person was going through.

The next time you see someone give you an irritated look, make a snappy remark, or cut you off in traffic, instead of being easily offended, give them the benefit of the doubt, and be kind, knowing that there's probably a very good reason for their actions, and chances are, it wasn't about you at all.

September 21

It Takes Courage

*Then Job answered the L*ORD *and said: "I know
that You can do everything, and that no purpose of
Yours can be withheld from You.*

Job 42:1-2 (NKJV)

If there is one thing we could use more of in order to face
each day, it is *courage!* Some days require more than others,
but without it, we would never leave the safety of our homes.
It takes courage to go out into the world and embrace new
opportunities. It takes courage to go for a job interview, make a
commitment of marriage, become a parent, discipline a child,
end a bad relationship, and so on. You especially need courage to
move forward after going through a painful experience because
the first human response is to run away from your problems.

But *running* never fixed anything and usually makes it
worse! The Bible says in Hebrews 10:19-20 (ESV), "Therefore,
brothers, since we have confidence to enter the holy places by
the blood of Jesus, by the new and living way that he opened
for us through the curtain, that is, through his flesh." You can
possess the courage needed for every life situation because God
will give it to you . . . all you need to do is ask! Psalm 138:3
(NIV) says, "When I called, you answered me; you greatly
emboldened me."

When tempted to run, remember you have nothing to fear.
Just run to Jesus! He will lift you up and fill you with power and
courage to face any situation!

Tooting Your Horn

For the day of the LORD of hosts shall come upon
everything proud and lofty, upon everything lifted up—
and it shall be brought low.

Isaiah 2:12 (NKJV)

God wants you to be kind, generous, loving, and helpful to others, but He wants you to do so for the right reasons. There are some who will run to open a door for someone, but only if they think someone is watching. Others will make a point of letting people know all their good deeds they have done, inwardly hoping to make a good impression. However, the Christian life is not about being a show-off, but rather extending lovingkindness from a pure heart and with the right motives.

When the preacher asks for donations to help a family in need, instead of being the first one to wave your hand that you'll gladly give, quietly give your financial gift to your preacher as you head out the door—without expecting *or* wanting any praise! The Bible says in Matthew 6:4 (NLT), "Give your gifts in private, and your Father, who sees everything, will reward you." There is no room for pride in a Christian's heart. Luke 18:14 (NIV) makes this very clear: "For all those who exalt themselves will be humbled, and those who humble themselves will be exalted."

Instead of trying to esteem yourself in the eyes of your friends, impress God instead by being humble, meek, and unpretentious. In other words, stop tooting your own horn and let your actions come from pure motives.

All About the Love

For we are His workmanship, created in Christ Jesus
for good works, which God prepared beforehand
that we should walk in them.

Ephesians 2:10 (NKJV)

God made you special, just the way you are, and yes, He *really* does love . . . you! It's God's unending, amazing, miraculous love that gives you the desire to surrender your heart and life to Him! It's all about the *love*, for unless you understand God's deep and abiding love for you, why would you ever want to serve Him? It's important to realize that God made you uniquely different from everyone else, with your own set of talents, gifts, and personality—so, never compare yourself to others!

When you focus on other people's expectations and not who God wants you to be, you will surely stumble and fall! Don't compare your journey with anyone else. God has a special plan . . . just for you! But don't get all puffed up with pride thinking you are more important, because you are not better or worse than anyone else! God made everyone equal, but with individual differences! He created *you* to be *you*! He has a purpose for your life, and He will give you everything you need to accomplish His plan for you! Best of all, God doesn't make mistakes! He intentionally made you and loves you more than you could possibly know or comprehend!

Sweet Peace

I have blotted out, like a thick cloud, your
transgressions, and like a cloud, your sins. Return
to Me, for I have redeemed you.

Isaiah 44:22 (NKJV)

Whenever we have done something that we know to be wrong, our conscience kicks in and triggers the guilty feelings that draw us to repentance. The only way to obtain real peace is to first acknowledge our sin and then to ask God for forgiveness. Without the Holy Spirit speaking to our hearts, we would never realize our need for forgiveness. Sin always separates us from God, and, if we want to restore the bond between us and our Lord and Savior, then we need to ask God to forgive our transgressions. Immediately, our burden is lifted and the sweet peace of forgiveness is restored in our hearts.

There is no better feeling in the world than being one with Christ! Sometimes, you may have a friend or family member that has sinned against God, but they are not willing to ask for forgiveness. Although we love them dearly, we cannot ask for forgiveness on their behalf. God does not hold us accountable for the choices of others—only for our own. Neither can we repent for them; they must want and ask for forgiveness for their own sins. However, we can lift them up in prayer that God will give them the strength to repent and send the Holy Spirit to speak to their hearts. We can always pray an intercessory prayer for our loved ones, especially when they are too weak to pray for themselves.

Side of Mercy

*For judgment is without mercy to the one who has shown
no mercy. Mercy triumphs over judgment.*

James 2:13 (NKJV)

Everyone has experienced mercy at some time in their lives, whether it's a parent who didn't give a harsh punishment, a teacher who allowed you to retake a test, a family member who took the blame for something you did, or perhaps a boss who let you keep your job when you clearly made a mistake. Mercy isn't a word that many people talk about today, but everyone knows the meaning: "withholding punishment from someone who deserves it."

The Bible tells a story in Matthew 18 of how God feels about an unmerciful heart. A master's servant who was shown mercy refused to extend mercy to his own servant, and in verses 32-35 (NIV), we're told, "Then the master called the servant in. 'You wicked servant,' he said, 'I canceled all that debt of yours because you begged me to. Shouldn't you have had mercy on your fellow servant just as I had on you?' In anger his master handed him over to the jailers to be tortured, until he should pay back all he owed. This is how my heavenly Father will treat each of you unless you forgive your brother or sister from your heart." Always remember if you're going to make an error, then err on the side of grace and mercy!

Attitude of Gratitude

*Giving thanks always for all things to God the Father in
the name of our Lord Jesus Christ.*

Ephesians 5:20 (NKJV)

No matter how discouraged you are today, take fifteen minutes to do nothing but praise Jesus! Start writing down all the things you're thankful for and then praise God for His blessings. Those fifteen minutes will change the whole course of your day, for when you concentrate on your blessings instead of your problems, your entire spirit is lifted! Your attitude of gratitude is infectious! People respond differently to a smile than they do to a pout, grumpy frown, or face of indifference! And not only will others be blessed by their interaction with you, but you'll be happier too!

When you start to realize how much God has given you and how blessed you truly are, it's life changing! You'll not only feel the warmth of God's love but your faith in Him will grow! With God's strength, you can trust whatever trials you are going through . . . to Him. And when you stop trying to fix your own problems, you'll no longer feel frustrated, abandoned, and all alone—because you'll realize God has never left you or forsaken you, and He's not going to start now!

God has your back! He loves you more than you could possibly know, and He is with you always! Begin your day with an *attitude of gratitude* and you'll enjoy God's sweet peace . . . all day long!

Turn to Jesus

*Why are you cast down, O my soul, and why are you
disquieted within me? Hope in God; for I shall again
praise him, my help and my God.*

Psalm 43:5 (NRSV)

When faced with a situation that is out of your hands
and you have no power to change it, the feeling of
helplessness is overwhelming. You sit there staring into space
in total disbelief asking yourself, *What just happened?* or *What
am I going to do now?* Whether you were denied entrance to
the college of your choice, you just lost your job, your house
burned down, a loved one died, a spouse announces they want
a divorce, or a million other heartbreaking situations, you are
not alone! God is with you to comfort you and to wipe away
your tears. And He is not only there to tell you *everything will
be okay*, He is there to lead, guide, and help you go down the
safe path that He has chosen for you.

Turn to Jesus, for He is the *only* one who can save you! Not
all the things we *think we want* are good for us! If we could
see into the future, we wouldn't want it any other way . . . than
God's way! Many times if God gave us what we asked for, we
would be absolutely miserable. You can trust God to know
what's best. Even when your life seems bleak and you can't see
through the fog, God is right there, gently nudging you in the
right direction! So when the door slams shut on your plans and
dreams . . . turn to Jesus!

Love as Jesus Loved

"For I have given you an example, that you should do as I have done to you."

John 13:15 (NKJV)

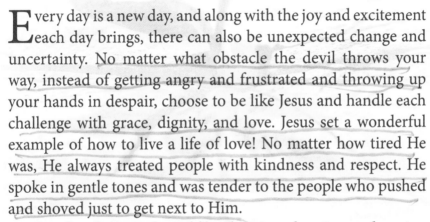

Every day is a new day, and along with the joy and excitement each day brings, there can also be unexpected change and uncertainty. No matter what obstacle the devil throws your way, instead of getting angry and frustrated and throwing up your hands in despair, choose to be like Jesus and handle each challenge with grace, dignity, and love. Jesus set a wonderful example of how to live a life of love! No matter how tired He was, He always treated people with kindness and respect. He spoke in gentle tones and was tender to the people who pushed and shoved just to get next to Him.

One day, the crowds could be clapping, cheering, and waving palm branches, and then just a short time later, throwing sticks, hurling stones, and yelling, "Crucify Him!" Whether the crowds loved Him or hated Him, He was always gracious, humble, and kind in return. He didn't just *preach* love, He lived it!

The Bible says in Ephesians 5:1-2 (ERV), "You are God's dear children, so try to be like him. Live a life of love. Love others just as Christ loved us. He gave himself for us—a sweet-smelling offering and sacrifice to God." What a beautiful way to describe God's love. Determine every day to love as Jesus loved.

Life Is Challenging

*My brethren, count it all joy when you fall into various
trials, knowing that the testing of your faith produces
patience. But let patience have its perfect work, that you
may be perfect and complete, lacking nothing.*

James 1:2-4 (NKJV)

Let's face it—life is challenging! There's no such thing as "easy
street," and it's not going to get any better until Jesus comes!
However, some days are worse than others, where the challenges
can seem more like a mountain than a molehill. But instead of
getting discouraged and overwhelmed, allow *faith* to help you
see the massive mountain in front of you as an opportunity to
grow. Sometimes growth can be uncomfortable, but the *faith-
producing* outcome is well worth the pain!

The Bible says in Matthew 17:20 (NIV), "If you have faith as
small as a mustard seed, you can say to this mountain, 'Move
from here to there,' and it will move. Nothing will be impossible
for you." Notice that this verse does not say *your personal
strength* can move a mountain; it clearly states that it's *faith*!
Simply put—it is faith in God's ability, not yours! With that
kind of faith, you can claim victory because God will give you
the strength you need to face any challenge the devil throws at
you! James 1:12 (NIV) says, "Blessed is the one who perseveres
under trial because, having stood the test, that person will
receive the crown of life that the Lord has promised to those
who love him."

Best Friends

With my whole heart I have sought You; oh, let me not wander from Your commandments!

Psalm 119:10 (NKJV)

If you really want to know Jesus as your *best friend*, then you must spend time with Him, and that doesn't mean just once in a while when you need something. All relationships require communication to survive. If you only talk to someone now and then, you will not be relevant in their life. You won't be the first person they think of when times get tough or when there is some amazing news to share, and the reason is, you are not close! Only friends who spend time together, communicate, and share details of their lives will be close friends, and so it is with God.

Our Heavenly Father is not looking for a casual friendship with you, but truly wants to be your best Friend! The Bible makes it very clear what will happen if you don't maintain a close friendship with God. John 15:6 (NLT) says, "Anyone who does not remain in me is thrown away like a useless branch and withers. Such branches are gathered into a pile to be burned." That's a very powerful verse about the importance of staying close to Jesus! He loves you more than you could possibly imagine, so don't ignore God's voice calling out to you. Instead, give Him your heart, share every aspect of your life, spend time in prayer and study of His Holy Word, and before you know it, you'll have become best friends.

When No One Notices

*And those who know Your name will put
their trust in You; for You, LORD, have not
forsaken those who seek You.*

Psalm 9:10 (NKJV)

W hy is it that no one seems to notice when you're in pain, sad, or hurting? You could be depressed for weeks and those around you are seemingly oblivious. But if you were to make a mistake, why, everyone seems to notice and are all too quick to point it out! Fortunately, God isn't watching you with devilish anticipation just waiting for you to mess up! He loves you so much that He is at your side the very second you call on Him, for He hears *and* responds to your cries for help.

The Bible says in Zephaniah 3:17 (NIV), "The Lord your God is with you, the Mighty Warrior who saves. He will take great delight in you; in his love he will no longer rebuke you, but will rejoice over you with singing." How wonderful to know that your Savior cares! He not only notices when you are sad, lonely, or suffering from a broken heart, but He lifts you up and gives you the strength, comfort, and courage you need to carry on. Psalm 37:24 (NKJV) says, "Though he fall, he shall not be utterly cast down; for the LORD upholds him with His hand." What a beautiful promise that you can claim! God will uphold you—He will lift you up!

When you are at your lowest and it feels no one notices whether you are dead or alive, remember that God not only notices, but He is ready to respond the instant you call.

Fake Friends

*Those who withhold kindness from a friend forsake
the fear of the Almighty.*

Job 6:14 (NRSV)

Real friends are an incredible blessing in your life. A true, trusted, and loyal friend is priceless! The Bible says in Romans 12:10 (NIV), "Be devoted to one another in love. Honor one another above yourselves." In other words, God is telling you how to be a friend—by loving and putting your friends' needs above your own. And in Proverbs 17:17 (NKJV), you are counseled about being a loyal friend: "A friend loves at all times."

It's important not to be a *wishy-washy* friend, where you are nice one moment and ignore them the next. God even gives advice on how to find a friend and how to be a faithful friend in Proverbs 18:24 (NKJV): "A man who has friends must himself be friendly, but there is a friend who sticks closer than a brother."

It is heartbreaking to find out someone you *thought* was your friend, really isn't! Especially when you have invested a lot of time in the friendship and you have trusted them with your heart. These kinds of friends are *fake friends*, and life's too short to have relationships with *zero* trust. It's important to choose friends who will be there for you through thick and thin! Jesus is a true friend and He will never throw you under the bus or turn His back on you! Seek godly friends, avoid *fake friends*, and choose Jesus to be your best Friend for life!

God's Job Requirements

*"You whom I have taken from the ends of
the earth, and called from its farthest regions, and said
to you, 'You are My servant, I have chosen you and
have not cast you away.'"*

Isaiah 41:9 (NKJV)

———◆———

This world keeps setting higher and higher expectations that it's no wonder so many people walk around feeling as if they just don't measure up. To enroll your child in private school requires an interview to determine if they meet the school's high standards. To get a job, you have to compete against other applicants who might have a more impressive resume. And sadly, there are even churches who want only the best and brightest to hold church leadership.

If you've convinced yourself that you have nothing to offer God and are waiting until you become *perfect* before you serve Him, think again! He wants you to work for Him based on *who you are* rather than *what you are not*! It may surprise you to know that God doesn't judge you on your *ability,* but rather what's in your heart. The Bible says in 1 Samuel 16:7 (NKJV), "Man looks at the outward appearance, but the LORD looks at the heart." It's not important if others think you are not worthy to serve, it only matters what God thinks. Pray and ask Him what He would have you do and then obey with Holy Spirit confidence. Remember, God's job requirements are different than man's, for He only asks for a heart full of love that is surrendered to Him.

Get-Well Plan

*The entrance of Your words gives light; it gives
understanding to the simple.*

Psalm 119:130 (NKJV)

When your past is troubled and you just can't get past the pain, your world becomes dark and dismal. The memories haunt you as you keep regurgitating past hurts over and over again in your mind. As long as you dwell on your troubled past, your world will continue to get darker and darker and will prevent you from experiencing the joy God wants to give you. You can ask yourself, *Why me?* all day long, but it won't bring you happiness, nor will it bring you the answers and peace you seek. You cannot change the past, but you can allow God to change you!

Whether the pain you experienced was from your own poor choices or no fault of yours at all, the *get-well plan* is the same: release your pain, heartache, bitterness, and horrible past . . . to Jesus! Today is a brand-new day to start over, allowing God to lead and guide. Give Him control of your life, and with Jesus by your side, you have nothing to fear. Ask Him to remove the painful memories and replace each distressing thought with His sweet peace. He will place His loving arms around you, and there is no place to be . . . than in the arms of Jesus! God's *get-well plan* is the only remedy that will bring lasting joy and eternal happiness!

Assassinated by Words

*A talebearer reveals secrets, but he who is of a
faithful spirit conceals a matter.*

Proverbs 11:13 (NKJV)

One of the fastest ways to self-destruct is to gossip! Yet, there are people who just can't seem to help themselves and feel the need to talk about everyone. They hear the slightest bit of news and simply can't wait to share it with the first person they meet. You might think as long as you are telling the truth, then it's okay—no harm done! Perhaps you saw a friend's spouse having what appeared to be an intimate lunch and you ran and told someone. Then that person told someone else and the incident was told over and over, ruining this man's reputation and causing pain to his wife, family, and others. But what you didn't know was that lady at the "intimate dinner" was actually his sister sharing personal heartache.

Make no mistake, the disease of *gossip* is real and deadly, not only for the people who are assassinated by words, but for you as well because there will be no gossipers in heaven! The Bible says in Psalm 101:5 (NKJV), "Whoever secretly slanders his neighbor, Him I will destroy." God makes it very clear over and over again that He has no tolerance for gossipers. People who get pleasure from discussing other people's problems are infected with a fatal illness! But praise the Lord, He has a cure! Pray David's prayer in Psalm 141:3 (NIV): "Keep watch over the door of my lips," and God will give you the victory over gossip!

Walking the Walk

*"If anyone serves Me, let him follow Me; and where I am,
there My servant will be also. If anyone serves Me,
him My Father will honor."*

John 12:26 (NKJV)

———◆———

Some people who profess to love God will go to church each week, sing praises, and even pray, but they don't have a clue who God really is! Once they walk out of the church doors, they barely think about God again, much less pray and worship Him—unless of course, they have a crisis that comes up. And *serving God* is not even on their radar because they are too self-focused on all the things *they* want to do. But just *going to church* is not going to save you; neither is going through the motions of being a Christian.

The Bible says in Matthew 7:21 (NKJV), "Not everyone who says to Me, 'Lord, Lord,' will enter the kingdom of heaven, but only the one who does the will of my Father who is in heaven." And in Colossians 3:23-24, (NIV) we're told, "Whatever you do, work at it with all your heart, as working for the Lord, not for human masters, since you know that you will receive an inheritance from the Lord as a reward. It is the Lord Christ you are serving." God makes it very clear in John 14:15 (NKJV): "If you love Me, keep My commandments." It is not enough to *profess* to love God—you must be obedient to His will. Now is the time to make a full commitment to Him. Start with examining your heart and ask, *Am I just talking the talk . . . or am I walking the walk?*

Don't Dance with the Devil

Repent therefore and be converted, that your sins
may be blotted out, so that times of refreshing may come
from the presence of the Lord.

Acts 3:19 (NKJV)

When you fall in love with Jesus, you just can't help but change, because . . . Jesus changes you! The old person that you once were is gone and your new life as a Christian now defines who you are. However, you cannot experience a vibrant life in Christ one moment and dance with the devil the next! You must take a side and choose whom you will serve, because you can only serve *one* master!

If you choose to *dabble* in sin, you will be absolutely miserable! You simply cannot lie, cheat, gossip, or commit any other sin and live a life of purity and commitment to your Lord and Savior. The Bible says in Joshua 24:15 (NKJV), "Choose for yourselves this day whom you will serve . . . But as for me and my house, we will serve the Lord." And in Romans 12:1 (NKJV), the apostle Paul pleads, "I beseech you therefore, brethren, by the mercies of God, that you present your bodies a living sacrifice, holy, acceptable to God, which is your reasonable service."

Make God first in your life and you will experience the real joy in living, for Jesus *is* the joy in life. It is not possible to be happy and serve Satan! Make your choice to serve Jesus and don't dance with the devil!

Best Friend Jesus

"For God so loved the world that He gave His only begotten Son, that whoever believes in Him should not perish but have everlasting life."

John 3:16 (NKJV)

───◆───

True friendship is to be cherished, valued, and treasured highly, for it is rare to find someone who actually deserves the title, *friend*. Finding someone who loves unconditionally, is there for you through thick and thin, and will never let you down is a special gift. And of course, a real friendship requires honesty, loyalty, and trust—traits that are even harder to come by these days. It seems that some friends are loyal until it serves their purpose not to be, while others pretend to be friends because of what you can do for them because of or something they need from you.

A sure time to find out if your friends are real is the moment tragedy or trouble strikes! Fake friends tend to disappear very quickly, and when the dust settles, it is your true friends that have weathered the storm with you. But of all the great friends you could possibly have, there is only *one* friend that you can always count on no matter what! He will never leave you or forsake you and always has your best interest at heart. He isn't jealous, spiteful, or dishonest, and best of all . . . He loves unconditionally! Yes, your best Friend, Jesus, loves you more than you could possibly imagine . . . more than anyone else ever could!

Activate Your Faith

Immediately the father of the child cried out and said
with tears, "Lord, I believe; help my unbelief!"

Mark 9:24 (NKJV)

Christians talk about *faith* but few truly understand the real meaning. As long as everything is going great in their life, their faith is strong, but at the first sight of trouble, they jump on the worry wagon and faith is thrown out the window! You simply cannot be pacing the floor, biting your nails, or spending sleepless nights weighed down with worry and have complete faith in God! Hebrews 11:1 (NIV) sums up the meaning of faith: "Now faith is confidence in what we hope for and assurance about what we do not see."

When your life is falling apart and you're helpless to make things better, that's when faith sustains you—knowing with absolute certainty you are in the hollow of God's hand! It's one thing to *know* you serve a trustworthy God, but when you actually witness faith in action, your love and trust goes off the charts! Someone once said, "When God pushes you to the edge of difficulty, trust Him fully because two things can happen. Either He'll catch you when you fall or he will teach you how to fly." That's a powerful reality because our God is trustworthy, loving, all-powerful, and wants what's best for us, so there's no need to worry when we allow God full control of our lives! Activate your faith today, and start by believing God will do what He says He will do . . . even in the bad times!

Life Lessons

*The LORD will fight for you, and you shall
hold your peace.*

Exodus 14:14 (NKJV)

Your journey here on earth begins the moment you are born until you breathe your last breath. And the beautiful thing is, each new day is a day to learn and grow in a constantly changing world. But your greatest *life lessons* won't happen when you are on top of the mountain and everything is going great in your life. No, not at all. Your most valuable lessons are learned when you are down in the valley—when your friends betray you, your marriage fails, your health diagnoses are grim, you are out of work, and you have no money to pay the bills, etc. And that's when you really find out who your *real friends* are. But more importantly, it is during hard times when you lean on Jesus the most!

If you are in the valley right now, remember you are not alone. Jesus is with you and will never leave you. He will give you comfort, support, guidance, and wisdom. He may speak to you when you're reading His Holy Word, or through the Holy Spirit speaking directly to your heart. Many times, God's answer comes through a friend, an unusual circumstance, divine intervention, or even a dream. God speaks to His children in many different ways, but the important thing is . . . to listen for His voice. No one likes to go through difficult times, but it is during our trials that we learn important life lessons, and in doing so, grow closer to Jesus.

Don't Be a Showoff

*And let us not grow weary while doing good, for in due
season we shall reap if we do not lose heart.*

Galatians 6:9 (NKJV)

Helping others is something God wants you to do, but He also wants you to do it for the right reasons. Giving money to a homeless man because you think someone is watching or serving food at a soup kitchen so you can brag to your friends is not what God has in mind. Jesus makes it very clear that when you help others, you do so with humility and without expecting anything in return.

The Bible says in Matthew 6:1 (NIV), "Be careful not to practice your righteousness in front of others to be seen by them. If you do, you will have no reward from your Father in heaven." When you unselfishly reach out to someone in need, you are putting God's love in action! And it doesn't matter that others notice; it only matters that God does. Above all, He knows your heart and He knows whether or not your motives are pure.

Hebrews 6:10 (NIV) says, "God is not unjust; he will not forget your work and the love you have shown him as you have helped his people and continue to help them." And in Proverbs 19:17 (NIV), we're told, "Whoever is kind to the poor lends to the LORD, and he will reward them for what they have done." More important than any earthly reward or gain is your *heavenly reward*. So, share God's love to others for the *right reasons* and . . . don't be a showoff!

The First Step

*But none of these things move me; nor do I count my
life dear to myself, so that I may finish my race with joy,
and the ministry which I received from the Lord Jesus, to
testify to the gospel of the grace of God.*

Acts 20:24 (NKJV)

There is only one way to experience all that life has to offer, and that is to follow God's plan for you. And there's only one way to know what *His plan* is and that is to communicate with Him directly. God will not force you to follow Him—it is your choice. But, without God's divine direction, there is no joy, and without joy, life is a drudgery, void of enthusiasm and purpose. Before you know it, one day just rolls into the next and life's problems become so difficult that your future seems hopeless.

Take the first step toward a joy-filled life by surrendering to Jesus! The only way to live an undefeated life is by allowing Him to take up residence in your heart, replacing all the selfishness, fear, anger, and pain with His peace, comfort, wisdom, and guidance. Maintain your close relationship with God by spending time with Him every day, in prayer and the study of His Word. Soon, you won't be able to imagine your life any other way than God's way and it will be impossible for the enemy to discourage you.

As long as you are walking with Jesus, you have nothing to fear! So, take that first step by reaching out and grasping His outstretched hand and never allow anything or anyone to come between you and your Savior!

October 13

Friendship Evangelism

*"But you shall receive power when the Holy Spirit
has come upon you; and you shall be witnesses to Me in
Jerusalem, and in all Judea and Samaria, and to
the end of the earth."*

Acts 1:8 (NKJV)

When you stop and think about God's incredible sacrifice for your salvation, you just can't keep this life-saving news to yourself! God is such an awesome God and the whole world needs to know! The best way to witness for Jesus is to live by example! Let every aspect of your life reflect God's character. You may feel shy, awkward, or unworthy to witness for Christ, but God isn't asking just the highly-educated and sophisticated people to witness. He wants everyone to share His love! Pray for insight and holy boldness to be an incredible soul-winning tool for God! The Bible says in 1 Peter 3:15 (NIV), "Always be prepared to give an answer to everyone who asks you to give the reason for the hope that you have. But do this with gentleness and respect." Pay especially close attention to the last line—*with gentleness and respect*.

Too many well-intentioned people try to argue religion! They go about it all the wrong way using the Bible as a *hammer* to let people know what they are doing wrong. But that is not the right way to witness, and more importantly, it is not God's way! The best way to win souls for Jesus is to *love them* to the Lord! Friendship evangelism is much more effective than criticism and harsh judgment, so reach out and be a friend!

Actor or Reactor

A hot-tempered man stirs up strife, but he who is slow
to anger quiets contention.

Proverbs 15:18 (ESV)

When things go wrong, it's easy to have a knee-jerk reaction and do or say things you shouldn't. Acting on impulse is rarely a good thing to do. Many times when reacting based on emotion, you can make a mountain out of a molehill and find yourself wondering why in the world you behaved in such a manner, not to mention regretting all the harm that was done. If you had only stopped to think and pray about the situation, friendships could have been salvaged, you wouldn't have made enemies, and disaster could have been avoided.

It takes little or no thought to *react*, but it takes Holy Spirit power to respond in a Christlike way, especially if your feelings have been hurt or someone you love has been mistreated. It is then that Satan really enjoys creating friction by stirring up anger and hurt feelings. The Bible says in Ephesians 5:16-17 (NRSV), "Making the most of the time, because the days are evil. So do not be foolish, but understand what the will of the Lord is." Pray the prayer of David in Psalm 141:3 (NKJV): "Set a guard, O LORD, over my mouth; keep watch over the door of my lips," and don't forget to ask God to give you more self-control so that all your actions can glorify Him. In other words, be an actor for God and not a reactor for the devil!

Your Church Family

How is it then, brethren? Whenever you come together, each of you has a psalm, has a teaching, has a tongue, has a revelation, has an interpretation. Let all things be done for edification.

1 Corinthians 14:26 (NKJV)

It's important to be a part of your church, whether it is holding an office, taking part in the service, or just knowing and loving your church family. There's nothing wrong with attending large churches, provided your choice is motivated by the right reasons. Sometimes people choose to attend large churches because they want to *blend in*, where they can come and go . . . unnoticed. The problem with just *blending in* is that you never really feel like you have a *church family*, nor do you feel the satisfaction and contentment of being a member of God's family. If there's no motivation to contribute, then it's easy to just drift away altogether. When you stop growing spiritually, you die spiritually.

It's a privilege to work for Jesus. The Bible says in 1 Timothy 1:12 (NIV), "I thank Christ Jesus our Lord, who has given me strength, that he considered me trustworthy, appointing me to his service." Everyone needs to take an active role in church duties. It's also important to love and embrace your church family, spending time together not just at church, but socially as well. Families should be there for each other in the good and bad times, and that includes *your church family* too!

Following God's Will

*Therefore do not be unwise, but understand what
the will of the Lord is.*

Ephesians 5:17 (NKJV)

Doing what *God* wants and not what *you* want is a lifelong struggle of your will versus God's will. Some people think that if they follow God's plan then there will never be any trouble, but the truth is, trials and tribulation will be with us until Jesus comes! What you can count on is that God will be with you through every storm—you don't have to face your struggles alone!

Sometimes God allows burdens to draw you even closer to Him, and it is through your trials that your character is perfected for heaven. God won't force you to serve Him. He wants you to *choose* to serve Him because you love Him. It is so very important that you are doing the will of your Father, for truly your salvation depends on it. In Matthew 7:21-23 (NKJV), we're told, "Not everyone who says to Me, 'Lord, Lord,' shall enter the kingdom of heaven, but he who does the will of My Father in heaven. Many will say to Me in that day, 'Lord, Lord, have we not prophesied in Your name, cast out demons in Your name, and done many wonders in Your name?' And then I will declare to them, 'I never knew you; depart from Me, you who practice lawlessness!' "Wow! It doesn't get clearer than that! Following God's will is critical . . . because your salvation depends on it.

Embrace Today

"Therefore do not worry about tomorrow, for tomorrow will worry about its own things. Sufficient for the day is its own trouble."

Matthew 6:34 (NKJV)

———◆———

The secret to having a *happy life* is to stay close to our best Friend, Jesus. No matter what trials we are facing, we don't have to get all stressed out, because we are never alone; Jesus is with us at all times! So many people dream of the day when they will finally be happy—when they reach financial success, when their children graduate from college, when they finally take that dream vacation, and so on. They spend so much time fantasizing that they let their whole life pass by in a meaningless state, living their lives just *waiting to be happy*.

But God wants us to be happy now! Instead of daydreaming our lives away, we need to embrace today and *live for Jesus*! The only way to truly experience real happiness is to live a life fully surrendered to Him, and then we will have joy such as we've never known. And the good news is, we won't have to wait until we've reached some self-appointed goal in our lives. God wants us to live each day as if it were our last, but plan for the future. Now, that doesn't mean planning all the details of our lives out, but rather trusting God to do amazing things through us. Planning is different than living in a fantasy world! God is not a fantasy. He is very real and He alone knows our future, so stop living for what might be . . . and embrace today!

Keep Getting Up

*For whatever is born of God overcomes the world.
And this is the victory that has overcome
the world—our faith.*

1 John 5:4 (NKJV)

Christians sometimes get discouraged when they pray asking God to lead and guide, and then not long after, stumble and fall. They may even consider just giving up since it seems that, no matter what, they always fall. But the difference between a Christian and a wicked man is this: a Christian keeps getting back up, but the wicked stay down! The Bible says in Proverbs 24:16 (NKJV), "For a righteous man may fall seven times and rise again, but the wicked shall fall by calamity." Notice how this verse first points out that *both* the wicked and the righteous *fall*, but *only* the righteous *keep falling*! That's because it's impossible to fall . . . if you are not standing up!

As long as you keep getting up, the Bible calls you *righteous*! If you just stay down, you will be lost! What truly matters is, not how many times you fall, but how many times you keep getting up! To give you strength and Holy Spirit power to *get up*, claim God's promise in Ephesians 6:13 (NIV): "Therefore put on the full armor of God, so that when the day of evil comes, you may be able to stand your ground, and after you have done everything, to stand." God *will* give you the victory—just keep getting up!

October 19

Prayer Partner

*"If you abide in Me, and My words abide in you,
you will ask what you desire, and it shall be done for
you. By this My Father is glorified, that you bear much
fruit; so you will be My disciples."*

John 15:7-8 (NKJV)

———◆———

If you want to draw closer to God, spend time communicating with Him through prayer and the study of His Word. There is no right or wrong way to pray, nor does God expect you to pray in an eloquent manner. He longs for you to let *Him* fix your problems, no matter how big or small, and He especially loves to hear your praises.

When we pray, we should align ourselves with God's purpose, leaving behind our own desires and trusting His perfect will. It's also good to pray with fellow believers. The Bible says in Matthew 18:20 (NIV), "For where two or three gather in my name, there am I with them." That's a powerful promise you can claim and is reason enough to take God at His word.

We can absolutely know that God will answer us, as confirmed in 1 John 5:14 (NIV): "This is the confidence we have in approaching God: that if we ask anything according to his will, he hears us." When you have a difficult decision to make or you're faced with a life-altering situation, instead of worrying yourself into a sick frenzy, ask a prayer partner to pray with you and then trust God to answer.

Criticizing Others

"Or how can you say to your brother,
'Let me remove the speck from your eye'; and look,
a plank is in your own eye? Hypocrite! First remove the
plank from your own eye, and then you will see clearly
to remove the speck from your brother's eye."

Matthew 7:4-5 (NKJV)

It's always easier to point out the faults of others than it is to see your own weaknesses. That's probably because it's painful to envision yourself less than who you think you are. It's much more comfortable to live in a self-imposed bubble, believing that you are better than everyone else. But criticizing others won't make your own faults disappear. Nor will you have the character God wants you to have. The Bible says in Matthew 7:4 (NIV), "How can you say to your brother, 'Let me take the speck out of your eye," when all the time there is a plank in your own eye?"

Always keep in mind—there is only one who can change hearts—and that is God and He is the only one who can "fix" people. Criticizing others will not only bring them down, but it will bring you down too! Instead of looking for the bad—look for the good in others—and you will find it! Ask God to help you face your own faults—so much so that you'll actually hate your own sins—more than you hate the faults of others. Then ask God to change *you* and help you be the person He wants you to be.

Death Trap

*Wrath is cruel and anger a torrent, but who is
able to stand before jealousy?*

Proverbs 27:4 (NKJV)

One of the fastest ways to lose your Christian experience is to allow seeds of jealousy to enter your heart. The devil wants you to compare yourself to those around you because, when you do that, you'll fall into his death trap. As long as you live on this earth, there will be injustices. There will always be those who seem to have it all—they live in nicer homes and are more popular, beautiful, and richer than you are. But, if you were to see inside their lives, you might feel differently about wanting to step into their shoes. The Bible says in Proverbs 14:30 (NIV), "A heart at peace gives life to the body, but envy rots the bones."

Money can't buy happiness. It's true, life isn't fair, but God's love is! He loves His children equally and the closer you draw to Him, the less you covet earthly pleasures. The only way to avoid the devil's death trap is to hold God's hand and allow Him to lead and guide you each step of life's journey. Continually dwell in His presence through praise, worship, the study of His Holy Word, and prayer.

When you commune with God throughout your day, you'll not only feel closer to Him but . . . your whole day will go better! You'll have joy, wisdom, strength, courage, and confidence you have never felt before!

Self-Centered Children

No discipline seems pleasant at the time, but painful.
Later on, however, it produces a harvest of righteousness
and peace for those who have been trained by it.

Hebrews 12:11 (NIV)

———◇———

The biggest problem with today's generation of children is that they are focused on *themselves*. Children are selfish, demanding to be the center of attention, believing that the world revolves around *them*. Even television sitcoms feature children making sarcastic remarks and the parents are made to look like foolish idiots. What is really happening is that the child has learned:

1. Parents don't mean what they say.
2. Respecting parents is not required.
3. Kids are in charge and can do whatever they want!

How sad it is that kids are growing up confused, lost, and disillusioned, often turning to drugs, alcohol, and other vices trying to *find themselves*. It's no mystery why they are leaving the church and turning their backs on God. Nowhere in the Bible does God recommend spoiling children. The Bible says in Ephesians 6:4, (NIV), "Fathers, do not exasperate your children; instead, bring them up in the training and instruction of the Lord." Parents should be encouraged by this promise in Proverbs 22:6 (NIV): "Train up a child in the way he should go, and when he is old he will not depart from it." Training your sons and daughters to love Jesus is the only way to avoid having *self-centered* children.

Okay to Be Different

I the LORD test the mind and search the heart,
to give to all according to their ways, according
to the fruit of their doings.

Jeremiah 17:10 (NRSV)

God made all of His children different. There are no two people exactly alike, not even identical twins! Think about the snowflakes that are too numerous to count, and yet science has confirmed there are no two snowflakes alike. So it is with humans—we are all created in God's image, but each of us have something special that no one else has! Not only are we uniquely different, but God treats each of us differently as well.

When Jesus was here on this earth, He didn't heal everyone in the same way. For instance, He put mud on one blind man's eyes, told him to rinse it off, and then he was healed, yet there is no record that he did this for every blind person He healed. Jesus healed many lepers by merely a touch or His spoken word, but He gave one group of lepers an assignment to do *before* they were healed.

God asked Abraham to kill his son, and He asked Peter to walk on water. You see, Jesus knows each of His children intimately and knows exactly what they need. What one person needs isn't the same as what someone else needs. We all have different personalities as well as different relationships with God based on how much time we spend with Him. Instead of judging, let's accept each others differences and remember that God loves all His children equally—it's okay to be different!

Mountain of Troubles

And my God shall supply all your need according to His riches in glory by Christ Jesus.

Philippians 4:19 (NKJV)

If you wake up in the morning feeling like you are facing the tallest, insurmountable mountain, you are not alone! There are many others that feel the same way! It may be a grim diagnosis, a stack of unpaid bills, a lost relationship, or something as simple as a pile of laundry that has you completely overwhelmed. Whatever it is, you cannot just *pray it away*, as if prayer was a *magic wand* you wave to get rid of all your troubles! The Bible says in 1 Corinthians 13:2 (NKJV), "And though I have all faith, so that I could remove mountains, but have not love, I am nothing."

This does not mean that if you have enough faith all your problems would be solved, for faith is not a tool that God gives to make your life easier. *Faith* is obtained by the love you have for your heavenly Father. The stronger your love for God, the stronger your faith! God wants you to love Him so much that you will trust Him with every aspect of your life—your joys, sorrows, worries, as well as your mountain of troubles! Jesus cares about even the tiniest detail of your life . . . yes, even your lack of energy to tackle your household chores, including the laundry! Pray and ask God to give you the strength to endure whatever mountain you are facing today!

October 25

Life of Love

*Beloved, if God so loved us, we also
ought to love one another.*

1 John 4:11 (NKJV)

The Bible has a lot to say about how God feels about human relationships. In Proverbs 17:17 (NKJV), we're told, "A friend loves at all times" and in 1 John 3:11 (NKJV), we're instructed, "We should love one another." God wants His children not only to *get along* with each other, but to *love* one another! And He is not just talking about people who are nice to us. God says in Matthew 5:43-45 (NKJV), "You have heard that it was said, 'You shall love your neighbor and hate your enemy.' But I say to you, love your enemies, bless those who curse you, do good to those who hate you, and pray for those who spitefully use you and persecute you, that you may be sons of your Father in heaven."

Pay special attention to those last words. If we want to be children of God, we must be loving! When someone is hateful, mean, and rude, the best advice comes from Ephesians 5:21 (NIV): "Submit to one another out of reverence for Christ." In other words, even though they don't treat you with respect, treat them like Jesus would—just love them! It's a lot easier being kind and loving to someone when your heart if full of God's love! Make Ephesians 5:2 (NKJV) your life's motto: "And walk in love, as Christ also has loved us and given Himself for us, an offering and a sacrifice to God for a sweet-smelling aroma."

No Goodbyes

*"Blessed are those who mourn, for
they shall be comforted."*

Matthew 5:4 (NKJV)

Having to say goodbye to friends or family can be downright heart-wrenching. Watching your little one leave for school that first day or dropping your teenager off for college makes you feel sad knowing your life will never be quite the same. Parting after a family reunion leaves you with a knot in the pit of your stomach. Watching your loved one disappear behind the security line at the airport brings tears to your eyes as you realize it may be a long time before you see them again. But the pain of being separated by death . . . is the worst goodbye of all! Knowing you will never hear the sound of their sweet voice or the gentleness of their touch seems too painful a burden to bear.

But don't despair, because the good news is, Jesus is coming again soon to take all those who have surrendered their hearts and lives to Him to live with Him in heaven forever. The Bible says in Revelation 21:4 (NIV), "There will be no more death or mourning or crying or pain, for the old order of things has passed away." And in 1 Thessalonians 4:17-18 (NIV), we can claim this promise: "After that, we who are still alive and are left will be caught up together with them in the clouds to meet the Lord in the air. And so we will be with the Lord forever. Therefore encourage one another with these words." Oh, what a glorious day that will be! Just imagine a life with no goodbyes, tears, sadness, or pain—but each day will be more wonderful than the day before!

Sinful Desires

*I acknowledged my sin to You, and my iniquity I have
not hidden. I said, "I will confess my transgressions to the
Lord," and You forgave the iniquity of my sin.*

Psalm 32:5 (NKJV)

Satan uses every possible tool to separate you from Jesus! He knows your weaknesses and he boldly exploits them to his advantage. Let's face it—Satan makes sin look very attractive, and he can take the ugliest parts of sin and make them appear to be fun, exciting, and downright enticing. He wouldn't be very successful at tempting you to sin if he didn't make it so alluring. Please note that it is not a sin to be *tempted*; it's a sin to *yield* to temptation. That's why it's best not to even allow yourself to be placed in a position where you are pushing your sinful desires to the limit! Walk away and say, "Get thee behind me, Satan."

Galatians 5:19-21 (NIV) tells us, "The acts of the flesh are obvious: sexual immorality, impurity and debauchery; idolatry and witchcraft; hatred, discord, jealousy, fits of rage, selfish ambition, dissensions, factions and envy; drunkenness, orgies, and the like. I warn you, as I did before, that those who live like this will not inherit the kingdom of God." It doesn't matter if your sinful desires are adultery, selfishness, pride, gossip, overeating, or murder—all sin will keep you out of heaven, period! But, praise the Lord! He has given a plan for salvation that none should perish!

God-Given Intelligence

For the LORD gives wisdom; from His mouth come knowledge and understanding.

Proverbs 2:6 (NKJV)

———◆———

When God created man, He thought of every detail that the human body would need to glorify Him, and the human brain is probably the most spectacular. He could have created us with a brain the size of a walnut with barely enough cognitive ability to function. But instead, God made humans the most intelligent living creatures on the planet! Our brains were not created to merely control our nervous system or perform superficial thinking. God blessed us with the ability to analyze situations and think deep, highly intelligent thoughts. *Thinking* spiritual thoughts is a way of showing God just how much we love Him.

The Bible says in Matthew 22:37 (NKJV), "You shall love the LORD your God with all your heart, with all your soul, and with all your mind." When we fill our minds with the devil's distractions—listening to or watching entertainment filled with violence, sex, vulgar language, and other evil vices of Satan—we are not only polluting our minds, but we are preventing our brains from thinking spiritual thoughts. It literally leaves us powerless and renders us like puppets in the devil's hands. Studying God's Word and learning more about our Lord and Savior gives us discernment to act on spiritual impulse and use all of our brain function to make informed decisions to live a life for Christ. Using *God-given intelligence* leads us to love God with our minds, thoughts, and actions.

Part-Time Christians

*But sanctify the Lord God in your hearts, and always be
ready to give a defense to everyone who asks you a reason
for the hope that is in you, with meekness and fear.*

1 Peter 3:15 (NKJV)

Being a Christian is not something that you turn off and on like a faucet deciding to play the *God card* whenever it's convenient, then do what you want the rest of the time. Nor is it *Christian* to be a kind, loving example of Christ when you are out in public, but then be grumpy and rude to your own friends and families. Some people attend church regularly, but, on their drive home, quickly forget all about being a *godly* person—driving like a maniac, honking the horn, and cutting people off in traffic, all because the person in the car in front of them is perceived to be going too slow. How quickly they forgot the spiritual message the pastor just preached moments before.

There are those who believe themselves to be living like Christ but have no clue how character-revealing it is the rude way they answer a phone. Being busy is no excuse to portray impatience or irritation when receiving an unexpected phone call! You are definitely not living the life of a committed Christian when you respond harshly, raise your voice, or take an authoritative tone when someone doesn't share your opinion. God doesn't want you to be a *part-time Christian*, He wants you to have a Christlike character and shine for Him—all the time!

Why Lord, Why?

*"And shall God not avenge His own elect who cry out day
and night to Him, though He bears long with them?"*

Luke 18:7 (NKJV)

Have you ever wondered why God doesn't intervene in our lives *before* life becomes a crisis? Why doesn't He just send a check in the mail instead of waiting until the cupboards are bare and the eviction notice is given? Better yet, why doesn't He just stamp out world poverty and hunger? Why does He allow the cancer to spread and leave little children without mothers? Why does He wait so long to answer prayers, stamp out corruption, end child abuse, and a million other *whys*!

And the answer is, we live in a sinful world and until Jesus comes, horrible things will take place. God doesn't force us to serve Him, nor does He *make* us live a godly life. God gave each of us the gift of *choice,* and we pay the heavy consequences of sin when we make bad choices! But let's be very clear: it's not God's will that we suffer or have a moment of pain. Quite the contrary, for the Bible says in John 10:10 (KJV), "I am come that they might have life, and that they might have it more abundantly." Because of God's amazing love for us, when we turn ourselves over to Him, He is able to pick up the broken pieces of our lives and will turn evil into good! Praise God we don't have much longer here in this wicked world of pain . . . for Jesus is coming soon!

Falling in Love

You shall love the LORD your God with all your heart,
with all your soul, and with all your strength.

Deuteronomy 6:5 (NKJV)

When you first fall in love, you're excited, energized, and eager to tell the world about how awesome your new mate is! You sing their praises to anyone who will listen. But over time, the excitement wears down. You start taking them for granted, and with all the hustle and bustle of life, distance grows between you, and you expect them to just understand when you no longer make them number one in your life. Then you wonder why your relationship just isn't as exciting and wonderful as it used to be and question what could have possibly gone wrong.

This scenario is the same for new Christians who fall in love with Jesus. They are so exuberant in their newfound faith that they share Jesus with everyone they meet. But as life gets busy and they slack off on their alone time with God, their love relationship with Him suffers. Before they even realize it, they no longer read their Bibles or even pray. The number one ingredient absolutely necessary to maintain any love relationship is communication! And your relationship with God is no different. The minute you stop communicating with your heavenly Father, you will start drifting away. Just like Peter who walked on water, the minute he took his eyes of Christ, he began to sink! Nurture your love relationship with Jesus by falling in love with Him every day . . . through prayer and studying His Holy Word.

Keep On Knocking

*For this reason we also, since the day we heard it,
do not cease to pray for you, and to ask that you may
be filled with the knowledge of His will in all wisdom
and spiritual understanding.*

Colossians 1:9 (NKJV)

Most Christians understand how to communicate with God, knowing prayer is not only a privilege but necessary for salvation! However, there are still many people in this world who don't even know who God is, and it is our Christian duty to be a daily witness for Him. It's also important to pray intercessory prayers. The dictionary defines the word "intercessory" as "the act of interceding or praying for others." The Bible says in 1 Samuel 12:23 (NKJV), "Far be it from me that I should sin against the Lord in ceasing to pray for you."

The Bible makes it very clear that it is not only necessary to pray for others—but it is a sin not to! Jesus not only prayed intercessory prayers for us when He was on earth, but He is still interceding on our behalf today! Satan knows full well the power of God, which is why he constantly attacks our prayer lives.

When tempted to be discouraged because your children, spouse, parents, and loved ones don't know Jesus . . . pray! Yes, love them enough to pray passionately that God will send the Holy Spirit to knock at their hearts' doors—and keep on knocking until they make a full surrender to God!

Repetitive Sins

*For the grace of God that brings salvation has appeared
to all men, teaching us that, denying ungodliness
and worldly lusts, we should live soberly, righteously,
and godly in the present age*

Titus 2:11-12 (NKJV)

———⋘⋙———

Why is it that there are some sins that no matter how much you try to give up, you tend to repeat over and over again. You go to the Lord with a sincere heart filled with remorse and ask forgiveness, but when the temptation rolls around again, you make the same mistake. It is then, with exasperation and despair, that you approach God's throne room—perhaps even somewhat embarrassed to ask God for forgiveness one more time.

If you are feeling as if you are the only one who has ever felt this frustration, read what the apostle Paul says in Romans 7:15-17 (ESV): "For I do not understand my own actions. For I do not do what I want, but I do the very thing I hate. . . For I have the desire to do what is right, but not the ability to carry it out." The secret to maintaining a life of righteousness is to always abide with Christ. The minute you take your eyes of Jesus, you will fall!

The Bible says in 1 John 3:8-10 (ESV), "Whoever makes a practice of sinning is of the devil . . . No one born of God makes a practice of sinning . . . By this it is evident who are the children of God, and who are the children of the devil: whoever does not practice righteousness is not of God." The only way to stop the cycle of repetitive sins . . . is to stay close to Jesus!

Cultivating Trust

Many sorrows shall be to the wicked; but he who trusts in the LORD, mercy shall surround him.

Psalm 32:10 (NKJV)

A child begins to learn about *trust* at a very young age—from the moment a little girl holds her daddy's hand crossing the street, she knows he's protecting her by the tight grip of his hand. When a father tells his son to jump from a tree, that little boy learned *trust* in his father's arms. And when his daughter is brokenhearted because her boyfriend broke up with her, it was her father's warm embrace that she trusted for comfort. Trust is *learned* and *earned*. Had the little boy fallen because his father failed to catch him, all trust would have been destroyed. That father earned his son's trust when he wrapped him in his arms of love!

So it is with our heavenly Father. God has *earned* your trust! You can share the details of your life with Him and know He not only listens, but He cares! You can trust that He will answer every prayer with your best interest in mind, and the more you communicate with Him, the more your faith grows. When the storms of life come—and yes, they will come—you'll be more equipped to handle whatever comes your way. Cultivating faith in God allows you to turn to Him without fear and cry out, "Father, help me! Hold me in your arms of love!"

Recognizing Unforgiveness

*Strive for peace with everyone, and for the holiness
without which no one will see the Lord.*

Hebrews 12:14 (ESV)

———◆———

There are some who *think* they have forgiven a past "wrong," but in reality, it is still lying dormant in their hearts, becoming more bitter, decayed, and smelly by the hour! People who won't forgive are miserable, and it affects every aspect of their lives, as well as those around them. If you hear something bad has happened to the person that hurt you and your heart wants to scream, "Yes, he finally got what he deserved!" then you really haven't forgiven, because when you truly forgive, you won't harbor bitterness, nor will you wish them harm.

Instead, you will love them with *God's love* even when it's impossible to love with *human love*. Sometimes the pain accumulates over time, and even though you've forgiven, a memory may come up again that's so painful, it creates the need to forgive all over again. If you choose not to forgive, there are deadly consequences, for the Bible says in Matthew 6:15 (NIV), "But if you do not forgive others their sins, your Father will not forgive your sins."

In other words, forgiving is so important to God that He has made it a requirement for your entrance to heaven! Pray and ask God to reveal any unforgiveness in your heart, and then to give you the strength and courage to forgive!

Helpless, Not Hopeless

For whatever things were written before were written for our learning, that we through the patience and comfort of the Scriptures might have hope.

Romans 15:4 (NKJV)

———◆———

Humans are limited by physical abilities, such as strength, endurance, and wisdom. There are emotional limitations too—for when someone steps on your last nerve, it could easily trigger an emotional eruption or even hinder your ability to love. Once you've exhausted your own physical and emotional limitations, you start to feel helpless and frustrated. But *helpless* doesn't mean you are *hopeless*. There's a big difference. Nothing is hopeless when God is with you, for when you are weak, He is strong. When you are discouraged, He will lift you up, and when you are brokenhearted, He will give you comfort. Jesus *is* your hope!

Don't wait until you have reached rock bottom to seek your Savior! Cry out to Jesus today and ask Him to come into your heart and life. The Bible says in Psalm 10:17 (NLT), "Lord, you know the hopes of the helpless. Surely you will hear their cries and comfort them." One of the many faith-building stories in the Bible is the story of Mary and Martha. They were both discouraged, angry, and frustrated with their Friend, Jesus, whose tardiness *caused* their brother to die—and yet, when Jesus finally arrived, He brought hope and joy! Remember, no matter how dismal life may seem . . . Jesus is your hope!

Protect Your Marriage

"So then, they are no longer two but one flesh. Therefore what God has joined together, let not man separate."

Matthew 19:6 (NKJV)

When most people get married, they do so with every intention of honoring their wedding vows. They don't *plan* to have an affair, yet why is it that so many couples fall into the bed of unfaithfulness? When this happens, most often it is because one or both spouses did not protect their marriage. If you want a happy, joyful marriage, there are three important rules that are absolutely necessary!

1. God must be the head of your home! Without His constant strength, power, guidance, and wisdom, this union is doomed for disaster!

2. Marriage is meant for *two*. The moment you form an intimate relationship with someone else, you allow a crack in the door for the devil to infiltrate your marriage. Whether it is an emotional affair or a physical one, it will destroy your holy union before God.

3. Honest, kind, and respectful *open* communication is necessary to resolve conflicts. Hold your spouse in high esteem and treat them as if they are the most important person in your life. And it's always good to practice this advice that has been passed on for generations: never go to bed angry!

Honor these rules to protect your marriage . . . and you'll experience the joy of godly companionship on life's journey.

God Is Enough

*The afflicted shall eat and be satisfied; those who seek
him shall praise the LORD! May your hearts live forever!*

Psalm 22:26 (ESV)

All too often, people go through life without any thought of the future—living in the moment and partying their life away. They are so focused on *self* that they become oblivious to the wants and needs of anyone else. But this is not only a meaningless and lonely existence, it is also a dangerous slippery slope. Before you know it, you become just like the prodigal son in the Bible who had to lose everything and hit rock bottom before he looked up and saw his need for a Savior. It's when you have nothing left that you realize . . . God is enough!

Only a life for Christ will bring everlasting happiness. Stop living for *self* and start living for Jesus! It is the only way to live a *joy-filled* life that God wants you to have! And when you make Jesus first in your life, you can't help but want to share Him with everyone you meet. Your own problems won't seem so big when you focus on helping others. You'll find that witnessing for Jesus not only blessses those you minister to, but you will be blessed as well.

So no matter how selfishly you have lived in the past, what mistakes you've made, or how long it has been since you attended church, it's not too late to give your heart to God. He loves you more than anyone else possibly could, and He is waiting to welcome you with open arms. Remember . . . God is enough—because He is your everything!

Holy Spirit Wisdom

*"But the Helper, the Holy Spirit, whom the Father will
send in My name, He will teach you all things, and bring
to your remembrance all things that I said to you."*

John 14:26 (NKJV)

God sends the Holy Spirit to light our way and keep us on the right path, for without guidance, we would be wandering aimlessly in darkness! He tenderly whispers when He sees us getting ready to make mistakes, and when we listen, we can avoid the dark pitfalls of certain destruction. It's when we ignore the nudges from the Holy Spirit that we get in trouble!

The Holy Spirit helps us understand Scripture, make wise decisions, and open our hearts to feel God's presence so that we may more fully comprehend God's amazing love for us! The Bible says in Ephesians 4:30 (KJV), "And grieve not the Holy Spirit of God, whereby ye are sealed unto the day of redemption." Wow! That is powerful! God makes it very clear the importance of listening to the Holy Spirit!

If we keep ignoring the Holy Spirit, at some point, God will say enough is enough and His Holy Spirit will be withdrawn. That's why the Bible pleads with us not to *grieve* the Holy Spirit. When we are discouraged, facing difficult trials, or responding to a task God has called us to, all we need to do is pray for an extra anointing of His Holy Spirit . . . and let God take over!

Jesus Saves

"Do I have any pleasure at all that the wicked
should die?" says the Lord God, "and not that he should
turn from his ways and live?

Ezekiel 18:23 (NKJV)

Martin Luther once said, "When I look to myself, I don't know how I can be saved. When I look to Jesus, I don't know how I can be lost." Sometimes when we look at our own faults and ponder the mistakes we've made, it is easy to believe the devil's lies and think, *I'm lost—I'm such a sinner.* But as long as we are remorseful, it doesn't matter what sin has been committed, because there is nothing that God can't forgive when we ask Him to. God doesn't base His willingness to forgive on *how we feel* about ourselves.

Some people look at God as a stern judge who is sitting in heaven just waiting for them to mess up. But that is not who God is at all! The Bible says in 2 Peter 3:9 (NIV), "He is patient with you, not wanting anyone to perish, but everyone to come to repentance." And Romans 3:23 (NIV) tells us, "All have sinned and fall short of the glory of God."

No one is perfect—we are all sinners, and the Bible confirms God's love for us in John 3:16 (NIV): "For God so loved the world that he gave his one and only Son, that whoever believes in him shall not perish but have eternal life." There is no greater love than that! God is not asking for perfection, He is asking you to *believe in Him.* Whenever you fall and the devil tells you that you're lost, remember, the devil is a liar—Jesus saves!

Straddling the Fence

*He who is not with Me is against Me, and he who does
not gather with Me scatters abroad.*

Matthew 12:30 (NKJV)

The devil wants you to believe you can experience all the evil pleasures of this world without painful consequences, but that couldn't be further from the truth. You can't have a foot in God's kingdom and the other one on the devil's playground. You must choose a side—you can not straddle the fence!

The Bible says in 1 John 2:15 (NIV), "Do not love the world or anything in the world. If anyone loves the world, the love of the Father is not in them." When you love the world, you care more about what people think of you, how much money you have, your status in the community, how well traveled you are, or how prestigious your job is. But when you fall in love with Jesus, you care more about what He thinks of you. You are motivated to serve God and to share His love with others and you would rather die than disappoint your Lord and Savior.

We're told in Romans 8:13 (NKJV), "For if you live according to the flesh you will die." And God gives each of us life saving advice in Haggai 1:5 (NKJV): "Now this is what the Lord Almighty says: 'Give careful thought to your ways.'" God imparts wisdom through His Holy Word so that you'll have all the information you need to make the right decisions along this difficult journey of life. Decide today to stop straddling the fence and choose God's kingdom . . . for your life depends on the choice you make.

Melt the Anger

Hatred stirs up strife, but love covers all sins.
Proverbs 10:12 (NKJV)

There are times when someone has hurt you so deeply that there is absolutely no desire within you to forgive. You start building a wall higher and higher, thicker and thicker, all because you don't want to give them the power to hurt you ever again. The fortress between you and your enemy provides the perfect environment for bitterness, anger, tears, and righteous indignation! You'll find it harder and harder to follow God's admonition in Matthew 18:21 where He says you should forgive seventy times seven!

But before you start feeling all justified for building your wall of defense, think about what Jesus would do. When He was here on earth, people lied about Him, spread rumors and gossip, and ultimately crucified Him on a cross for something He was not guilty of. Yet, through it all, He bore the pain in loving silence. Even as He hung on the cross, He prayed in Luke 23:34 (ESV), "Father, forgive them, for they know not what they do."

Instead of falling prey to the bondage of a heart hardened by hurt and betrayal, reach out to Jesus and ask Him to set you free by putting forgiveness in your heart. The Bible says in Matthew 6:15 (NIV), "But if you do not forgive others their sins, your Father will not forgive your sins." That's very serious because if God doesn't forgive your sins, you will miss out on eternal life! Absolutely nothing is worth missing out on heaven! Pray that you will love as God loves and allow Him to melt the anger in your heart and enjoy the sweet peace of forgiveness!

Burden-Lifter

"Peace I leave with you, My peace I give to you; not as the world gives do I give to you. Let not your heart be troubled, neither let it be afraid."

John 14:27 (NKJV)

During those dark days when everything seems to go wrong, instead of feeling sorry for yourself, trust God! Go to Jesus and tell Him all about it, praying, "Thank You, Lord, for this life lesson and the opportunity to trust You more. Show me what to do and give me more faith."

Trusting fully in Jesus is the only way to experience His sweet peace that will satisfy the longing in your heart. Knowing and believing that God has it all figured out and you don't have to worry about a thing . . . is such a burden-lifter! God has promised in Isaiah 26:3 to keep you in perfect peace, but in order to receive it, you must trust Him!

Satan would have you believe that peace is obtained through material possessions or human intervention. However, that is just another one of the devil's lies because real peace comes only from trusting your life to God and knowing He will work out all things for your good. Everyone talks about world peace, but that won't happen until Jesus comes. Until then, we can have *God's perfect peace* in our hearts!

Life is too short to live in fear, afraid for what tomorrow may bring. Leave the worrying to God and allow Him to be your *burden-lifter*. And don't forget to pray for more faith so that you can live each day with the full assurance that God has you covered—your life belongs to Him.

A Servant's Heart

Be of the same mind toward one another. Do not set your
mind on high things, but associate with the humble.
Do not be wise in your own opinion.

Romans 12:16 (NKJV)

Have you ever felt that there are some people who are just plain difficult to *love*? Perhaps you've encountered a demanding diner at a restaurant who yells at the waiter, commanding that his food be prepared to his liking. Usually, the person sitting across that table is cringing with embarrassment and would like to be anywhere but there! And then there is that person in line at the checkout counter who is loudly making known her displeasure that she must stand in line. The clerk can't bag up her purchases fast enough just to get her out of the store. And sometimes it's just more comfortable to write a check for the needy than to get sweaty, dirty, and tired helping those less fortunate.

Let's be honest—some people are easier to like than others, and it's much more difficult to be gracious when you are serving someone who thinks they are better than everyone else. But Jesus performed the ultimate act of humility when He knelt down and washed the dirty feet of His disciples—and in doing so, gave the best example of how to serve. There's no better example than that—of truly having a *servant's heart*. Let no job be so demeaning that you feel it is beneath you to help others. If the toilet needs unclogging, plunge it! If the floor is dirty, scrub it. And if the garbage is overflowing, throw it out! God created us to be equal. No one is better than anyone else, so be humble and always maintain a servant's heart!

Self-Loathing

*For You formed my inward parts . . . I will praise You,
for I am fearfully and wonderfully made; marvelous are
Your works, and that my soul knows very well. My frame
was not hidden from You, when I was made in secret,
and skillfully wrought in the lowest parts of the earth.*

Psalm 139:13-15 (NKJV)

Sadly, many people spend much of their lives hating themselves because they are not who they *wish* they were. Some resent the family they were born into or the color of their skin, while others want to be taller, skinnier, or better looking. Some are despondent and even angry because they have physical disabilities, while others blame God for not giving them good health. Others fall into despair thinking that when they lose weight, get a better job, or suddenly develop a dynamic personality, then they'll be happy.

Self-loathing is never productive, and, as long as Satan can keep you in a state of torment, then he wins! Instead of spending time hating all your shortcomings, embrace the person God made you to be! The Bible says in 2 Corinthians 10:12 (NKJV), "But they, measuring themselves by themselves, and comparing themselves among themselves, are not wise." Simply put, God doesn't make mistakes, and He loves His children all the same. Instead of wallowing in self-pity, put an end to self-loathing and learn to love the person God created you to be and then praise Him for His wonderful works.

God of Compassion

*As a father has compassion on his children, so the L*ORD
has compassion on those who fear him.

Psalm 103:13 (NIV)

Parents who love their children are full of compassion. If their child falls down, they comfort them, giving not only first-aid, but reassuring hugs as well. If a friend or family member calls with devastating news, you're quick to offer sympathies, consoling them with expressions of love, assuring them of how much you care, and offering to help. These are natural human responses toward those you love. The key word here is "love."

God loves *you* more than anyone else ever could, and He is longsuffering, gracious, loving, and compassionate toward you. When you're having a bad day or facing a crisis, God wants you to run to Him first! He alone is able to comfort you, restore you, and give you the strength that you need. And here's a big bonus: you can tell God anything, without fear of condemnation, abandonment, or worry that He will stop loving you. He is full of grace and mercy and offers not only comfort but promises of a better life with Him in heaven for all eternity! No one other than God can do that!

Whenever your heart is breaking, don't sink into depression or start playing the *blame game*. Instead, give your burden to Jesus and allow Him to heal your heart—for He is a *God of compassion* who loves you more than you could possibly know or comprehend!

Friendship with Jesus

"No longer do I call you servants, for a servant does not know what his master is doing; but I have called you friends, for all things that I heard from My Father I have made known to you."

John 15:15 (NKJV)

———◆———

Friendships are missing a key ingredient these days, and that is *loyalty*. It's harder and harder to find friends who you can trust and who are truly loyal—someone who will stick by you through thick and thin. So many people are just looking out for *number one*.

The Bible says in Proverbs 18:24 (KJV), "A man that hath friends must shew himself friendly: and there is a friend that sticketh closer than a brother." In other words, friendship is a give and take. If you want a friend, you must be friendly and have a kind, generous spirit towards the person you want to be friends with. God likens this kind of friendship as the kind of bond that siblings share—even closer than a family bond! Friends like this are to be treasured and valued.

Unfortunately, there are too many *fair-weather friends*—the kind of friend who is only your friend when things are going smoothly, but quickly turn on you at the first bump in the road. Thankfully, everyone can have the best friend ever . . . and that is Jesus Christ! He is loving, loyal, trustworthy, and will never turn His back on you. He will never leave you or forsake you for a moment! Oh, what a friend we have in Jesus!

Surviving the Storm

We are hard-pressed on every side, yet not crushed;
we are perplexed, but not in despair; persecuted, but not
forsaken; struck down, but not destroyed.

2 Corinthians 4:8-9 (NKJV)

Life is not perfect and never will be here on earth. As long as we breathe, we will go through trials and struggles and that won't change until we get to heaven. There are many promises in God's Word for us to claim as our own, but you won't find one promise where God says we will never experience heartache. However, the Bible does shed light on just how to survive any storm, no matter how severe.

Scripture tells of two different men on two different occasions who slept through a storm. One was Jonah—who was hiding in the bottom of a boat because he was running from God. When he awoke, his shipmates were running around in a panic, frantically trying to survive, and terrified that they would all die at sea. The other man asleep on a boat was Jesus— only He slept peacefully, fully secure that He was safe in His Father's care.

We can't stop or control the trials of life, but we can survive each storm by putting our faith and trust in our heavenly Father. The Bible says in Joshua 1:5 (ESV), "I will never leave you or forsake you." That is a promise we can claim! When we fully trust in God, we don't have to run around in a panic, but will experience a peace and calm . . . even in the middle of the most dangerous storm!

Holier than Thou

*You, therefore, have no excuse, you who pass judgment
on someone else, for at whatever point you judge
another, you are condemning yourself, because you who
pass judgment do the same things.*

Romans 2:1 (NIV)

God requires a clean, pure heart when serving Him, not
one filled with judgment, self-righteousness, pride, or
contempt. Sadly, all too often, well-meaning Christians actually
turn people away from God—all because their own hearts are
not filled with His love! Bottom line—you cannot share what
you do not have! If you really desire to serve Jesus, then you
need a *humble* heart! Pray as David did in Psalm 51:10 (KJV):
"Create in me a clean heart, O God; and renew a right spirit
within me." When you are witnessing, act as Jesus would—with
love, kindness, and mercy. The only way this is possible is when
you are filled with the Holy Spirit!

Always keep in mind that it is not *your* job to convict hearts.
It is God's job! A selfish, prideful spirit never draws people
closer to God! Just because you give generously to the church,
go to prayer meeting each week, or eat a vegan diet . . . does
not make you holier or better than anyone else! Approaching
someone with a *holier than thou* attitude will not only push
them further away from God, but you will be lost as well! There's
no such thing as *salvation by works*, for only Jesus can save you!
Remember, people don't need to *be like you* to be saved, they
need to be . . . *like Jesus!*

When God Says Yes

For the eyes of the Lord are on the righteous, and His ears are open to their prayers; but the face of the Lord is against those who do evil.

1 Peter 3:12 (NKJV)

The main reason for *prayer* is not to get things or for divine intervention in our lives. The most important reason to pray is to get to know God better. Keeping the lines of communication open with our heavenly Father is the key to a close relationship with Him, and the more we linger in His presence, the happier we will be.

However, many people pray only when they want something! Even if they haven't talked to God all year, they quickly drop to their knees when faced with a crisis, such as when a loved one becomes ill, when they are so financially strapped they don't know where to turn, or for a million other reasons. And as long as God says *yes* and their prayer is answered in the way that they want, they rejoice. But if their prayer isn't answered the way they want, then all of a sudden they are angry with God, even questioning His love for them! How sad it is that Christ's amazing act of love on Calvary is so quickly forgotten.

Instead of praying to *get things*, pray to *know* God. And don't forget to pray with complete faith that God will answer your prayer with your best interest in mind. Always pray for God's will to be done and thank Him for His answer—not just when He says *yes*, but all the time!

The Right Thing

But do not forget to do good and to share, for with such sacrifices God is well pleased.

Hebrews 13:16 (NKJV)

When life is overwhelming and it seems like the whole world is against you, cling to Jesus! Don't worry about what people are saying about you or what *others* are doing—just concentrate on how you are living *your* life and let your actions reflect Jesus. God gave a specific instruction on how to live a godly life and it is known as the "Golden Rule." You can find it in Matthew 7:12 (NKJV): "Therefore, whatever you want men to do to you, do also to them, for this is the Law and the Prophets."

When people are mean, be kind. When friends hurt you, forgive. Be honest, even when others have cheated you. Ignore gossip with loving silence. Choose to be happy, even on a bad day. Do your best, even if others criticize you; and love others, even if shown hatred. No matter what the devil throws at you, choose to be like Jesus. You'll always be doing the right thing when you take the *high road* because that is what God wants you to do.

Keeping Jesus in your heart will reflect His light to all those around you, even on your worst day. It's good to follow the counsel in Galatians 6:10 (ESV): "So then, as we have opportunity, let us do good to everyone." You'll not only be doing *the right thing*, but you'll be happier too, and best of all, others will see Jesus in you!

Stay Faithful

He heals the brokenhearted and binds up their wounds.
Psalm 147:3 (NKJV)

———◆———

God never promised that if you would follow Him, your life will be perfect. He never promised the sun would always shine or that you would never experience pain. The truth is, this journey here on earth is difficult and challenging. There are so many twists and turns to life, and through it all, it is critically important to stay focused on Jesus. The devil would like nothing better than to separate you from the only one who can save you, and he will stop at nothing to get your attention. Satan loves to plant seeds of doubt, especially when you are going through a crisis and are the most vulnerable. He loves to whisper his lies, encouraging you to blame God for your troubles. But Satan is the creator of sin and he gets all the credit for pain and heartache . . . not God!

Stay focused on your heavenly Father who loves you more than anyone else ever could! When you are in trouble, call upon Him for help. The Bible says in Psalm 34:17-19 (ESV), "When the righteous cry for help, the LORD hears and delivers them out of all their troubles. The LORD is near to the brokenhearted and saves the crushed in spirit. Many are the afflictions of the righteous, but the LORD delivers him out of them all." You don't have to be afraid of life's challenges, heartache, or pain, because you are never alone! Stay faithful and stay focused on the only one who can save you from all your trials, misery, and suffering . . . Jesus Christ, your Lord and Savior.

Silent Treatment

*Set a guard, O Lord, over my mouth; keep watch
over the door of my lips.*

Psalm 141:3 (NKJV)

There are some relationships that experience the *silent treatment* whenever one of the partners is not happy with the other. Instead of talking it out and reaching an understanding, they choose to *punish* their mate by not communicating with them. Sometimes this can go on for hours, days, or even weeks. Of course, the longer the silent treatment lasts, the more dangerous it is to the relationship. It's okay to take a break, think things through, and pray about it—but then open the door of communication as talking things out is always the best plan! It's never good to speak in anger, because, once spoken, those hateful words can never be erased.

There are times when silence is welcomed, as it gives each other a chance to cool off and think more clearly. Before Christ's crucifixion, when He was being accused of things He was not guilty of, He remained silent and never uttered a word to defend Himself. This is hard to comprehend, as it is human instinct to want vindication whenever falsely accused! We can learn a lot from Christ's example. Instead of defending ourselves with righteous indignation, we can pray silently for strength to see us through. It is through the quiet moments that we can feel God's presence the most. Set aside time to be silent—to meditate on God's Word, pray, reflect, and listen to the still, small voice of our Savior.

Emotional Roller Coaster

In the multitude of my anxieties within me,
your comforts delight my soul.

Psalm 94:19 (NKJV)

There are days when you just don't *feel* like your connection with God is what it should be. Perhaps you've slacked off on your prayer and worship time, or, for whatever reason, you're discouraged and feel like God is a million miles away. But, praise the Lord, you can rest assured that God's love for you and your love for Him is *not* based on feelings! When your emotions are like a runaway horse, pull back on the reins and refuse to let that horse get the best of you! Tell God what's on your heart and ask Him to help you—He will! Believe what God says and not what your fickle emotions are telling you, because your feelings are not an accurate measurement of reality.

When most people ask, "How are you?" they don't really want to hear anything other than, "Fine, thank you!" But God is not like *most* people! He is a God of love, and He truly cares and wants to hear more than a casual response. He is interested not only in *how you are*, but also *how you are feeling*!

Never feel embarrassed or awkward sharing your heart with your heavenly Father, for He loves you more than anyone else ever could. He not only cares—He has all the answers and is willing to meet your every need! You don't have to rely on your *feelings* to know if God is there, because He has promised in Joshua 1:9 (NKJV), "The LORD your God is with you wherever you go," and He always keeps His promises!

Strength of Gentleness

You have given me the shield of your
salvation, and your right hand supported me,
and your gentleness made me great.

Psalm 18:35 (ESV)

———◆———

Gentleness is often spoken about in the Bible and is one of the words used to describe Jesus' character. Yet, in today's society, being gentle is sometimes viewed in a negative way—as if you're weak or possibly even cowardly. But gentleness is a trait we should all strive for. It takes a lot of strength to respond with a gentle voice when someone is screaming at you. Gentleness is really *strength* that is released in an appropriate, controlled manner. It's especially important to be gentle when sharing your faith. No one wants to listen to someone pushy who comes off as a *know-it-all*!

Jesus was never a bully, nor did He preach in a loud, bossy, authoritative voice. He simply told the truth and allowed others to choose whether or not they would follow His teaching. The Bible says in Philippians 4:5 (NIV), "Let your gentleness be evident to all. The Lord is near." And in Colossians 3:12 (NIV), we're told, "Therefore, as God's chosen people, holy and dearly loved, clothe yourselves with compassion, kindness, humility, gentleness and patience." Determine today to be more like Jesus and treat others with courtesy, kindness, thoughtfulness, and respect—it is then that you'll discover the strength of gentleness.

Persevering Under Trials

Oh, give thanks to the LORD! Call upon His name;
make known His deeds among the peoples!

Psalm 105:1 (NKJV)

When things are going smoothly in your life, it's easy to praise Jesus! But when something earth-shattering shakes your world, the first human response is to cry, get discouraged, and blame God! Instead of falling apart and bursting into tears, the best thing to do is to praise God for all His goodness! When you step back and count your blessings, you see things from a different perspective and realize how much you have to be thankful for, in spite of all your troubles.

The Bible says in 1 Thessalonians 5:18 (NLT), "Be thankful in all circumstances." And in James 1:12 (NIV), we're told, "Blessed is the one who perseveres under trial because, having stood the test, that person will receive the crown of life that the Lord has promised to those who love him." Wow! God even calls it a blessing when we go through trials and stand faithful through the test.

It is during the tough times that you lean on Jesus the most! No matter what you're going through, if you look around, you'll see that you have much to be thankful for and life really isn't *that* bad after all! You'll also discover that someone else always has it worse than you do. So, the next time you find yourself in the midst of a storm, remember what God says about persevering under trials and instead of feeling sorry for yourself . . . count your blessings!

Not About Stuff

"Take heed and beware of covetousness, for one's life does not consist in the abundance of the things he possesses."

Luke 12:15 (NKJV)

When you are nearing the end of life's journey and you look back over the years thinking about all that you accomplished and regretting the things you wish you had, it becomes crystal clear what really matters most. It's really not important how fancy your house was, what kind of cars you drove, how prestigious the job you had, or how much money you had in the bank. Bottom line—it's not about *stuff*! When you're young, you think you've got your whole life in front of you and there's no sense of urgency about the importance of how you spend your time. But make no mistake—life is short. Before you know it, you will blink and find that you're the one looking back wondering how life went by so quickly.

The only way to ensure peace and satisfaction at the end of your days is to have lived your life surrendered to God. There's no better place to be than following God's plan for you—He knows your wants, dreams, and desires even more than you do. The Bible says in Jeremiah 29:11 (NIV), "'For I know the plans I have for you,' declares the LORD, 'plans to prosper you and not to harm you, plans to give you hope and a future.'"

It just doesn't get better than that! Make sure your future is secure by giving God control of your life starting today, because everlasting joy is all about trusting Jesus . . . and *not about stuff*!

Our Savior Lives

*"I am He who lives, and was dead, and behold,
I am alive forevermore. Amen. And I have the
keys of Hades and of Death."*

Revelation 1:18 (NKJV)

It's hard to imagine the depth of God's love for us. To think that He loved us so much that He sent His *only* Son, Jesus, to come to this earth to die on a cross, so that we might have eternal life with Him—*that* kind of love is unfathomable! And Jesus led a life without sin. His every thought, deed, and action were all because of His deep and abiding love for mankind. He gave and gave and gave—never asking for anything in return. He healed the sick, comforted the brokenhearted, and gave hope to the hopeless. He was gentle and kind to everyone, including those who lied about Him, mistreated Him, and betrayed Him. His heartfelt desire was that *no one* should perish, but that all would live in heaven with Him forever!

Jesus certainly did not deserve to be treated as a common criminal who was beaten unmercifully, ridiculed through the streets, and mocked even as He hung on the cross. Jesus could have changed His mind at any point, but He chose us! He chose to die so that we could live! He loved us *that* much!

When they laid Him in the tomb, His enemies thought they had won! But praise God, Jesus arose victorious from the tomb! Not even death could keep Him in the ground! Our Savior *lives*, and because He lives, we have a future in heaven with Him forever!

The Greatest Physician

"Those who are well have no need of a physician, but those who are sick. I did not come to call the righteous, but sinners, to repentance."

Mark 2:17 (NKJV)

When people become ill, the first thing they do is make an appointment with their doctor. And if the doctor doesn't know what's wrong, more than likely they'll call in a specialist. Sometimes it takes several different appointments at many different offices to determine the correct diagnosis, and it may take weeks or even months to get an appointment with just the doctor you need.

There is, however, *one* doctor who has a *no waiting* policy! You don't have to make an appointment in advance and no referrals are needed. No patient goes unseen and no insurance is required. In fact, all treatment is free of charge. But, the best news is . . . He is the greatest physician of all! He knows absolutely everything and has all the answers to whatever is ailing you!

Who is this incredible Physician, you ask? Well, His name is Jesus! Be sure and get a daily spiritual check up by spending time with Him. Tell Him all about how you are feeling—not just physically, but emotionally and spiritually as well. But don't just seek God when you are sick. Maintain a healthy, happy life by receiving His energizing boost of Holy Spirit power with your daily check up. It will give you the strength and courage to face whatever life brings. In fact . . . it's just what the doctor ordered!

Content with Uncertainty

He who is in you is greater than he who is in the world.

1 John 4:4 (NKJV)

———◈———

Living in a state of limbo takes a lot of patience and strength that can only come from God. Human weakness demands to know what is happening and when, but a real test of your faith comes from trusting God in all things—especially uncertainty. Not knowing what tomorrow will bring and being totally okay with that requires true faith and trust in God. The Bible even gives the secret to reaching this level of contentment in Philippians 4:11-13 (NIV): "I am not saying this because I am in need, for I have learned to be content whatever the circumstances. I know what it is to be in need, and I know what it is to have plenty. I have learned the secret of being content in any and every situation, whether well fed or hungry, whether living in plenty or in want. I can do all this through him who gives me strength."

You may not know what the future holds, but you do know who holds the future. So then you have nothing to fear! When you are walking close to Jesus, you can be spontaneous, joyful, excited, and content with uncertainty because your heavenly Father is with you every moment of the day. Claim His promise in Hebrews 13:5 (NIV): "Keep your lives free from the love of money and be content with what you have." Reach out and take God's hand today, trust Him with every aspect of your life, and be content with uncertainty.

Blocked by Fear

> " 'You will not need to fight in this battle.
> Position yourselves, stand still and see the salvation
> of the LORD, who is with you, O Judah and Jerusalem!'
> Do not fear or be dismayed; tomorrow go out against
> them, for the LORD is with you."
>
> 2 Chronicles 20:17 (NKJV)

One of the main reasons people do not accomplish their goals comes down to one word—fear! Sometimes just the mere thought of speaking out, getting up in front, meeting new people, applying for a job, or even asking for a raise is so far out of their *comfort zone* that fear shuts them down completely. There's no need to live in fear as it zaps your energy, keeps you locked in a prison of self-doubt, and prevents you from being all that God wants you to be! But there is a way of getting rid of all those *butterflies* fluttering in your stomach, and that is to give your fears to God. In return, He will give you His strength and confidence to go forward.

When you're blocked by fear, pray and ask God for an extra measure of courage to take on any task He gives you. You'll be surprised at how quickly fear will hastily retreat! Immediately, God will surround you with His sweet peace and all fear will melt away. Whenever you're afraid, claim Isaiah 41:10 (NKJV): "Fear not, for I am with you; be not dismayed, for I am your God. I will strengthen you, yes, I will help you." Help is only a prayer away!

With God's Love

"And whenever you stand praying, if you have anything
against anyone, forgive him, that your Father in heaven
may also forgive you your trespasses."

Mark 11:25 (NKJV)

When someone has mistreated you, hurt your feelings, or has wronged you, the best thing to do is forgive. Don't wait a year, a month, a day, or even an hour. Ask God to put forgiveness in your heart . . . immediately. The longer you harbor unforgiveness in your heart, the more miserable you will be! But even worse, if you don't forgive, you will lose all happiness on this earth and in the earth to come, because you won't be there. Jesus said in Matthew 6:15 (NIV), "But if you do not forgive others their sins, your Father will not forgive your sins." It doesn't get clearer than that!

Sometimes, the pain of injustice is so great that it is not humanly possible to forgive, much less love that person. Yet the Bible says in Luke 6:27 (NKJV), "But I say to you who hear: Love your enemies, do good to those who hate you." God wants you to love your fellow man . . . and not just those who are nice to you! He wants you to *love* your enemies too! So how can you possibly forgive when you've been hurt so deeply? The answer is . . . by asking God to put *love* in your heart, and then, love them with *God's love*! Yes, you can have the courage to forgive by claiming God's promise in Philippians 4:13 (NKJV): "I can do all things through Christ who strengthens me." God will give you the strength to forgive and love your enemies with His love.

Garbage In, Garbage Out

*Let us draw near with a true heart in full assurance of
faith, having our hearts sprinkled from an evil conscience
and our bodies washed with pure water.*

Hebrews 10:22 (NKJV)

———◆———

Do you find yourself in a *spiritual rut*—with your wheels spinning in one place and you just can't move forward in your walk with God? When that happens, it's usually because our hearts are filled with garbage! You know, the garbage of sin, otherwise known as the devil's tools of discouragement, such as anger, jealousy, resentment, unforgiveness, selfishness, or self-pity. All of that is just garbage in our hearts, weighing us down . . . and for some crazy reason we want to hang on to!

It just doesn't make sense why we have such a hard time letting go of the very things that separate us from God. The old expression "garbage in, garbage out" is so true. If we fill our hearts with resentment and anger, then that is what is going to come out in all our deeds and actions!

The Bible tells us how to keep our hearts pure in Psalm 119:9 (NIV): "How can a young person stay on the path of purity? By living according to your word." In other words, read God's Holy Word for strength to abide by His guidance. Pray David's prayer in Psalm 51:10 (NIV): "Create in me a pure heart, O God, and renew a steadfast spirit within me." Once we allow God to clean our hearts, we experience such an amazing transformation that no words can describe—true joy such as we have never known!

Decisions! Decisions!

Your word is a lamp to my feet and a light to my path.
Psalm 119:105 (NKJV)

Every day, we are faced with making decisions—some more critical than others. We usually don't get too stressed out about the insignificant ones, such as which parking spot to choose or what to eat for supper. But when faced with one of those life-changing decisions, then what are we to do? Of course, we discuss it with our spouse, family, or friends, but the *first* person we should go is to God! He alone knows the future, and more importantly, what is best for us!

The Bible says in James 1:5 (NKJV), "If any of you lacks wisdom, let him ask of God, who gives to all liberally and without reproach, and it will be given to him." In other words, God is telling us that we can come to Him for wisdom, guidance, and direction without fear of Him scolding us for bothering Him! God *wants* us to come to Him!

No need to spend sleepless nights worrying and pacing the floor in a fit of anxiety. You have full assurance that whatever happens, God's in control, and He will never let you down. Of course, it's up to you to follow where God's leading. In Psalm 32:8 (NKJV), we're told, "I will instruct you and teach you in the way you should go; I will guide you with My eye." It really doesn't get any clearer than that! We don't have to make decisions blindly—hoping that we make the right one! We can get the answers we need directly from our heavenly Father. And the best part is . . . God doesn't make mistakes!

Root of All Evil

No one can serve two masters. Either you will hate the one and love the other, or you will be devoted to the one and despise the other. You cannot serve both God and money.

Matthew 6:24 (NIV)

There's a Bible text about money that some people misunderstand the meaning of, simply by skipping over one little word . . . which totally changes the whole meaning! That very significant word is *love* and it's found in 1 Timothy 6:10 (NKJV): "For the love of money is a root of all kinds of evil." Now, here is where the confusion exists. Some Christians read this and say that money is a sin! But that is not what God is saying at all. It clearly states that the *love* of money is the root of all evil—not money itself. Hebrews 13:5 (NIV) tells us, "Keep your lives free from the love of money and be content with what you have."

It's impossible to have a close walk with Jesus if wealth is more important to you than anything else. In other words, how you value money and what you do with it is critically important spiritually. Truth is—you can find out quite a bit about a person by just looking at their checkbook! Now, of course, no one would ever dare to do that, but if you did, you would learn what's really important to that person. Do they spend it on video games, lottery tickets, movies, etc. or do they pay tithes and offerings, give to church evangelism, support Christian education, and donate to charities. Matthew 6:21 (NKJV) says, "For where your treasure is, there your heart will be also." Ask God to guard your heart so you won't develop a *love* of money.

A Broken Heart

"I will turn their mourning into joy; I will comfort them, and give them gladness for sorrow. . . . and my people shall be satisfied with my goodness, declares the LORD."

Jeremiah 31:13-14 (ESV)

When you are sad, discouraged, or brokenhearted, it's human nature to reach out to a friend for comfort. Somehow, just telling someone who cares about you seems to make things a little better. It doesn't mean your faith in God is diminished because you reached out for human comfort. There's nothing wrong with sharing your troubles and receiving support from earthly friends. In fact, the Bible encourages it. But don't replace God's comfort for that of others, because the comfort that God provides is so much more satisfying than anything a friend on earth can provide. Jesus is both our Savior and our friend.

Keep in mind that God sees the *big picture* and knows what is best for us. Don't get discouraged when going through life's trials—for being a Christian doesn't mean you'll never feel the pain of a broken heart. The Bible says that even Jesus "wept."

Although Jesus knew the future, He had complete faith in His heavenly Father and He knew God would win the battle— yet Jesus still grieved for his children. Jesus is the only healer of hearts and the only one who can give real and lasting peace, joy, healing, and happiness.

Freedom of Choice

"Behold, I stand at the door and knock. If anyone hears My voice and opens the door, I will come in to him and dine with him, and he with Me."

Revelation 3:20 (NKJV)

The main reason for prayer is to have a personal relationship with our heavenly Father. Some people pray only when they are in trouble or when they want something. If God doesn't answer just the way they think He should, they feel He isn't real, or He doesn't care, or that prayer *doesn't work*! But It doesn't mean that God didn't hear you or doesn't love you. Sometimes, no matter how hard we pray, things don't turn out the way we hoped!

For instance, if we are praying for a loved one to give their heart to Jesus, we must remember that God will not change another person's will. He has given all of us *freedom of choice* and that person is free to choose whether to do right or wrong. No amount of praying will make God *force* His will on them! But we can continue praying intercessory prayers for the Holy Spirit to keep working on their heart!

Adult parents who have prayed for years for the salvation of their children may never see their prayers answered in their lifetime. But keep praying, because God will honor those prayers long after they have passed away. It won't be until Jesus comes that they learn their children gave their hearts to Jesus! So, be faithful with your prayers and don't forget to trust God with the answers . . . for He alone knows what's best.

Quit Complaining

*If then you were raised with Christ, seek those
things which are above, where Christ is, sitting at the
right hand of God. Set your mind on things above,
not on things on the earth.*

Colossians 3:1-2 (NKJV)

Have you ever heard someone go on and on about how terrible their life is? They have nothing positive to say and no matter how encouraging you try to be, they insist on seeing the dark side of life, as if they enjoy wallowing in their misery. After a while, no one really wants to be around all that negativity! Christians should be the most positive people on the planet! We have the blessed hope of a soon coming Savior . . . and eternal life with Jesus! Now that's something to get excited about and look forward to!

No matter how bad it gets, we have no reason to feel sorry for ourselves, because God has everything under control, and He has a better life planned for us! Even the person who seems to have lost everything still has *something* for which to praise Jesus! Most people if given the chance to swap out their problems for someone else's, would say, "No thanks! I'll keep my own." There's always someone who is dealing with a whole lot more heartache than we are. Learn to be grateful for the things we often take for granted such as God's love and protection, His faithfulness, and most of all, for sending His Son, Jesus, to die on a cross so that we might have eternal life with Him! So let's quit complaining . . . and start praising Jesus!

Throw Out Legalism

*Therefore by the deeds of the law no flesh will be justified in
His sight, for by the law is the knowledge of sin.*

Romans 3:20 (NKJV)

There are some Christians who worship God because they are trying to work their way to heaven. Bible study and prayer become something obligatory to do in order to prove to God they deserve to be saved. *Good deeds* becomes a check-off list they can proudly show to the King of the Universe. Some even think if they eat a vegan diet, *then* . . . they will for sure get their personal ticket to eternity! But there's no such thing as *salvation by diet*!

Once our spiritual life becomes *legalistic*, we are lost. In this misguided state, it becomes easy to view God as a harsh judge, just waiting to sentence us to eternal damnation. But God is not a gloating, legalistic God who cheers when we fall. Nor is He expecting us to be perfect. We are all sinners. Our Lord and Savior doesn't want anyone to perish! This is confirmed in John 3:16 (NKJV): "For God so loved the world that He gave His only begotten Son, that whoever believes in Him should not perish but have everlasting life."

We need to understand that we can't *earn* or *buy* our way to heaven! There is only *one* way and that is through the blood of Jesus Christ! Do the right thing . . . for the right reason! In other words, we should serve God because we love Him—throwing legalism out the window!

In Christ Alone

Nor is there salvation in any other, for there is no other name under heaven given among men by which we must be saved.

Acts 4:12 (NKJV)

The lyrics to a song written in 2002 by Stuart Townend and Keith Getty beautifully express the reassurance we have when we belong to Jesus Christ, our Lord and Savior. "In Christ alone my hope is found; He is my light, my strength, my song; this Cornerstone, this solid ground, firm through the fiercest drought and storm. . . . No guilt in life, no fear in death—this is the pow'r of Christ in me; from life's first cry to final breath, Jesus commands my destiny. No pow'r of hell, no scheme of man, can ever pluck me from His hand; till He returns or calls me home—here in the pow'r of Christ I'll stand."

There are people we have looked up to as pillars of our church, but when they were faced with hardship and trials, they crumbled beneath the load. We are crushed when we learn that a Christian brother or sister submitted to the temptations of Satan, but the truth is, we are all human and make mistakes—no one belongs on a pedestal except God! Christ and Christ alone is our hope and strength . . . and our only example of how to live a godly life! When we place our faith and trust in humans, we will be disappointed, but God will never let us down or forsake us! God's love is eternal and unchanging—unaffected by what is happening in the world around us! Our security rests firmly *in Christ alone.*

Enjoying Your Work

*This is what I have seen to be good: it is fitting to eat
and drink and find enjoyment in all the toil with
which one toils under the sun the few days of the life
God gives us; for this is our lot.*

Ecclesiastes 5:18 (NRSV)

God is pleased when you work hard, but He doesn't base His love for you on how much you make or how prestigious your position. Instead, He values your honesty, integrity, patience, and trustworthiness. God looks inward, because a heart filled with joy produces peace and fulfillment in all aspects of your life—including in your work! The Bible says in Philippians 4:11 (NKJV), "Not that I speak in regard to need, for I have learned in whatever state I am, to be content."

Although work is needed to provide income for daily living, God doesn't intend for it to be a drudgery. When you allow Jesus to dwell in your heart, no matter the task, there is joy. Whether deadlines, household chores, exams, or an endless to-do list, do everything to the glory of God. You'll find your day will go a whole lot better with a song in your heart, even in spite of a demanding boss, irritating co-workers, or an unpleasant task.

Instead of dreading getting out of bed in the morning, take time for spiritual food. Pray and ask God to fill you with His joy, then follow God's advice in Ecclesiastes 9:10 (NKJV): "Whatever your hand finds to do, do it with your might; for there is no work or device or knowledge or wisdom in the grave where you are going."

Family Love

Love suffers long and is kind; love does not envy; love does not parade itself, is not puffed up . . . does not rejoice in iniquity, but rejoices in the truth; bears all things, believes all things, hopes all things, endures all things.

1 Corinthians 13:4-7 (NKJV)

How we live our lives each day has a big impact on all those around us, especially our families. It makes sense because they are the ones that we spend the most time with. If we want to shine for Jesus, we need to first start at home! Our attitude, the decisions we make, and how we react to day-to-day situations show whether or not Christ is living in us.

Sometimes we make an effort to be kind to strangers, but then come home and act quite differently with those we claim to love the most. Living a Christ-centered life doesn't mean that you act like a Christian all day long, and then when you get home, you throw your *Christian cap* on the hook and become grumpy and rude!

God wants you to shine for Him all the time, especially at home! How you treat others defines your character, so ask yourself, *Am I kind and thoughtful or am I quick to respond in an irritated tone?* When arguments and tempers start to rise, call on Jesus to give you the strength to respond in love. With Christ as the center of the home, family ties are the strongest and so is family love!

December 12

Trials and Troubles

*Be still, and know that I am God; I will be exalted among
the nations, I will be exalted in the earth!*

Psalm 46:10 (NKJV)

There seems to be no way to escape the daily pressures of life—too much work to do, too many bills to pay, too many heartaches, too much conflict . . . and on and on! There's just no end to the busy hustle and bustle and the constant struggles of never having enough money in the bank and never being able to *get a break*. Is every cell in your body pleading for relief from all the stress? Do you long for quietness and peace? Jesus is ready and willing to give you the peace that you seek. His arms are open wide just waiting for you to run to Him.

No matter how much stress is in your life, don't allow it to pull you away from the awareness of God's love. The Bible says in Romans 8:38-39 (NIV), "For I am convinced that neither death nor life, neither angels nor demons, neither the present nor the future, nor any powers, neither height nor depth, nor anything else in all creation, will be able to separate us from the love of God that is in Jesus Christ our Lord."

Whatever trials or troubles are increasing the stress in your life, don't go running for the anti-anxiety pills. The best stress reliever of all is *Jesus*! He alone knows the future and what is best for you, so you have nothing to worry about—God's got you covered. Give Him all your worries as well as your wants and desires. Then, relax and trust Jesus to do what's best.

Heart to Heart

Jesus said to him, "If you can believe, all things are possible to him who believes."

Mark 9:23-24 (NKJV)

Too often we pray without faith. Instead, we pray *hoping . . . hoping . . . hoping . . .* that God will answer our prayers, but not fully believing that He will! Some question why there is a need to pray at all because God *knows* our thoughts. And this is true—God does know our thoughts, but He *responds* to our prayers!

It is an incredible privilege that God has made it possible to speak to Him directly. We don't need to have anyone else talk to God *for* us, since God has made provision to talk with Him heart-to-heart, one-on-one! How amazing that we can communicate so closely with the King of the Universe! But when we pray, we need to pray with faith, believing that God hears, listens, and answers!

The Bible says in Matthew 21:22 (NKJV), "And whatever things you ask in prayer, believing, you will receive." And in Hebrews 11:6 (NKJV), we're told; "But without faith it is impossible to please Him, for he who comes to God must believe that He is, and that He is a rewarder of those who diligently seek Him."

God wants us to come to Him with our praise, as well as our burdens and heartaches, and the best part is that He is trustworthy! We can tell God things that we wouldn't dream of telling anyone else, and He will lead and guide us in the right way. Always pray believing— with God all things are possible!"

God's Affirmation

*But encourage one another daily, as long as it
is called "Today," so that none of you may be
hardened by sin's deceitfulness.*

Hebrews 3:13 (NIV)

———◆———

An encouraging word goes a long way in lifting the spirits
of others. Whether you are affirmed by a friend, family
member, or even a stranger, there is power in encouragement!
Everyone needs to know they are doing a good job, that they
matter, and that they are loved! Feeling *needed* and *useful* are
important ingredients for healthy self-esteem. Without them,
you become extra critical of yourself, start doubting your
abilities, and begin feeling useless, wondering why you even
exist in this world! Soon your imagination runs wild and you
spiral out of control!

Letting others know that you appreciate them is an
instant morale booster. However, it's important to give honest
compliments as being *fake* will not only backfire, but make you
untrustworthy, and pretty soon no one will believe you . . . even
when your comments are made with sincerity. It's good to have
a strong support system of friends who you can count on to
always be there for you and lift you up. But never forget that
God is the best friend you could possibly have.

When you are filled with self-doubt wondering if you
matter, look to Jesus. He will give you the encouragement you
need so that the ice of self-doubt will melt away! God's healing
balm of affirmation is better than any compliment you could
ever receive!

Garden of Hurt

See to it that no one fails to obtain the grace of God;
that no root of bitterness springs up and causes trouble,
and through it many become defiled.

Hebrews 12:15 (NRSV)

There's only one remedy for removing bitterness and pain from your life and that is *forgiveness*. Living with resentment and anger is a miserable existence, and, if left to grow, destroys your very soul. It ruins all relationships, including current *and* future ones, and leaves you lost and empty. Holding on to *justified anger* will choke the very life right out of you. It doesn't matter if you *don't deserve it* or *it wasn't fair*—that's not an excuse to be bitter.

The truth is, God loves you even more than you could imagine and He wants to give you His sweet peace that you seek. But in order to receive it, you must plow under that *garden of hurt* and ask God to replace it with His sweet forgiveness. The Bible says in Colossians 3:8 (NRSV), "But now you must get rid of all such things—anger, wrath, malice, slander, and abusive language from your mouth."

Sometimes the pain is so deep, it's not humanly possible to let go. If that is how you're feeling, run to Jesus' outstretched arms and receive His love and forgiveness. He is able to take away all hatred for even your worst enemies and replace it with a godly love. And here's the good news: instead of pain and bitterness, you'll experience God's perfect peace, and the garden of hurt in your heart will be replaced with beautiful, fragrant flowers of love!

December 16

True Humility

When pride comes, then comes disgrace, but with
humility comes wisdom.

Proverbs 11:2 (NIV)

———◆———

God wants us to be humble. Ephesians 4:2 (NIV) says, "Be completely humble and gentle; be patient, bearing with one another in love." Yet there are some people who think if they are humble, then they are in a position of weakness. But true humility is just the opposite—it is a position of strength, because it takes Holy Spirit power to remain humble.

However, it does not mean that to be humble you must grovel or enable and endure cruelty. There is a huge difference between humility and groveling. For instance, when Jesus performed the first ordinance of humility, He *washed* the disciples' feet, He didn't lick them! God doesn't expect His children to be doormats or to be bullied. There are some men in this world who mistake their Christian duty as *head of the household,* and instead of leading in a Christlike manner, they are demanding, arrogant, pushy, and abusive.

It is not God's plan for wives to take such abuse, although there are many precious women of God who endure the suffering because they mistakenly feel it is their Christian duty to do so. How sad that they are so deceived. Jesus was humble, yet strong. He faced His enemies with a silent, kind, and gentle manner, all the while standing firm and strong. Even during the events leading up to His crucifixion, He took each blow with quiet dignity—never once raising His voice in anger. Follow Christ's example and experience *true humility*.

Heart Changer

What causes fights and quarrels among you? Don't they come from your desires that battle within you? You desire but do not have, so you kill. You covet but you cannot get what you want, so you quarrel and fight. You do not have because you do not ask God

James 4:1-2 (NIV)

Any long-term relationship will experience difficult times. It's inevitable that you will not always see things eye-to-eye. It doesn't matter whether it's a family member, long-time friend, roommate, coworker, or a spouse, there will be times of disagreement. That's because we all have our own agendas, dreams, and goals, and then when you add selfishness to the plate . . . it is a recipe for trouble! The only way to get through these times of stress is to lean on Jesus! He *is* the only real *heart changer* because only God can change hearts!

The only way to get beyond competing desires . . . is prayer! Ask God to give you more love in your heart for those you are experiencing conflict with. You can also pray and ask God to change the hearts of those you are praying for—because God is the one and only, Heart Changer!

The Bible says in Ephesians 4:3 (NIV), "Make every effort to keep the unity of the Spirit through the bond of peace." Our God is a God of love, and He wants His children to be like Him—reflecting His love to others! Why not call on the Heart Changer . . . today!

A Stumbling Block

"Let your light so shine before men, that they may see your good works and glorify your Father in heaven."

Matthew 5:16 (NKJV)

People make choices every day but seldom stop and think about the effects their decisions will have on those around them. When you choose a wrong path, you are not the only one who will get hurt, for others will suffer because of your mistakes as well. The Bible says in 1 Corinthians 12:26 (NKJV), "If one member suffers, all the members suffer."

As a follower of Christ, your life should always be a living example of His love, and God wants you to be a witness to all those you come in contact with. When you fall, it will cause others to fall too. There's an incredible responsibility that comes with being a Christian. Acts 1:8 (NKJV) says, "You shall be witnesses to Me." and in Romans 14:7 (NKJV), we're told, "None of us lives to himself." God wants us to love, support, and encourage each other. It's not enough to accept Christ for your Savior and then just keep Him all to yourself! God wants you to share His love with others, and that is pretty tough to do if you are living a life with one foot in the church and the other one on the devil's playground.

Choose to live a godly life and don't allow spiritual weakness to cause your brother to fall. It's very clear in 1 Corinthians 8:9 (KJV): "But take heed lest by any means this liberty of yours become a stumbling block to them that are weak." When you are weak, God is strong. He will defeat your enemies and give you wisdom to make the right choices.

Move Your Feet

"The sheep hear his voice; and he calls his own sheep by name and leads them out. And when he brings out his own sheep, he goes before them; and the sheep follow him, for they know his voice."

John 10:3-4 (NKJV)

When you are trying to make an important decision and you don't know which way to turn, drop to your knees and pray for wisdom. If you are sincerely wanting your prayer answered, you need to be willing to listen for God's direction, and then go where He tells you to go. You can't expect God to guide your footsteps if you are unwilling to move your feet! In other words, you need to follow where God is leading.

Too many times people pray and ask for *God's direction*, but what they expect is for God to give them what *they* want. Standing still and hanging on to what *you* want to do is not going to take you in the direction where God is leading. And never forget that God will never take you down the wrong path! You are always safe when following Jesus! The Bible tells us in Proverbs 3:5-6 (NASB), "Trust in the LORD with all your heart and do not lean on your own understanding. In all your ways acknowledge Him, and He will make your paths straight."

Pray as David did in Psalm 143:10 (NKJV), "Teach me to do Your will, for You are my God; let Your good Spirit lead me on level ground." This journey on earth is a dangerous one, filled with the devil's evil distractions, and the only way to survive is by following where our Savior leads.

Totally Committed

*But God, who is rich in mercy, because of His great
love with which He loved us, even when we were dead in
trespasses, made us alive together with Christ
(by grace you have been saved).*

Ephesians 2:4-5 (NKJV)

Our God is 100% totally committed in His love for us. When He gave His only Son to come to this earth and die so that we might live, He didn't just die for *some* of His children, or for just a few of His favorites. He loves us all unconditionally and with His whole heart! He doesn't do anything halfway! He doesn't listen to just a few of our prayers whenever He feels like it or protect us only half the time! Jesus didn't come to this earth, look around, and say, "Nope, I changed my mind. I'm going home." Had He done that, all of us would be eternally lost—with absolutely no hope for a future!

God loves us with an everlasting, unending, and amazing love that is far beyond our comprehension. He doesn't just love us *part-time*, when we are doing everything He wants us to do. No, He loves us, even when we mess up, do the wrong thing, and get into trouble, for God hates the sin, but loves the sinner! You see, He loves us *no matter what*! Just as God loves us, He wants us to return His love and give our hearts completely to Him! He doesn't want us to love Him with half our hearts, choosing to sin part of the time and serving God whenever we *feel* like it! Choose today to give God your whole heart and be 100% totally committed to Him!

The Rule Book

For whatever things were written before were written for our learning, that we through the patience and comfort of the Scriptures might have hope.

Romans 15:4 (NKJV)

Whenever playing a new game, it's necessary to read the rule book in order to know just how to play the game. If you don't know the rules, your chances of a successful outcome are pretty slim. This journey of life is a difficult one, but fortunately, God wrote the "Rule Book," which sets the guidelines for a joy-filled, meaningful life.

When you read God's Holy Word, you learn what dangers to avoid, how to make good choices, and avoid disaster. But even more important, you learn how to live a life that leads to eternal life with your Lord and Savior. Without God's Rule Book, you would never know right from wrong, or how to avoid the things that hurt yourself or endanger others. God's Word has the answer for every situation. If you're confused the Bible brings clarity. When you're broken hearted—His Words bring comfort and when you don't know which way to turn—the Holy Scriptures provide wisdom and discernment.

Understanding God's Rule Book requires prayerfully spending time pondering and digesting each word and when you do—you'll become more balanced, enlightened, strengthened and walk with new purpose—because the Bible is God's guiding light, and nourishment for your soul.

Envy Rots the Bones

You are still worldly. For since there is jealousy and quarreling among you, are you not worldly? Are you not acting like mere humans?

1 Corinthians 3:3 (NIV)

———◆———

Sometimes people are so unhappy with their own life, they become jealous of all the good things happening to everyone else. The green-eyed monster appears when their neighbor comes home with an expensive car, a friend buys a beautiful home, or a family member gets a big promotion at work. Before long, they get downright resentful, actually believing it should have happened to them instead. They begin to question God, demanding to know why they were not blessed like everyone else. Jealousy is a dangerous, slippery slope! It brings misery, heartache, pain . . . and even worse—it will separate us from Jesus!

Bottom line—there's no room for jealousy in a Christian's life! The Bible makes it very clear how God feels about jealousy. Proverbs 14:30 (NIV) says, "A heart at peace gives life to the body, but envy rots the bones." There's no reason to envy anyone, for God made each of us special and unique. We can shine for Him just the way He made us . . . for we are all beautiful in His eyes! The only way to eliminate envy is to ask God for a clean pure heart and to replace all jealousy with His perfect love.

Let It Go

A fool vents all his feelings, but a wise man holds them back.
Proverbs 29:11 (NKJV)

———◆———

When someone has treated you unfairly or done something to hurt you or someone you love, your first response is usually fueled by fiery rage! The sting of injustice immediately reaches out to push your anger button—but before you do, remember that how you respond is a choice. Ephesians 4:26 (NIV) says, "In your anger do not sin." And in verse 31, the message is clear: "Get rid of all bitterness, rage and anger, brawling and slander, along with every form of malice."

You can choose to get mad and lie awake at night thinking of ways to even the score—or you can just *let it go*. The Bible says in James 1:19-20 (NIV), "My dear brothers and sisters, take note of this: Everyone should be quick to listen, slow to speak and slow to become angry, because human anger does not produce the righteousness that God desires."

It not only displeases God when you let your temper flare, but it won't make you feel any better either! When you find yourself in a situation that takes every ounce of strength not to explode with anger, stop . . . take a breath, and then just let it go! Give all your hurt and pain to Jesus, and ask Him to put forgiveness in your heart for those who did you wrong. You'll be surprised at how much better you'll feel without carrying around that heavy burden. And best of all—you'll be pleasing God!

Pity-Party Train

*Then Jesus said to His disciples, "If anyone desires to come
after Me, let him deny himself, and take up his cross, and
follow Me. For whoever desires to save his life will lose it,
but whoever loses his life for My sake will find it."*

Matthew 16:24-25 (NKJV)

Everyone has a *down day* now and then—the kind of day
when everything goes wrong and nothing turns out quite
the way you had hoped. And when discouragement sets in, self-
loathing seems to comes along for the ride as well. But your
emotions don't determine the kind of person you are and your
feelings about yourself are rarely an accurate measurement of
what is *real*.

When the pity-party train rolls in, resist the urge to jump
aboard! Instead, cling to Jesus, who loves you even when you're
having a down day. Just one second in God's presence will calm
your nerves and lift your spirits. The Bible says in Joshua 1:9
(NIV), "Do not be afraid; do not be discouraged, for the Lord
your God will be with you wherever you go." And in John 14:1
(KJV), we're told, "Let not your heart be troubled: ye believe in
God, believe also in me."

Don't beat yourself up because you're discouraged! You're
human, and it's only natural that there will be times when you
just don't like yourself very much. Someone once said, "A minor
setback is preparing you for a major comeback!" Whenever the
dark fog of discouragement begins to roll in, just remember
that even on your worst day . . . Jesus loves you!

The Perfect Gift

"For the Son of Man has come to seek and to save that which was lost."

Luke 19:10 (NKJV)

———⟨◆⟩———

Christmas is a day that young and old look forward to—eagerly anticipating the long tradition of opening presents! Each beautifully wrapped box represents hours of thought, preparation, and shopping—all with the hope that it will be just the perfect gift for their loved one. However, even though the act of gift giving is motivated by love, it is often not received in the way we would hope, as evidenced by the long lines at the return counter the day after Christmas. Those lines tell the story that, for many, it was the wrong gift!

God gave us the ultimate gift when He sent His only Son to this earth as a tiny baby. He grew up sinless and without fault, but died on a cross for our sins so that we could have eternal life with Him. There is no greater gift than the gift of *salvation*! But there is one gift we can give, and it's such a perfect gift. That gift is *our hearts*. But God won't force us because He wants us to willingly surrender to Him. And once we give our hearts to Jesus, one way to let Him know how much we love and appreciate Him is to *thank Him*.

God loves to hear our praises, our gratitude, and our acknowledgment that He is our Lord and Savior and King of the Universe. He also loves for us to talk with Him, telling Him our needs, wants, and desires. Won't you give God the perfect gift today?

What a Day!

Nevertheless we, according to His promise, look for new heavens and a new earth in which righteousness dwells.

2 Peter 3:13 (NKJV)

When you are going through the deepest valley of your life and it seems as if your heartache will never end, remind yourself that this world is not your home. Life here on earth . . . is temporary! Whatever is causing your pain won't last long because Jesus is coming soon and will put an end to all sorrow, tears, heartache, and death!

The words to the familiar hymn "What a Day That Will Be" by Jim Hill expresses so beautifully how wonderful it will be when we get to heaven. The words go like this: "There's coming a day when no heartaches shall come; no more clouds in the sky, no more tears to dim the eye; all is peace forever more, on that happy golden shore; what a day, glorious day that will be. What a day that will be when my Jesus I shall see, when I look upon His face, the one who saved me by His grace; when He takes me by the hand and leads me to the promised land; what a day, glorious day that will be. There will be no sorrows there, and no more burdens to bear; no more sickness and no more no pain; no more parting over there; and forever I will be with the one who died for me; what a day, glorious day that will be."

So no matter what the devil throws at you, don't be discouraged or even entertain the idea of giving up, because soon and very soon, we will be in heaven forever with our Lord and Savior . . . and what a day that will be!

God's Gift of Grace

*You therefore, my son, be strong in the grace that is in
Christ Jesus. And the things that you have heard from
me among many witnesses, commit these to faithful men
who will be able to teach others also.*

2 Timothy 2:1-2 (NKJV)

God's amazing grace cannot be purchased, won, bartered, or
earned. It is a gift that God gives freely to all His children,
even though none are deserving. The Bible says in Ephesians
2:8-9 (NKJV), "For by grace you have been saved through faith,
and that not of yourselves; it is the gift of God, not of works,
lest anyone should boast." Upon receiving His grace, God wants
you to extend that same mercy to others.

Whenever someone has done you wrong, it is human nature
to want revenge. But when Christ lives within you, there is no
need for a *human-instinct* response, because as a child of God
you have access to the supernatural powers of the King of the
Universe, which transcends all natural human emotions, deeds,
or actions. Once the Holy Spirit has worked within you to show
undeserved kindness to your fellow man, you will experience
incredible joy, peace, and happiness which supersedes any
"good" feeling that revenge could possibly bring.

No matter what the circumstance, God will give you
sufficient *grace* for you to lavish on even your worst enemy! You
can claim God's promise in Psalm 84:11 (NKJV): "The LORD
will give grace and glory; no good thing will He withhold from
those who walk uprightly."

Doubting Thomas

"And this is the will of Him who sent Me, that everyone who sees the Son and believes in Him may have everlasting life; and I will raise him up at the last day."

John 6:40 (NKJV)

———◆———

When Jesus arose from the tomb, it was Thomas, one of Jesus' disciples, who could not bring himself to believe that Jesus was indeed alive! Even though his fellow disciples testified that *they* had actually seen Him, Thomas refused to believe. In John 20:25 (NKJV), Thomas declared, "Unless I see in His hands the print of the nails, and put my finger into the print of the nails, and put my hand into His side, I will not believe." It wasn't until eight days later, when Jesus appeared in a room full of His disciples, that Thomas believed. Jesus walked over to Him and said, "Reach your finger here, and look at My hands; and reach your hand here, and put it into My side. Do not be unbelieving, but believing."

Immediately, Thomas cried out, "My Lord and my God!" His declaration was personal! Instead of just being *someone's* Lord, Thomas claimed Jesus as *his* Lord. When you call Jesus "Lord," you are surrendering to Him, showing respect and recognizing His position as *Lord of your life*! Jesus wants all His children to believe in Him as our Savior and follow Him as our Lord! Don't be a doubting Thomas; instead, trust fully in Christ. There is plenty of biblical evidence to support that our God is real, and He died on a cross so that we can spend all eternity with Him in heaven.

God's Perfect Timing

To everything there is a season, a time for
every purpose under heaven.

Ecclesiastes 3:1 (NKJV)

It's human nature to be impatient, not wanting to stand in line at the bank or sit in the waiting room wondering when your name will be called. It's can be frustrating when sending an email and then having to wait for a response. And when you have to wait for a test result that will determine your fate, ten minutes can seem like a lifetime!

But God's timing is perfect, for, after all, He is the Creator of time! He alone knows the end from the beginning and what will make us happy. He also knows when our hearts are ready to receive the blessings He has in store for us. The Bible says in Ecclesiastes 3:11 (NKJV), "He has made everything beautiful in its time. Also He has put eternity in their hearts, except that no one can find out the work that God does from beginning to end." It's not our job to *know* the future—it's our job to *trust* God to do what's best for us. Many times if God gave us *what* we wanted *when* we wanted, it would be a disaster!

God's Holy Word makes it very clear that man's timing and God's timing is completely different! In 2 Peter 3:8 we're told, "But, beloved, do not forget this one thing, that with the Lord one day is as a thousand years, and a thousand years as one day." The best thing to do is trust God in all things—and yes, that includes His perfect timing!

Open My Eyes, Lord

*"Let not your heart be troubled; you believe
in God, believe also in Me."*

John 14:1 (NKJV)

———◆———

Sometimes we are so blinded by our own pain that we don't see God's blessings, and, worse, we often miss out on opportunities God gives us. Many times we get frustrated and even angry when life doesn't work out the way we want. But the Bible says in James 1:2-4 (NKJV), "My brethren, count it all joy when you fall into various trials, knowing that the testing of your faith produces patience. But let patience have its perfect work, that you may be perfect and complete, lacking nothing." It's easy to be so focused on our own problems that we can't see what God is trying to show us.

Even the disciples struggled with this, for when Jesus hung on the cross, even though He warned them his time on earth was short, they were completely shocked and devastated when He died! When their eyes were opened to the truth, they realized that Jesus' death wasn't the worst thing that could happen—it was the *best*, because Jesus paid the price for sin and made it possible to have eternity with their Lord and Master.

It's so important to spend time with God each day, because when we do, He allows us to see beyond our own trials and heartache to the beautiful plan He has for our lives. So, pray each day, "Open my eyes, Lord."

Time for Reflection

Only be careful, and watch yourselves closely so that you do not forget the things your eyes have seen or let them fade from your heart as long as you live. Teach them to your children and to their children after them.

Deuteronomy 4:9 (NIV)

Today is a good day to look back over the year and take stock of how you spent the last twelve months. It's good to savor the memories of all the special moments, as well as think about what you could have done differently during all the difficult ones. Sometimes, looking back can be painful, especially if there was the loss of a loved one, the end of a relationship, or a particularly sad event that took place—but even in those dark times, it's still good to think about and remember how God carried you through every trial.

Once you have walked down memory lane, it's time to make your resolutions for the coming year. Determine with *God's help* not to make the same mistakes as in the past and ask Him to guide your every step going forward. Make a commitment to spend more time each day worshiping and praising God. Prayerfully lean on the Holy Spirit to guide all of your actions, and don't forget to pray for strength—because without God's power, you will fail miserably. When you are powered by the Holy Spirit, you will face each trial differently. You'll have strength to remain calm in the midst of each difficult challenge, kind when faced with harshness, and forgiving when mistreated. So, go forward into the new year resolving to draw even closer to your Lord and Savior, giving Him your whole heart.

Index

Other books by Brenda Walsh available at
www.brendawalsh.com

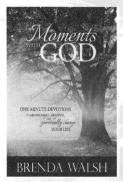

Moments with God
Brenda Walsh / Hardcover / 384 p.

This daily devotional book by Brenda Walsh is filled with timeless inspirational messages that you can read from cover to cover or use the index to choose a topic that speaks to your life for that day. Each page flows with encouragement, hope, and love that will lift your heart toward heaven. **(Also available in audiobook.)**

Battered to Blessed
Brenda Walsh with Kay D. Rizzo / Paperback / 222 p.

Brenda Walsh tells a gripping and powerful story of her personal experience with domestic violence and amazing grace. Battered to Blessed is Brenda's amazing journey from pain to peace and living a whole new life of incredible joy in Jesus! **(Also available in Spanish and an audiobook version.)**

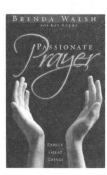

Passionate Prayer
Brenda Walsh / Paperback / 331 p.

Brenda Walsh is one who has learned by experience the power of passionate prayer. This book is filled with miracle stories of God's intervention in her life and the lives of those for whom she has prayed. **(Also available in audiobook.)**

Other books by Brenda Walsh available at
www.brendawalsh.com

Passionate Prayer Promises
Brenda Walsh and Kay Kuzma
Paperback / 230 p.

Do you sometimes have the feeling your prayers are boring and repetitious, or you don't know how to pray? If you want a more exhilarating personal and passionate prayer life, Passionate Prayer Promises is the resource you've been waiting for. **(Also available in sharing and Spanish versions.)**

Prayer Promises for Kids
Brenda Walsh and Kay Kuzma / Paperback / 128 p.

Prayer Promises for Kids is a colorful prayer book of over 100 sample prayers on topics that school-age kids deal with everyday, such as being afraid of bullies, rejection, failure, coping with bad habits, and making friends.

Miss Brenda's Bedtime Stories
Brenda Walsh / Hardcover / 128 p.

Miss Brenda's Bedtime Stories is a collection of five hardcover volumes, each filled with more than twenty-five delightful stories that you will never forget. Each book is filled with exciting character-building stories that teach valuable life lessons. Some stories take you halfway around the world and others will seem as if they could have happened in your own backyard. These true stories are sure to be loved by children and treasured by parents and grandparents as well. Perfect for reading together before bedtime—or anytime—these stories will warm your heart and draw your family closer to Jesus! **(Also available in audiobook.)**

Additional Devotional Resources

For more devotions like these, download Brenda Walsh's free app, *Sharing God's Love*, available on the App Store® for the iPhone or iPad or on Google Play™ for Android devices.

A new devotion will be available to read each day, with the added option of listening to Brenda's audio version.

You can also connect with
Brenda Walsh on: